Rhetorical Homologies

Rhetorical Homologies

Form, Culture, Experience

Barry Brummett

The University of Alabama Press

Tuscaloosa

Typeface: Minion

∞

The paper on which this book is printed
meets the minimum requirements of
American National Standard
for Information Science–Permanence of Paper
for Printed Library Materials,
ANSI Z39.48–1984.

Brummett, Barry, 1951–
Rhetorical homologies : form, culture, experience / Barry Brummett.
p. cm. — (Rhetoric, culture, and social critique)
Includes bibliographical references (p.) and index.
ISBN 978-0-8173-1423-1 (cloth : alk. paper)
ISBN 978-0-8173-5570-8 (pbk. : alk. paper)
1. Rhetoric—Philosophy. 2. Communication—Philosophy. 3. Form (Aesthetics) 4. Mass media—Aesthetics. 5. Symmetry (Art) 6. Popular culture. 7. Experience. I. Title. II. Series.
PN175.B73 2004
808′.001—dc22

2004002835

For Jennifer Betancourt, Susan Corbin,
Aida Gonzalez, Deanna Matthews, and Margaret Surratt:
Leaders, helpers, friends, wonderful counselors,
princesses of peace

Contents

1

Rhetorical Homologies

Everything has shape, if you look for it. There is no escape from form.
—Salman Rushdie, *Midnight's Children*

Some strategies for understanding discourse and how it works in human affairs are very broadly shared across the humanities. Among these strategies is the principle of metaphor—the idea that one thing can stand in for, or represent, another; or the idea of linguistic structure—language forms a structure of oppositions and associations within texts that imply motivational structure; or the strategy of personae—authors take on certain personae, texts imply certain kinds of authors and likewise call upon readers to take up certain subject positions, readers may accept, refuse, or negotiate the stances they take in relationship to texts, and so forth. We find such strategies, often called by different names, at the heart of many methods and schools of thought. They are widely adaptable to different approaches and philosophies, and are likely to resonate with fundamental, even transcendent forms of thought, text, and communication.

Among these widely used strategies is the idea of *homology*. Although this principle takes on new meanings and connotations in its different applications, we will begin with an understanding of homology as a formal resemblance. A homology is a pattern found to be ordering significant particulars of different and disparate experiences. Because homologies are formal they are, as Michael Lane noted, "not on the surface, at the level of the observed, but below or behind empirical reality" (14). A homology is a formal structure that must be identified, described, and shown to be manifested in the particular content of texts and experiences. If A is like B on significant dimensions of form, to that extent the two are homologous. That it is formal makes a homology no less "real."

To illustrate: an extremely capable administrative associate in my department had spent a good hour dealing with an obstreperous faculty member who did not want to hear "no," who could not understand the nature of budgetary limits, and who reacted to anything but total acquiescence with pique, suspicion, and stubbornness. Once the faculty member had left, I observed to this administrator that she could not do her job if she were not the experienced, battle-tested mother of two little boys—an observation with which she heartily agreed. I had asserted a homology between her home life and her work life. The faculty with which she must deal are not little boys and girls but often their behavior is formally similar to the behavior of children. A child will not understand why he cannot simply have that expensive toy; a professor will not understand why she cannot simply take that trip at department expense to a far corner of the earth. A general formal pattern of "self-centered greed with no understanding of the principle of limited resources" underlies both sets of behavior.

Homologies may also undergird the kinds of experiences that are thought of as primarily textual, and it may bring texts into the same pattern as extratextual experience (we may modify these distinctions later, but they serve for the moment). Back home in the evening, the administrative associate might calm her frazzled nerves by reading a book or watching a television show in which the story line likewise embodies a pattern of "self-centered greed" as well as suggesting a cure for the affliction of greed in others. The text of the book or show would be homologous with the experience she had during the day, and *because* it would be homologous (linked, relevant) it could thus speak to her and advise her as to what to do and how to feel. Such a homologous text would have *rhetorical* power.

Homology is most interesting when it is observed as a linkage among *disparate* orders of experience, such as texts, media, different kinds of material experience, and so forth. The more disparate, the more interesting and insightful is the homology. If I had observed the administrative associate's skillful handling of two young girls in a playground squabble, my comment about her qualifications as a mother of two young boys would not have asserted an interesting homology, since managing two young boys and managing two young girls are not disparate orders of experience, and thus, although the link between the two sets may well also be formal, the shared content of dealing with real little children is as important and relevant as is any kind of shared form. Homology is interesting and worth investigating when a pattern of behavior on the battlefield is the same as a pattern of behavior in the living room, or in the theater, or while grocery shopping. If a common pattern is found across experiences like that, a homology worth investigating exists; what that means, why it is interesting, and why homology is rhetorical are the subjects of this book.

In the following pages I will explain the virtues of homology as a widely used methodological strategy across the humanities, and will then focus on the more specific idea of *rhetorical homology*. A rhetorical homology is a special case of formal resemblance, grounded in discursive properties, that facilitates the work of political and social rhetoric, or influence. Attunement to rhetorical homology through methods of rhetorical criticism allows one to track lines of rhetorical influence that might otherwise be obscured. To understand how rhetorical homologies are created among different classes of experience can be a useful way to understand how power is created, managed, or refused rhetorically in human affairs.

To begin this discussion, let us note that the idea of a formal resemblance calls up a distinction between form and content, itself a venerable staple of textual analysis. The distinction needs to be revisited and reconsidered. I will argue that the distinction between form and content is continuous and variable rather than sharply dichotomous, an insight that will help us understand how rhetorical homologies work.

What Is Form, What Is Content?

A simple distinction that might be made between form and content holds that content is the information conveyed by a message whereas form is either the pattern that orders the content or the physical manifestation of the message. Both distinctions are hard to maintain. Suppose I want to tell you the combination to a safe. The numbers to which one should turn would be the content of such a message. But the ordering of those numbers is surely just as much a part of the message; it does make a difference whether one turns to 15 first or to 6. Order and pattern are inseparable from the bare articulation of the content in the first place; it makes a difference whether I put a 1 first or a 5 if I want to convey the idea of the number 15.

When we say "form" and mean the physical manifestation of a message, we are also speaking of patterns and regularities. If I give you the combination of the safe "in the form of" a song, we know it is a song because it follows the pattern of other messages we call songs. To be apprehensible, a physical manifestation of any message must be a recognizable type of thing, and thus follows a form. If I say, "This radio station must be country-western," it is because I recognize the forms that make the one song I am now hearing representative of a type of music. But this idea of form as a physical manifestation that conforms to a pattern is likewise difficult to separate from the idea of content, as form so often works to convey information on its own terms.

If you and I are dining and I want you to pass me the salt, I might say, "Pass the salt, please," or I might say, "Praise Jesus! And thank God, that I may receive the salt today," or I might say, "If you would be so kind, my dear Arbuthnot, to help me to the salt when entirely convenient, I would be most appreciative." One might say that the content in each utterance is the same (I am expressing a desire for salt) but that in each case the utterance follows a different form that is shared by other utterances in other contexts, respectively: ordinary social interaction, the evangelist's tent revival, and a conspicuously mannered, formal style.

But the distinction here between form and content is not so simple, for surely into each simple content of a request for salt the formal resemblance to another kind of utterance has also injected the content of ordinary interaction, religion, or mannered formality. If we insist on a conceptual distinction between form and content we find that new content piggybacks in on the form that is being used. My use of a religious form of address sneaks into our conversation the odor of candles and incense. Form is thus a bridging device, using a shared pattern to facilitate the mixing, shifting, and associating of content across different dimensions of experience. To make distinctions between form and content may thus be largely conventional, as in fact they are both intertwined. We will examine the work of Kenneth Burke later, but here let us note that he is likewise of this opinion, for he argues in *The Philosophy of Literary Form* that his method (which I shall argue is often homological) "integrates considerations of 'form' and 'content'" (90).

An even deeper reason why form and content are inherently inseparable has to do with the idea that unless content or information is patterned, it cannot be part of human consciousness. One of the clearest explanations of this claim comes from I. A. Richards, who argues in *The Philosophy of Rhetoric* that even our most basic perceptions are structures of sensations, and that we do not "have" such experiences until they are ordered and structured:

> I can make the same point by denying that we have any sensations. . . . A sensation would be something that was just *so*, on its own, a datum; as such we have none. Instead we have perceptions, responses whose character comes to them from the past as well as the present occasion. A perception is never just of an it; perception takes whatever it perceives as a thing of a certain sort. (30)

The idea of the "sort" is key in Richards, and it is a thoroughly formal term. He argues that "a particular impression is already a product of concrescence. Behind, or in it, there has been a coming together of *sortings*" (36). Writing with C. K. Ogden, Richards argues that "whenever we 'perceive' what we name 'chair,' we are interpreting a certain group of data (modifications of the sense organs), and treating them as signs of a referent" (22). This means that all of experience is formal, patterned, before it enters our consciousness at all: "experience has the character of recurrence, that is, comes to us in more or less uniform contexts" (55). Other thinkers such as Susanne Langer agree in arguing that "sense-data and experiences . . . are essentially meaningful structures" (266)—note that formal term, *structures*. Running throughout all these observations by Richards, Ogden, and Langer is the paradox that formal thinking asserts a similar structure underlying dissimilar experiences. To see many different experiences as of the same sort merges the disparate into the same formal order. That is the role of homology: not to unite what is already the same, but to link disparate orders of experi-

ence by way of the same form. Of course, since nothing in everyday experience is ever exactly the same as anything else, homology must be the
engine of stable categories in our consciousness.

These observations may be found throughout the humanities among
many different thinkers. The implication is that even the simplest piece
of information or "content" is already patterned, formal; indeed, it is
present to us in the form of content or information precisely because it
is formed. Yet there remains an intuitive sense of something we would
call form, which works palpably in a different way and at a different
level from content, even if it is inseparable from it. The content of the
idea that "a tree is a beautiful thing" can be conveyed in discourse that
follows the form of a lyric poem, or in discourse that follows the form
of a technical report, and so forth. What are we attuned to in thinking
about form as something distinct from content, even in principle, when
we make such a distinction?

I propose thinking of form and content as shifting positions on a
continuum of abstraction. Key to the idea of perceptions as sortings
or structures, explored previously, is the idea of abstraction. The simplest physical perception is already at some level of abstraction "up"
from the level of raw, immediate physical sensation. Every sensation is
experienced as a sensation of a particular "sort," and is thus always already abstract as it reaches human consciousness. Note that abstraction
is a kind of formal linkage. This particular pain is experienced as a pain
of some sort, as linked to, as like, other pains of this sort that I have
experienced in the past. To abstract is to assert a resemblance that cuts
across specific local experiences; those resemblances across experiences
constitute form.

An experience can be, among other things, kinesthetic, such as walk-
ing down the street, or it can be textual, such as viewing a film. Any
particular experience thus has information or content: something happens, a difference is made, some new shift in one's view of the world
occurs; and it also has form: a pattern or structure that makes it like
other experiences and links it to those experiences. Those are but different points on the continuum of abstraction. In all experiences, we receive content or information and we also experience patterned linkages
from the experience to other experiences of the same sort. The dimension of experience that is relatively more immediate and local is content;

the dimension of experience that is relatively more patterned and connected to other sorts of experience is form. The news broadcast I watch right now brings me information or content about a specific murder that has just occurred, but as I process that information in increasingly higher levels of abstraction I likewise move toward increasingly wider circles of connection to see this murder as being of the same sort as other murders, this news broadcast as being of the same sort as other broadcasts—in other words, as having form and formal connections.

But what makes a "sort"? This is a crucial question. Sorts of experiences, groups of experiences linked together formally, need not be the same orders of experience. If we think of films as naturally being in formal linkage to other films, we may be trying to trace formal linkages by following content (the content of film). The "form and genre" line of research in rhetorical studies is strong and venerable, and often takes this approach, as in Karlyn Kohrs Campbell and Kathleen Hall Jamieson's seminal study. Grouping films together as a form because they are all about, say, war, or because they all respond to predictably recurrent contexts is certainly a way to identify formal patterns creating a "sort," but there may be wider and more inclusive sorts yet. A film about alien space invasions may at some level of abstraction share patterns or forms with my experience of office life at work, or with the form of a family conflict, or the form of a news story about a political convention. As we slide on the scale of abstraction from the content of the immediate to the formal sortings found higher up that scale, we must be prepared to jump the tracks laid down by the lower, content-heavy levels of abstraction and find higher level formal links among all sorts of experiences— or should I say, all kinds of experiences within a sort. "Sorts" may thus be understood as increasingly wide circles of formal resemblance, of abstraction, that continue moving outwards until at some point the formal linkages break, or become less interesting and compelling than narrower linkages. "Things appear, they change, they disappear" may be the widest homology of all, but you can't use it to get published.

Form and content are thus continuous rather than distinct. They are arrayed on a scale of abstraction, which is a scale of connections and linkages through sortings. A usage that treats form and content as distinct is quite widespread, but as we explore those usages among other scholars, or as we express such a distinction here, we will need to bear in mind the artificiality of the difference being asserted. As noted earlier, a term that is very widely used to mean formal linkages is the word *homology*. Let us review some of the ways that term has been used in many different scholarly literatures.

Some Views of Homology

The assertion of a homology is taken to be the discovery of important connections among different orders of experience, revealing new information about those orders and about the underlying form that connects them. As Fredric Jameson notes, homology is "a term currently in wide use in a variety of literary and cultural analyses" (43). Michael Lane describes homology as "correspondences in structure" among different experiences (16), a view shared by Pierre Maranda (30). Claude Lévi-Strauss, whose controversial work purported to equate myths around the world at a very deep level of formal structure, saw homology as "orderly correspondence" among texts or experiences (*Symbolic*, 232), and Lucien Goldmann saw homology as a "deep level of coherence" as well (129). Many scholars use the term *homology* explicitly; others write in ways completely consistent with that usage even if they do not employ the precise term. Researchers in the natural sciences, social sciences, and the humanities use the idea of homology in a wide range of ways. Some see strongly deterministic, lawlike power for homologies while others observe formal linkages but claim no kind of causal relationship. For a survey of how the idea of homology is used across many disciplines, see the Appendix.

A few theorists are more directly relevant to our current subject of rhetorical homologies in their attention to texts and the effects of texts in managing ideas and perceptions. John Fiske identifies homologies ordering texts and experiences as a source of the *rhetorical* effectiveness of texts, claiming that "making sense of a text is an activity precisely parallel to making sense of social experience, and . . . it is the mutually validating fit between textual experience and social experience that accounts for the popularity of specific texts" ("Discourses," 139). Fiske and John Hartley argue that homologies between texts and experiences enable texts to influence audience perceptions of the experiences directly, at a formal level: "the more closely the signifier reproduces our common experience, our culturally determined intersubjectivity, the more realistic it appears to be" (38).

Bill Nichols's idea of "pleasure-in-recognition" is homological and rhetorical, for he claims that the recognition of formal links between text and experience is motivating to an audience (40–41). Similarly, Robert Sklar argues that successful television texts "need to express, in their various conventional and stylized ways, some of the real feelings and concerns of their audience," which would be a homological linkage between text and experiences that accounts for achieved popularity or rhetorical success (82). Dennis Porter argues that one way success can be achieved is when television soap operas come to structure the other experiences of the day, when they "occupy a structuring place at the center of an active day. Looked forward to beforehand, [the soap] reverberates suggestively afterwards" (345). Mary Piccirillo suggests a similar relationship between television and experience: "Collected instances of intimacy allow viewers to share a common history with a television series, one which parallels the history imbedded in the practice of everyday lived experience," a structuring relationship that is thoroughly homological (345).

Dick Hebdige argues that homologies among texts, cultural artifacts, and the life situations people confront form homologies that enable texts to address life's problems rhetorically (113–14). He claims that British subcultures such as West Indians, Teddy boys, punks, and others use those homological links to fashion rhetorical responses to life's dangers and frustrations. Similarly, Paul Willis argues that homologies structure texts and behaviors in a society along similar patterns (201–03). For instance, he identifies formal linkages between the boisterous style of behavior among British "bike-boys," the loudness of their motorcycles, and broad patterns of behavior linked to class (52–53). Control over behaviors that are patterned by class is a way of controlling what class means and how it affects people. These homologies then help people live through the hardships imposed by class structure.

Different Kinds of Magic

The theorists and critics reviewed here and in the Appendix would not by any means be pleased to find themselves tucked into this rather large bed together. Although I believe the idea of homology to be widely shared and wide-ranging, each study that uses homology must give or imply an answer to a key question: What is the nature of the connections among experiences and experiences, or experiences and texts (when some experiences are of texts)? The answers given or implied vary widely, and are not always compatible with one another.

One of the most contentious sites of battle, for instance, is among theorists of different Marxist persuasions (whose fights and resentments are no less bitter or less minute than are the disagreements among the many tribes of Lutherans). Goldmann's work is attacked, for example by Jameson, as reflecting a kind of "vulgar Marxism" in which an economic base simplistically generates a cultural, social superstructure. The base, in that view (and whether anyone recently, even Goldmann, really defends this position is arguable) works as a homology underlying the superstructure. There are many varieties of Marxist takes on homology, including objections to its very idea, but they all address the key question asked earlier: What is the nature of the connections among experiences and experiences, or experiences and texts? That question implies that there are such "real" connections with patterned regularities that can be studied and explained, and it suggests that the nature of the connection is systematic and theorizable.

Gavin Kendall and Gary Wickham develop a theory informed by Michel Foucault's work to argue that "ordering" is a key social function and thus should be part of any method intended to reveal social conditions. They do not use the term *homology* focally, but their approach is nevertheless thoroughly homological as they follow Foucault's lead in identifying structures that order together widely disparate realms of experience. Their argument, then, takes Foucault's vision of structures of power as connecting disparate experiences at a bedrock level.

Making such systematic theories is perhaps the greatest challenge of the humanities, even the social sciences. The natural sciences observe that an action *here* has an equal and opposite reaction *there*. The bedrock grounding for that relationship is a physical law. There are many formally parallel actions and reactions studied by those in the humanities and social sciences. When it comes to homology, what seem to be significant or at least interesting formal parallels pop up here and there in

social life. What connects them? What social parallel to a law of thermo-
dynamics can be offered to explain how formally similar experiences get
to be that way?

I have come to the conclusion that theorists answer those questions
by asserting a kind of magic at work in the social field. This social assertion parallels the assertion of the natural science that "gravity" connects
disparate objects or experiences; gravity is a kind of scientific magic in
that sense. It just works that way, the assertion goes, and then evidence
is marshaled to fit the theory (the marshaling and fitting of which is
itself a kind of homology). A "vulgar" Marxist who thinks the base patterns the superstructure will just assert that a magical influence is at
work to connect base and superstructure. Lévi-Strauss suggests a different kind of magic at work ordering myths all over the world in the same
way, a magic of fundamental structures in human nature. When bell
hooks observes that "where there are communities of people of African
descent, there is a deep structure" she identifies some notion of culture
as the magic that manifests similar ways of living across time and space
(*Art*, 161). A traditional rhetorician offers up the magic of rational appeal as the reason why people are induced to order their lives to match
patterns suggested in discourse. A theologist offers the will of God as
the magic connecting this with that.

By using such an outrageous term as *magic*, I mean to say that the
nature of the connections among formally similar experiences is arguable but not absolutely, transcendently provable. One asserts a kind of
social, discursive, perhaps even physical "force" governing those connections. But the nature of the force asserted is, I believe, akin to a leap of
faith. To say that one experience is formally similar to another *because*
of economic structuring, or common ancestors, or rationality, or cogni-
tive structures, or the will of God, or what have you finally comes down
to what kind of world one thinks one lives in, and what is the Great
Engine that turns its wheels.

The Great Engine in this book is not primarily an answer provided by
Marxism, theology, structuralism, or traditional rationalistic rhetoric; it
is a magic grounded in the rhetorical nature of discourse. The *rhetorical
homologies* we examined a few pages ago, and the rhetorical homologies
I identify here, are grounded in the "magic" of discourse, or how lan-

guage works. I will end up arguing that homologies connect disparate experiences because of the nature of how discourse works—discourse understood as a social phenomenon in part, but a phenomenon that also follows the logics of its own structures and imperatives. Such a stance makes use of other "magics" but subordinates them to its own spells.

A clear, insightful example of this discursive grounding for homologies is Kathryn M. Olson's recent insightful study asserting a homology undergirding sport hunting, hate crimes, and stranger rape—surely an eclectic blend of disparate experiences, nevertheless all ordered together by the magic of discursive structures. Olson grounds the homology in the power of discourse itself. Her stance positions her to advise the public as to how discourse might be altered so as to alter the behaviors that it grounds.

One excellent way to understand that kind of discursive magic is, I believe, to consult the works of Kenneth Burke. The approach to homology that I propose here is not exclusively Burkean but it is strongly informed by his theories and by his overall perspective on the irreducibility of discourse as a grounding for human experience. Let me now turn to some works of Burke as a springboard for the approach I wish to develop here.

Kenneth Burke as Homology Theorist and Rhetorical Theorist

Although I am not aware that he ever used the term, I will claim that one of the great theoreticians of homology in the twentieth century was Kenneth Burke. The assertion of formal structure was a preoccupation in most of his works. I examine what I will read as homological theories in four of his books: *Counter-Statement, Attitudes toward History, The Philosophy of Literary Form,* and *A Grammar of Motives.* Burke's interests in form are vast and varied, but a theme that recurs throughout his work is the problem of how form works rhetorically so as to influence an audience, to create attitudes and motivations, to address problems and frame situations in particular ways. In pursuing that theme Burke shows the connectedness of experience via the discourses we use to manage experience. Burke is our entrée into understanding homology more fully as a rhetorical device.

Counter-Statement

In his early book *Counter-Statement*, Kenneth Burke has much to say about form and pattern in art and literature. Early in the book, he distinguishes between "form and subject-matter," or "technique and psychology," and identifies the "breach" between the two as a development of late modernism (31). But Burke immediately complicates his use of that term "psychology," for there is more than one type. Burke identifies a common use of "psychology" that seems consonant with our earlier use of "content" or "information" as a dimension of texts that stands in contrast to formal patterns. "Psychology has become a body of information (which is precisely what psychology in science should be, or must be). And similarly in art, we tend to look for psychology as the purveying of information" (32). Burke bemoans trends in art that call for the artist to "lay his emphasis on the giving of information," and refers to Cézanne's landscapes as "tainted with the psychology of information" (32).

In contrast to a psychology of information-giving, Burke aligns "the psychology of the audience" with form: "form would be the psychology of the audience" (31). He likewise defines form in terms of audience expectations, for "form is the creation of an appetite in the mind of the auditor, and the adequate satisfying of that appetite" (31), later expressed as, "*Form* in literature is an arousing and fulfillment of desires" (124) or "the creation and gratification of needs" (138). At a stroke, Burke has accomplished two useful tasks for our purpose. First, he has located form in the discursive manipulation of human motivations and perceptions. Such a grounding need not deny any other ontological status to form conceived in other ways, biologically or mathematically, for instance. The kind of form he will discuss is grounded in something that texts do in the minds of an audience. Second, he has placed form within the order of erotics, of desire and appetite, of the pleasing of an audience—and that means he has made form inherently rhetorical. As we follow Burke into more developed explanations of how form connects discourse and experience, we must bear in mind form's grounding in rhetoric and in the psychology of the audience.

The relationship among audience, text, and the creator of the text in terms of form is intricate. Burke argues that "the audience dreams, while the artist oversees the conditions which determine this dream" (36). Note that the artist but "oversees" while the "conditions . . . determine" the audience's experience of form; this is a language in which the creator of a text is manipulating artistic elements that create what the audience experiences. Form seems to be a property of the text that is realized in the audience's experience. Writing of music as a highly formal medium, Burke notes that "in the opening lines we hear the promise of the close," another way of saying that audience desires or appetites are created with the expectation of their satisfaction—created by the text but experienced by the audience (35). This experience of form Burke describes as "eloquence," and he contrasts it to the "facts" that information gives us.

What eloquence, a property of texts, does for Burke is to exercise the human faculty of experiencing form in such a way that a particular form is laid down in the consciousness. People have the potential to experience form, and the particular artistic experience makes a particular form present as a structuring device in the consciousness: "art has always appealed, by the changing individuations of changing subject-matter, to certain potentialities of appreciation which would seem to be inherent in the very germ-plasm of man, and which, since they are constant, we might call innate forms of the mind" (46). Similarly, he later claims that "the formal aspects of art appeal in that they exercise formal potentialities of the reader" (142). For example, to experience the formal property of contrast, "there *must be* in my mind the sense of contrast" (48). That formulation sounds very close to the grand structuralisms of Freud, Lévi-Strauss, and others, but we must remember that Burke is speaking very generally in terms of potentialities for formal appreciation, not in terms of specific formal structures (e.g., specific contrasts, which may well vary in history). Burke can be read as supporting the view that the potential for form is actually experienced in history, where culture-specific forms are created, shared, and struggled over. Later in the book Burke explicitly sidesteps this issue of whether form is biological or cultural by saying, "Psychology and philosophy may decide whether they are innate or resultant; so far as the work of art is concerned they simply *are*" (141).

The tickling of those formal potentials in localized experiences of art creates localized, historically situated perceptions of particular forms in life and in art. In Burke's terms, "Truth in art is not the discovery of facts, not an addition to human knowledge in the scientific sense of the word. It is, rather, the exercise of human propriety, the formulation of symbols which rigidify our sense of poise and rhythm" (42). The term "rigidify" is telling: he appears to be saying that a text runs an audience through experience of a particular form, which then reifies (rigidifies) that form in the consciousness as a way to manifest art and experience in history. Form thus seems to be a property of discourse, or more fundamentally a property of symbolizing, that is transferred to consciousness in the act of appreciating the text. While form may be a way of conveying some kind of emotion or insight, its induction in the consciousness of the audience is also an end in itself; Burke describes this as a process in which "the artist's means are always tending to become ends in themselves" (54–55).

One of the key ideas in Burke's development of form in *Counter-Statement* is the idea of the Symbol. Burke capitalizes the term in the essay "Lexicon Rhetoricae" in that book, but his earlier references to a lowercased symbol are consistent with his later thought. The symbol appears to be a property of a sign within a text or of a whole text itself. It is a predicate of the object produced by the artist. Burke says of the artist, "The poet steps forth, and his first step is the translation of his original mood into a symbol." But the symbol is within four sentences also described as form: "he has attained articulacy by linking his emotion to a technical form" (56). Arguing explicitly for the symbol as an instrument of "technical form," Burke says that "the technical appeal of the symbol lies in the fact that it is a principle of logical guidance, and makes for the repetition of itself in changing details which preserve as constant the original ratio" (60).

Here is a description of form in homological terms. A particular play, character or image in a play is understood not primarily as that particular character but as the sort of character it is the present embodiment of. Note that description of the symbol as an instrument of logical guidance parallels Burke's earlier description of the artist manipulating materials so as to "determine" the way in which an audience "dreams," or experiences a text; here the artist "guides" the audience. But it is form within texts, not the information or content presented, that does the guiding. Burke refers to an artist's "revelation" as "belief" or "fact," but explains that "art enters when this revelation is ritualized, when it is converted into a symbolic process," in other words, when content is ordered by form (168). That form may underlie and cross over many different times and places ("the repetition of itself in changing details"), but the form remains influential upon the audience in more or less "the original ratio." So when he describes the character Falstaff as a nearly perfect symbol (58–59), we might imagine the form beneath the particular instantiation that is Falstaff in Shakespeare's plays re-emerging in "the original ratio" in other characters flung far and wide in time and space. Those characters are, we might say, homologous with one another as different instantiations of the same form.

Burke's idea of the symbol, he argues, "faces two ways, for in addition to the technical form just mentioned (an 'artistic' value) it also applies to life, serving here as a formula for our experiences" (61). Neither the technical form of expression in art nor the "real life" experience exhausts what the Symbol is; it "faces" both at the same time and is the form that makes them homologous. This seems to me to be a clear expression of how form, and homology, serves not only as art for art's sake (technical form) but also as a formula for the manifestation of experience. We use formulae as guides to help shape, create, and manifest certain experience: the formula for compound interest will produce a specific calculation of today's interest; the formula for water will produce water. This is rhetorical language, in the vein of determining and guiding what we have seen presented here. A homology guides an audience, it advises them, and is thus rhetorical. Art, and the form it embodies, will not only " 'reflect' a situation [but is] a way of dealing with a situation" (80) rhetorically.

Burke's discussion of technical form in the "Lexicon Rhetoricae" expresses the idea of material that the artist manipulates so as create and gratify audience needs. In the "Lexicon" he says, "A work has form in so far as one part of it leads a reader to anticipate another part, to be gratified by the sequence" (124). Homology is the dimension of form that cuts across many such a work, experience, time, or place. When Burke identifies "five aspects of form as progressive (syllogistic and qualitative), repetitive, conventional, and minor or incidental, we can understand him as identifying forms that might also link together different texts and experiences (124–28).

Burke urges us to consider "the single poem or drama as an individuation of formal principles" (143). It is in specific local experiences that we see any form being manifest to us. Burke argues that "a form is a way of experiencing; and such form is made available in art when, by the use of specific subject-matter, it enables us to experience in this way" (143). The contrast between form as a "way" of experiencing and the specific, local "experience in this way" is telling, for it suggests form as a structure homologously cutting across many specific experiences. These repeated experiences are the "re-individuation of forms" (148). This phenomenon is perhaps nowhere as clear as in television, where the insatiable demand for programming leads to one individuation after another of the same handful of plots. Television shows may thus be understood as appealing in large part depending upon the form they instantiate, the form that makes them homologous with other shows. Burke clearly prefers the appeal of form to that of information, regarding the latter as a "'disease' of form" (144) that "tends to interfere with our enjoyment in the repetition of a work" (145) since form may be enjoyed again and again but information once mastered is old news.

Burke's postulation is not exclusively formal. He discusses "what the reader considers desirable," or matters of fact, under the heading of "form and ideology" (146). A story that featured conversion of pagans to Catholicism would not be appealing to a Protestant, he notes (147). The formal pattern of conversion might of course be the same in each case, but the content or information of religious difference would be telling. Burke thus reminds us that form and homology are not "everything." On the other hand, ideology, or "the nodus of beliefs and judgments" of an audience (161), may be indispensable in giving the elements of an experience or text their characters so that they may participate in formal patterns in particular ways. One cannot follow the form of a tragedy without invoking an ideology to say which qualities in a person are heroic and which are not, and thus ideology may help to shape the elements that are ordered in form (162).

It is in discussing the Symbol (now capitalized) late in *Counter-Statement* that Burke is most suggestive regarding homology. That discussion occurs in the context of an explanation of "patterns of experience," wherein Burke asserts the existence of "universal experiences" that "all men, under certain conditions . . . are capable of experiencing" (149). Such a grand, seemingly ahistorical statement must be understood in terms not of specific experiences but of forms, patterns, or types of experiences. There is no specific "attack" experienced by "all men," but there are basic forms of attack (sorts) that all might experience. This assertion of such a fundamental formal pattern opens the possibility for widely disparate experiences across time and space to be linked formally—in our terms, homologously.

Close upon this discussion of universal patterns of experience comes Burke's introduction of the Symbol, which "is the verbal parallel to a pattern of experience" (152)—and we might say that there could be non-verbal or kinesthetic parallels to such patterns as well. Note that the Symbol does not parallel an experience but rather a *pattern* of experience. We must understand the Symbol not as a particular collection of words or images but as the pattern underlying words or images, a pattern that parallels a pattern of experience.

Burke begins with an image of a poet who "pities himself for his undeserved neglect" (152) so much so that "self-pity assumes enough prominence in his case to become a pattern of experience (153). The poet "converts his pattern into a plot," in other words, a pattern of experience is turned into a discursive pattern, suggesting a homologous relationship between two separate orders (153). Burke suggests several such "plots," such as "The King and the Peasant" or "The Man Against the Mob" or "A Saint Dying in Neglect," suggesting by this profusion of "plots" that a basic form may underlie many different texts as well as the original experience of neglect that prompted the poet to write. Note the generic, formal nature of the plots he suggests; none are specific individuations of plots in a particular play. These plots all suggest a particular play that will individuate the underlying basic form. In *The Tempest*, Burke suggests that the Symbol, the underlying form, being expressed is "a complex attitude which pervades the setting, plot, and characters" (153). It is not the specific things that happen in the play; likewise, such a complex attitude might pattern another play or a real experience.

That basic form is described as a formula: "The Symbol is a formula" (153), a formula for how to experience. But it would appear as if it guides the audience in experiencing both life and text, for Burke says that "the

Symbol is perhaps most overwhelming in its effect when the artist's and the reader's patterns of experience closely coincide" (153). Note he does not say when their experiences coincide, but when the patterns of experience are homologous. And note that Burke describes the attainment of this homology in specifically rhetorical form, as "overwhelming in its effect."

Insofar as it is a formula for experience, we would expect the Symbol to suggest what sort of experience one is having. Burke makes precisely that move in arguing that "a Symbol appeals" in several ways, "as the interpretation of a situation . . . by favoring the acceptance of a situation . . . as the corrective of a situation . . . as the exerciser of 'submerged' experience . . . as an emancipator . . . as a vehicle for 'artistic' effects" (154–56). But how does it do so? It is clear that the Symbol, as any homology, is a bridging device. And the bridging among experiences is a precondition for rhetorical effect. But how can embodying a formal pattern that underlies many texts and experiences advise an audience in how to live through this particular experience?

We will need to interpret Burke for our own purposes to some extent here. He argues that the Symbol is a "generating principle" or "a guiding principle in itself" (157). "Ramifications" of the Symbol arise (157–58); if one embodies a general pattern of neglect in The King and the Peasant, Burke notes that this individuation of the form of "neglect" will call forth a Queen and a Peasant's wife. Some of these will be relevant to the formal linkage established and some will not; as Burke says, "These secondary or ramifying Symbols can be said to bear upon the underlying pattern of experience only in so far as they contribute to the workings of the key Symbol" (157).

I want to stress two things here. First, a Symbol may suggest all those different responses to an audience because most situations are amenable to being ordered within more than one pattern, even at the same time. The creator of the text suggests one form through which an audience may see a situation, but the audience may well read a text so as to discover another form. Skillful creators of texts may be able to predict which forms an audience will use to connect text with experience, but audiences are famously active and cannot be assumed to roll over and accept the formal offerings of the poet. As a "generating principle," different forms may align different experiences homologically with the text. This makes the rhetorical effect of homologies a site of struggle and complex, not reducible to always and only *single* homological structures.

Second, the "ramifications" to which Burke refers are results of the particular individuation of the Symbol, the fact that any basic form must be expressed through a particular information-laden manifestation that will be compared to particular information-laden experiences. The Christ myth, for instance, is surely a fundamental formal pattern with which many texts and experiences may be found to be homologous. But suppose among the many texts that individuate the Christ metaphor, we find some in which the Christ figure is female, as in the film *Resurrection,* or played by an African American actor, as in the film *The Brother from Another Planet,* and so forth. Content or information piggybacks into audience reception of texts on the back of homologies. An audience responds to a given film because it embodies the Christ myth, yet there cannot help but be a rhetorical effect from individuating the form of Christ in this particular female or dark-skinned body. These are some principles that we may excise out of Burke's discussion of form that help us to understand how homology might operate rhetorically.

Burke argues that "a theoretically perfect Symbol would, in all its ramifications, reveal the underlying pattern of experience" (158). This is also described as a Symbol having power "in proportion as it limits its ramifications to a strict reinforcement of the poet's underlying pattern" (160). Such a Symbol might be theoretically perfect, and it might well induce an audience to accept the Symbol because the audience resonates so powerfully with its clean, unencumbered form. But such a "perfect" symbol would have limited rhetorical power to introduce *new* attitudes and motives to an audience through the mechanism of a form. Likewise, Burke says that "the underlying pattern is best observable when words refer to no specific thing—as 'liberty, equality, fraternity'" (159). Again, that kind of content-less Symbol would have limited rhetorical ability to use form to introduce content. Conversely, Burke says that a Symbol is complex "in proportion as its ramifications follow the 'logic' of the Symbol rather than the emotions of the underlying pattern" (160). In other words, the text calls attention to the particular individuation of form that it is rather than the form itself. Rhetorical power can be lost by going too far in this direction as well, for it attenuates the formal connections that link the Symbol to other texts and experiences homologously.

Burke argues that "intensity in art may be attributed sometimes to form, sometimes to the Symbol, sometimes to both. Symbolic intensity arises when the artist uses subject-matter 'charged' by the reader's situation outside the work of art" (163). This kind of "charging" may be understood as rhetorical power, but as we have seen, it cannot be had through content alone. The bare news that there is a tiger behind you is unlikely to move you unless it is expressed through recognizable patterns of alarm, wonder, humor, and so forth. Texts cannot be effective simply by reporting a subject matter experienced by an audience, which would be largely information; texts must join that subject matter homologously with a pattern; texts must say that the situation is not only familiar but is of this *type*, and the linkage to type is part of the rhetoric of homology.

Burke provides a great deal more detailed analysis of the Symbol than can be reported here. He discusses factors affecting the appeal of the Symbol, ways in which variations in experiences between artist and audience might affect the Symbol's reception. For our purposes, the basic structure of the Symbol as facing toward form and toward experience is key, for it suggests homologies underlying text, context, and experience. In discussing the rhetorical appeal of what we might call popular culture, Burke says, "A work deals with life for a great many people when it symbolizes such patterns of experience as characterize a great many people and ramifies the Symbol by such modes of experience as appeal to a great many people" (191). Here again we see the Symbol linking patterns of experience with the ramifications of particular texts and experiences. Much of the rhetorical power of homology lies in the connection between the two.

Attitudes toward History

Burke's *Attitudes toward History,* originally published in 1937, explores the intersection between politics and art, which is in and of itself suggestive of homologies linking disparate orders of experience. Burke explains that "by 'history' is meant primarily man's life in political communities. The book, then, deals with characteristic responses of people in their forming and reforming of congregations" (i). Burke presents a grand view of Western cultural history, divided into stages of "Evangelical Christianity," "Mediaeval Synthesis," "Protestantism," and "Early Capitalism" (ii). Burke seeks the means by which people form attitudes in response to types of historical circumstances, "kinds of quandary that *mutatis mutandis* recur under various historical conditions. That is, though every historical period is unique as regards its particular set of circumstances and persons, the tenor of men's policies for confronting such manifold conditions has a *synthesizing* function. For instance, if we feel happy on three different occasions, these three occasions are in a sense attitudinally united" (iii). Note how homological that way of thinking is. Burke is not as concerned with specific historical situations as with *kinds* (sorts) of recurring problems, and with the ways in which "policies for confronting" those types are also synthesizing. The attitude of happiness as being a "united" one despite occurring on three different occasions is likewise homological thinking. Burke offers his own "attitude of attitudes," which he identifies as "the 'comic frame,' the methodic view of human antics as a comedy," which is likewise a homological structure through which he will equate many different attitudes (iii).

Turning his attention toward the problem of acceptance or rejection of particular historical circumstances within the larger frames of form, Burke claims that,

> One constructs his notion of the universe or history, and shapes attitudes in keeping. Be he poet or scientist, one defines the "human situation" as amply as his imagination permits; then, with this ample definition in mind, he singles out certain functions or relationships as either friendly or unfriendly. If they are deemed friendly, he prepares himself to welcome them; if they are deemed unfriendly, he weighs objective resistances against his own resources, to decide how far he can effectively go in combating them. (3-4)

This language puts particular historical circumstances into larger frames, seeing them in terms of those larger frames, and is thus homologous thinking. One literally puts situations "in terms of" larger, homologous frames, for "action requires programs—programs require vocabulary. . . . We must name the friendly or unfriendly functions and relationships in such a way that we are able to do something about them. In naming them, we form our characters, since the names embody attitudes; and implicit in the attitudes there are the cues of behavior" (4). The naming of situations is an act of abstraction, for it is a simplifying of situations: "Our philosophers, poets, and scientists act in the code of names by which they simplify or interpret reality" (4), in simplifying one way or another one likewise interprets. But let us also recall that abstraction, form, and simplification are part of the same process. So what Burke's philosopher, poet, or scientist does is to suggest a formal structure by which a situation may be understood. But such a formal structure, embodied in a vocabulary, is also the grounding of a homology among other situations that share the same structure.

The linguistically grounded attitudes that rhetors—philosophers, poets, and scientists—formulate in response to types of situations comprise a "frame of acceptance." Burke says, "By 'frames of acceptance' we mean the more or less organized system of meanings by which a thinking man gauges the historical situation and adopts a role with relation to it" (5). As examples of "the three most well-rounded . . . frames of acceptance in American literature" Burke offers William James, Whitman, and Emerson (5). A review of their work leads Burke to suggest that there are general frames of "acceptance" of adverse situations that are manifest in different subforms such as "the Pollyanna solution," the fable of the fox and grapes, "trench humor," and other similar strategies (20). By enrolling many different such strategies together as frames of acceptance, Burke implies that they are to that extent homologous; by extension, the situations they name would then be homologous. Burke likewise treats frames of rejection as "but a by-product of 'acceptance,'" since such frames counsel acceptance of some other frame besides that offered by a dominant "orthodoxy" (21).

We have noted earlier the homologous way of thinking that sees forms cutting across both discourse and material experience. Burke's thinking in *Attitudes toward History* suggests a similar homology. The frames of acceptance and rejection by which people name and react to their particular situations are encoded in the formal patterns that are

"poetic categories": "each of the great poetic forms stresses its own peculiar way of building the mental equipment (meanings, attitudes, character) by which one handles the significant factors of his time" (34). For
Burke the classic genres of poetry, literature, and art are not merely discursive forms but also forms by which experience is ordered; they thus
cut homologically across both discourse and experience.

Burke introduces the general sorts of frames suggested by major,
standard literary types. For instance, he presents "the epic as a typical
frame of symbolic adjustment under primitive conditions" (34) for it
"makes men 'at home in' those conditions. It 'accepts' the rigors of war
(the basis of the tribe's success) by magnifying the role of the warlike
hero" and so on (35). Tragedy, on the other hand, counsels "resignation"
to life's problematic situations by suggesting a "scheme of causal relationships" (37). "Comedy, humor, the ode" are also explained (39). Burke
argues that "comedy warns against the dangers of pride, but its emphasis
shifts from *crime* to *stupidity*" (41). People are pictured "not as *vicious,*
but as *mistaken*" (41). Burke goes on to explain the dynamics of complaint underlying all uses of the elegy (44–49) and the ambiguities of
gratification and punishment present in satire (49–52). He formulates
the ways in which burlesque (52–56) and the grotesque (57–69) manage
distance between an audience and some object. The process of "*coaching
the imagination in obedience to critical postulates*" Burke describes as
the didactic, a category in which he places traditional rhetoric (75–86).

Having established the kinds of forms for structuring frames of acceptance and rejection found in the poetic categories, Burke spends
much of the rest of the book surveying history in grand sweeps, identifying whole philosophies and eras as formed around patterns grounded
in different discursive forms. We need not examine that work in detail
here. It is sufficient to note for these purposes that in putting discourse
and the formation of reactions to material existence on the same formal
grounds, Burke is offering homologous ways of thinking. A poetic category such as the epic or the ode then becomes a way to structure not
only how we symbolize experience but experience itself, since our reactions to situations always involve the naming and thus shaping of those
situations. These processes of formal alignment are clearly rhetorical,
for rhetoric (conceived broadly, not just as didactic) is precisely that
process of advising an audience as to how to accept or reject a situation,

and in accepting or rejecting, to construct the situation one way or another.

The Philosophy of Literary Form

Burke's *The Philosophy of Literary Form* originally appeared in 1941, with a third edition published by the University of California Press in 1973. This work also points to homology, without ever using that term. In this work Burke is concerned with "internal structure and act-scene relationships," or with the idea that a discourse has an internal structure or form that connects to the scene of which it is a part. He bases the work on the claim that "words are aspects of a much wider communicative context, most of which is not verbal at all. Yet words also have a nature peculiarly their own" (xvii). Bridging the discursive and the scenic, the verbal and the nonverbal, through form is one of the main and most interesting things that homologies "do."

The ways in which act-scene relationships and internal form relate are important in this book. Burke observes that "an act may be placed in many contexts, and when the character of the context changes, the character of the act changes accordingly" (xix). To be placed in one context as opposed to another, such that the very character of the act so placed changes, suggests that a given act, event, sign, and so forth may be placed in different patterns or forms. On the one hand, the form in that event is the context. The scene suggests the pattern into which the particular act is enrolled. A dropped handkerchief may be understood within the pattern of a love story, a spy story, or an athletic contest depending upon the scene and thus the form into which it is put. Homologies may thus be multiple and simultaneous, and their different forms may affect the way in which the elements ordered within a homology are themselves structured and understood.

On the other hand, specific circumstances may urge the use of one form over another to craft responses to the situation. It is form that changes and not merely content: "we may properly expect a form to function differently when it is part of one context than when it is part of some other context" (xxii).

Early in *The Philosophy of Literary Form*, Burke expresses an idea that is widely found throughout his works: "Critical and imaginative works are answers to questions posed by the situation in which they arose.

They are not merely answers, they are *strategic* answers, *stylized* answers"
(1). "Stylization is inevitable" in crafting symbolic responses to situations (128). Burke urges us to think of discourse "as the adopting of
various strategies for the encompassing of situations" (1), and he argues
that "every document bequeathed us by history must be treated as a
strategy for encompassing a situation" (109). Burke's view of art, of any
discourse, as inherently rhetorical in that it formulates for its creator and
its audience a response to a situation is central to his thinking.

But here we also find evidence to encourage us to think of this crafting of response as occurring at a formal level that cuts across and links
many different specific situations, for "in so far as situations overlap
from individual to individual, or from one historical period to another,
the strategies possess universal relevance" (1). By way of illustration he
cites the proverb, "Whether the pitcher strikes the stone, or the stone the
pitcher, it's bad for the pitcher." This proverb is presented formally as a
discursive structure that might underlie a wide range of situations that
Burke suggests, from a protestor against Hitler to Aristophanes to a local
clerk (2). We might then say that those situations are homologous with
one another, on the ground of the formal pattern expressed in the proverb. Later Burke gives another glimpse of elements (he does not say
whether they are textual or material, so we may assume either/both) in
a formal structure: "if A is in the same chordal structure with B and C,
its kindred membership must be revealed by narrative arpeggios. That
is, its function as an associate will be revealed by associational progres-
sions in the work itself" (58–59). The same chordal structure may be
found in different works of music, of course; the metaphor suggests homologies based on a shared discursive form underlying different texts
and experiences. We can pursue this homological thinking in at least
two ways: we can examine the particular attitudes that a given discourse
suggests to its audience for confronting a type of situation and think
about what other situations are formally patterned in this same way—
what other situations are homologous with it. Or we can identify a formal pattern that we believe to be found widely across many particular
experiences, homologically linking them, and then examine the specific
texts and situations that participate in that homology.

If we are on the lookout not just for homology but for rhetorical
homologies, Burke provides a clear rationale for seeing form's suasory

dimension. He offers "three subdivisions for the analysis of an act in poetry," which are "dream," "prayer," and "chart" (5–6). Prayer he describes as "the communicative functions of a poem, which leads us into the many considerations of form, since the poet's inducements can lead us to participate in his poem only in so far as his work has a public, or communicative structure" (5–6). Form is public, Burke thus argues, and the ground for communication (which of course subsumes rhetoric), because form provides the structure that gives people common ground and shared ways of communicating. Someone assembling a structured discourse is using a form that will have an effect on others: "if we try to discover what the poem is doing for the poet, we may discover a set of generalizations as to what poems do for everybody" (73). Burke is insistent on putting form at the heart of discourse, for he advises that "you approach the work as the *functioning* of a structure" (74). Such generalizations are homologies that "do something for" people in structuring experiences for them. Homology, because it links in a particular way, directs the attention of people in that particular way and is thus inherently rhetorical.

The particulars with which any work of art, any discourse, are concerned may thus be seen in terms of the widespread patterns in which they are homologously enrolled. A poet writes about her burdens, Burke notes (17). For example, he offers the hypothetical Mr. Q who writes a novel about "a deserving individual in conflict with an undeserving society" (18). But Burke notes that there is a whole class of such novels, and that each is "but different individuations of a common paradigm" (19). The paradigm may be thought of not only as a homology enrolling both the novels about the unappreciated deserving but also as the material experiences of Mr. Q and others like him. It is the presence of that form within the cultural repertoire that allows a sort of discourse to appeal to a sort of experience; homology makes the rhetoric possible.

Throughout Burke's work, we find invitations to see links from discourse to experience and across disparate kinds of experiences. He argues that

> the work of every writer contains a set of implicit equations. He uses "associational clusters." . . . Afterwards, by inspecting his work "statistically," we or he may disclose by objective citation the structure of moti-

vation operating here. . . . The interrelationships themselves are his motives. For they are his *situation*, and *situation* is but another word for
motives. (20)

Burke's own equations in that passage are remarkable, for a structure of
signs within a text is equated both with a structure of motives and with
a situation. Likewise, he later claims that "the motive of the work is
equated with the structure of interrelationships within the work itself"
(267). Situation for Burke is not then made exclusively of material or
symbol but is the symbolic assessment and naming of a situation so as
to create motives for response to it. He describes proverbs, which tell us
how to respond to situations, as names for "typical recurrent situations"
as well (293). That naming of situations is what artistic, political, in fact
any sort of discourse does, and it does so with clear social and political
effect in advising an audience how to live: Poetry "is undertaken as
equipment for living, as a ritualistic way of arming us to confront per-
plexities and risks. It would *protect* us" (61). And later he explains in
more detail how literature is "equipment for living" (293–304). All discourse may be understood "in terms of a situation and a strategy for
confronting or encompassing that situation" (64). This naming and confronting of situations is for Burke a primarily formal process; the structure offered by a text is a structure for encompassment. When he offers methodological advice for analyzing texts, therefore, he argues that,
"First: We should watch for the dramatic alignment. What is vs. what"
(69). From there "you propose your description of this equational structure . . . you offer your evidence for them and show how much of the
plot's development your description would account for" (89). This may
be read as the comparing of a text's or experience's particulars with a
structure suggested as a homology underlying several such texts or experiences.

But this naming, framing, advising function is asserted at the level of
perceptions and basic language use as well. Burke echoes Richards's
thinking in arguing that perceptions are already structured, a blend of
the material and symbolic in that they are of a class of experiences, at a
certain level of abstraction, rather than of any particular experience: "A
tree, for instance, is an infinity of events—and among these our senses
abstract certain recordings which 'represent' the tree. . . . In so far as we

see correctly, and do not mistake something else for a tree, our perceptions *do really* represent the tree" (26). A structure underlying discourse and experience is a homology, and here it is described as explicitly rhetorical in its ability to shape reality. Burke claims that "it is the moral impulse that motivates perception, giving it both intensity and direction, suggesting *what to look for* and *what to look out for*" (164). A moral impulse at the heart of perception, an impulse that advises people, is an engine of rhetoric.

In identifying "levels of symbolic action," Burke suggests different bases for homological groundings, and his descriptions are appropriately abstract. He describes "the bodily or biological level. Kinaesthetic imagery. Symbolic acts of gripping, repelling, eating, excreting" and so forth. Next, "the personal, intimate, familiar, familistic level. Relationships to father, mother, doctor, nurse, friends, etc." Finally, "the abstract level. Here we move into the concern with the part played by *insignia* in poetic action, their use by the poet as ways of enrolling himself in a band" (36–37). Thus, when bell hooks identifies some kinds of intercultural relationships as "eating the other," she is asserting a homology across disparate orders of experience based on bodily imagery (*Black*, 21–39). A political style in which a leader acts like a father establishes a homology between the family and politics on the personal level. The Christian practice of communion asserts an abstract level of homology linking together social dining, bloody death, and expiation of sins by way of a single ritual (insignia).

Burke often describes abstract patterns that we may understand as homologies ordering material experiences and discourses across wide ranges of life. In *The Philosophy of Literary Form* he introduces a discussion of the scapegoat, which he also pursues in other works (39–51; see also the *Grammar*, 406–08). Later in the book he will show how that formal pattern of transformation and expiation underlies Adolph Hitler's discourse in his famous essay, "The Rhetoric of Hitler's Battle" (191–220). The scapegoat is a worthy representative of certain sins or evils perpetrated by some person or group; the sins are symbolically loaded upon the scapegoat, which is then symbolically, ritually, or actually destroyed, destroying the sins along with it. This simple form underlies all manner of material experience and may be found in a wide range of discourse. In my own work I have found it ordering experience and discursive responses to experience in the arrest of John DeLorean ("Burkean Comedy"), presidential campaign rhetoric ("Burkean Scapegoating"), and San Francisco's "Zebra" murders ("Symbolic"). We might then say that these disparate experiences and texts are homologous in that they share the same important formal patterning described as scapegoating.

In discussing his methodology, Burke touches upon an interesting question having to do with the ontological status of homology, which we shall examine in more detail later on. The issue is, "where" do these forms exist? How are we to understand their status? Are they inventions of the scholar/critic, or is there some sense in which they are "real"? Of course we may want to refuse these distinctions later, but Burke himself is somewhat ambiguous on the question. In examining the structure of a work, he argues, we should not "help the author out" by suggesting structures and equations that are not "there" (69). He uses the loaded term "statistical" to describe this approach (69). Yet in proposing a perspective on discourse based on the idea of ritual drama as the "hub" of all symbolic activity (103), Burke argues that such a perspective is brought by the critic to the situation: "we are not upholding this perspective on the basis of historical or genetic material. We are proposing it as a *calculus*—a vocabulary, or set of coordinates, that serves best for the integration of all phenomena studied by the *social* sciences" (105). There is some sense that the "charts of meanings" suggested by the critic or by those who use them in life need to come *close* to meanings that are in some sense really there: "they are relative approximations to the truth" (108).

For Burke, the manipulation of form is not only a critical method but also a social intervention. He asks, "Are not wars what we make of them —like stones and trees, like Napoleon and the history of Greece?"—this in 1941 (238). Burke discusses different ways to feature war, as "hideous" or as a "thoroughly human" enterprise (239). Advocating the latter route, he advises, "let war be put forward as a *cultural way of life, as one channel of effort in which people can be profoundly human,* and you induce in the reader . . . precisely such a response as might best lead one to appreciate the preferable ways of peace" (240–41). Might not we read these musings on war as a consideration of which homological structure into which it should be put? Perceive war as homologous with other experiences on a formal pattern of "heroism" and it becomes one thing; perceive it as homologous with the more domestic and mundane "cultural way of life" and it becomes another. Choice of homologies thus becomes a rhetorical choice of homologies given the effect that different formal alignments will create.

A Grammar of Motives

The last of Burke's books that we shall explore for references that may be linked to homology is *A Grammar of Motives*, considered by many to be his crowning achievement along with *A Rhetoric of Motives*. The *Grammar* addresses the central question, "What is involved, when we say what people are doing and why they are doing it?" (xv). His answer will be to elucidate what he takes to be "the basic forms of thought which, in accordance with the nature of the world as all men necessarily experience it, are exemplified in the attributing of motives" (xv). It is an interesting grounding, for note that he not only intends ambitiously to explain "the basic forms of thought" but he also believes that they are fundamentally embodied not in religious or political thinking or any other system of thought but in the ways in which people discursively attribute motives. The structure for Burke's presentation of those basic forms of thought will be his famous pentad: "any complete statement about motives will offer some kind of answers to these five questions: what was done (act), when or where it was done (scene), who did it (agent), how he did it (agency), and why (purpose)" (xv). The pentad itself is already a kind of homology, for its terms are the structure one might use in describing any action, and it is offered as a grand scheme underlying and ordering all the attributions of motives that anyone might make. The pentad is thus a sort of grand homology on which widely different texts might be compared in terms of its terms. Burke urges us to think of these terms, of "the Grammatical resources as *principles,* and of the various philosophies as *casuistries* which apply these principles to temporal situations" (xvi). One can think of these terms as homologies; there are a number of different philosophies that follow a formal pattern of attributing motive to *act* or to *scene,* for instance, and each such philosophy individually is a more focused form that supports casuistries (in which, I think, Burke's old term from *Counter-Statement* of *reindividuation* is reborn) in which the formal pattern of the grammatical term is applied to particular historical situations. Burke spends much of the book reviewing "the philosophic schools" grounded by each pentadic term, showing the range of related but different philosophies brought together by each term (127–322).

Earlier observations about the variability of homological structures may find support in the *Grammar* as well. Not only does Burke identify different philosophies with different terms of the pentad, but he also notes that the terms are ambiguous in that they tend to merge into one another. It is difficult to refer to an act without talking about an agent who is doing it, in some sort of scene, and so forth. But if we can see these terms as homologies, this means that within a given casuistry, or specific historically grounded reindividuation of the homology, lies the potential to see that specific historical circumstance as ordered by another homology grounded in a different pentadic term. This flexibility, this mutability from one homology to another, is a linguistic resource arising from the terms themselves: "what we want is *not terms that avoid ambiguity*, but *terms that clearly reveal the strategic spots at which ambiguities necessarily arise*" (xviii). A given historical situation, a given text, may thus be ordered within different homologies because both situations and texts are at heart linguistic, and language admits of being structured within different patterns: "certain formal interrelationships prevail among these terms, by reason of their role as attributes of a common ground or substance. Their participation in a common ground makes for transformability" (xix).

Certain kinds of material experience as well as texts will attribute motives according to a logic of *ratios:* combinations of two or more terms of the pentad. Burke argues that fitness or appropriate linkage among the terms of a ratio is important for both the logical, narrative consistency of attribution of motives and for rhetorical effect. He begins the *Grammar* with a focus on the scene-act ratio: "It is a principle of drama that the nature of acts and agents should be consistent with the nature of the scene" (3). We might see at least some of that consistency in terms of homology. Offering examples from Ibsen's *An Enemy of the People* as good illustrations of a scene-act ratio, Burke notes that "the correlations between scene and act are readily observable, beginning with the fact that this representative middle-class drama is enacted against a typical middle-class setting" (3). Although there may be specific signs of the middle class in both scene and act, there may also be forms or patterns that might be summed up under the heading "middle class": structures of social relationships that follow a pattern of "respectability," forms of everyday life involving office work, and so forth. That kind of formal linkage would be one way to meet Burke's dictum that "from the motivational point of view, there is implicit in the quality of a scene the quality of the action that is to take place within it" (6–7). Let us not forget that such ratios are themselves homologous with forms experienced by the audience in its material experience, and the homology between play and experience allows the play to speak to experience rhetorically.

A given ratio can itself be a homological grounding among different kinds of experiences and texts. Reviewing a wide range of examples of the scene-act and scene-agent ratios, Burke argues that "variants of the scene-agent ratio abound in typical nineteenth-century thought, so strongly given to the study of motives by the dialectical pairing of people and things" (9). Although there are likely to be several patterns that express a scene-act or scene-agent ratio, the idea of the ratio itself can work as a kind of methodological guide for finding such forms homologously linking different texts and experiences. Burke reviews ways in which different philosophies and political commentaries use terms such as "ground" or "situation," which he argues indicates a discourse linked to scenic thinking (12–13).

Burke explores the long philosophical tradition of "substance" as an ontological category (21–33). He suggests that there are different ways to define an entity so as to suggest different kinds of substance, such as geometric, familial, or directional substance (29–33). Of interest to us in this project is his description of his own method of dramatism as "dialectic substance" (33–35), within which he subsumes the other categories of substance. Dialectical substance is the symbolic dimension of human nature: "men are not only *in nature*. The cultural accretions made possible by the language motive become a 'second nature' with them" (33). Of course, where there is language there is form, and thus Burke's idea of substance is a justification for thinking about homology as fundamental and formative of human existence—as being at the heart of our "substance." The reason why formal linkage is so important is because it is the sharing of substance, of fundamental alignment and identity. Substances are "names for motives" and thus homology is an engine for the generation of shared motives (43). Comparing the uniqueness of each person's situated historicity with the shared substance of *ways of talking* about those *types* of situations, Burke observes that "each man's motivation is unique, since his situation is unique. . . . However, for all this uniqueness of the individual, there are motives and relations generic to all mankind—and these are intrinsic to human agents as a class" (103–04).

If we may think of the pentad and its ratios as groundings for homologies, Burke has some advice for us on the ontological status of homology. He argues that "men's linguistic behavior here reflects real paradoxes in the nature of the world itself" (56), not the physical world alone but the world of people's actions and attributions of motives for the actions of others. Also, "the transformations which we here study as a Grammar are not 'illusions,' but citable realities," for "nothing is more imperiously there for observation and study than the tactics people employ when they would injure or gratify one another" (57). A homology is based in symbolic behavior but no less "real" since the symbolic is a major dimension of human existence. The discovery of a homology, supported by ample evidence, is thus not a figment of the critic's imagination but a discovery of the intersection between the word and the world.

Burke's discussion of the representative anecdote is likewise a merger between a methodological calculus and a statement about how people behave symbolically. It is both a means of searching for symbolic action and the symbolic action for which we search. Burke begins his discussion nonmethodologically by discussing how people in general, not the critic, behave:

> Men seek for vocabularies that will be faithful *reflections* of reality. To this end they must develop vocabularies that are *selections* of reality. And any selection of reality must, in certain circumstances, function as a *deflection* of reality. Insofar as the vocabulary meets the needs of reflection, we can say that it has the necessary scope. In its selectivity, it is a reduction. Its scope and reduction become a deflection when the given termi-

nology, or calculus, is not suited to the subject matter which it is designed
to calculate. (59)

Burke then argues that his method of "dramatism suggests a procedure
to be followed in the development of a given calculus, or terminology. It
involves the search for a 'representative anecdote,' to be used as a form in
conformity with which the vocabulary is constructed" (59). He is not
specifying whether it is the general run of "men" who use a representative anecdote in making a vocabulary, or the critic who would use such
a thing in discovering the vocabulary used by others. I think that ambiguity is strategic; it is both, and when a critic suggests a representative
anecdote underlying experience or discourse, the ambiguity suggests
that the anecdote is in some sense "really" being used by a community
of speakers and actors to order their experience.

   Note that in the previously cited passage, Burke describes the representative anecdote as a "form." I have earlier explored the ways in which
critics might use the representative anecdote as a method for exploring
formal patterns that are ordering different discourses, although I did not
use the term *homology* ("The Representative" and "Burke's Representative"). Nevertheless, the method is thoroughly homological. It involves
identifying an abstract, formal story form and then showing how that
form is manifest across different discourses. For instance, this story, "A
stranger comes among us, showing strange powers. The stranger is persecuted. The stranger is utterly changed, and in the process changes
us," is a representative anecdote underlying quite a few films, television
shows, plays, and novels. It is, of course, the Christ myth, and is a useful
critical device for showing how those films, shows, plays, and novels appeal because of their participation in that myth.

   Burke's ambiguity as to who uses, discovers, or generates the representative anecdote in constructing discourses strengthens the hand of
the critic, for if one finds sufficiently strong evidence of discourse following the form of an anecdote in "real life," one is justified in saying
that the anecdote identifies a form that was "really" generative of that
discourse, whether intentionally or not. The critic's explicit articulation
of the anecdote helps critic and audience to *see* the form that was "really
there" all along. The more discourse is brought into alignment with the
anecdote, the stronger the influence of the form that it suggests.

The representative anecdote is clearly formal. We see in the quoted passage that it is a "reduction" of complexity, as is all abstraction and all form. As a generator of more elaborate symbolic structures, the "calculus" that is the anecdote "must also possess simplicity, in that it is broadly a reduction of the subject-matter" (60). In simplifying, the anecdote "is in a sense a *summation*, containing implicitly what the system that is developed from it contains explicitly" (60). The particular vocabularies that are reindividuations of an anecdote are thus elaborations upon it, and at a lower level of abstraction. Locating a specific vocabulary within the abstract form described by an anecdote is also a choice of *circumference*. Burke suggests that "the choice of circumference for the scene in terms of which a given act is to be located will have a corresponding effect upon the interpretation of the act itself" (77). This is clearly true in terms of everyday life: it makes a difference whether one sees one's actions as "feeding Jane, this homeless person" or as "doing God's work," a difference based on different circumferences. A homology then suggests a wide, and a formal, circumference within which to understand particular acts, whether material or discursive.

We need not review all of Burke's explanation of "the philosophic schools" and how they feature terms of the pentad. By way of example, we might note that Burke equates "scene" with the general philosophy of materialism (128). A scenic orientation is shown to ground the thinking of a wide range of thinkers, as different as Hobbes, Spinoza, and Darwin, yet united by their shared substance of a featuring of scene. The core of this homology is described as "explaining the *internal* in terms of *external* conditions" (134). The "external" is actually a formal pattern underlying the state, nature, God's will, or anything else that is conceived of as external to the individual's action, lying outside the agent's intention and motivation. All of the terms of the pentad are considered in this way, as extended in forms that homologically undergird and thus link different thinkers into five "philosophical schools."

Picking up the theme of the representative anecdote again late in the *Grammar*, Burke discusses the idea of *constitutions* as documents embodying the will of groups of people, underlying social and political structures (323). His purpose here is not merely to discuss constitutions but to discuss those discursive structures underlying human relations, and thinking of such discursive structures as if they were constitutions helps us to understand how the structures work.

A constitution is a kind of representative anecdote, he argues, "some anecdote *summational* in character, some anecdote *wherein human relations grandly converge*" (324). A constitution is a calculus for naming and defining particular situations insofar as it suggests "what coordinates one will think by" (367). This is homological language, for it suggests the idea of a constitution as an anecdote—which as we discussed earlier can be understood as a homological structure—underlying many different laws and enactments of laws across time and space in a given society. In his usually self-reflective manner, Burke considers other anecdotes he might have used to describe a structure underpinning the acts of an entire society. He considers the railroad terminal (326–27) and total war (328–30) as candidates but rejects them as insufficiently representative and complete.

The constitution is also preferable as an anecdote, though, because it is "admonitory" (330–31). It is in the form of being "addressed" from one person to another (360). It embodies "a set of motives" (342). It is an "agonistic instrument" and thus names an "opponent" (357). In expressing all these characteristics, let us remember that Burke is in effect arguing that the discursive structures underlying human relations are rhetorical. Such rhetorically addressed, admonitory structures must underlie relations across time and space, just as the United States Constitution undergirds legal relationships across time and space. To sum up in homological terms, Burke is arguing that homological structures with rhetorical (admonitory) power undergird organized human relations. Such relations may be on the level of a marriage, a family, an organization, a city, or a whole nation. The discursive structure that holds those relationships together, conceived of as a constitution, is a formal structure that orders relationships along shared patterns. We are justified in this homological thinking by one of Burke's several overlapping meanings of the constitution as "that form of being, or structure and connection of parts, which constitutes and characterizes a system or body" (341). Note that the constitution is not the body itself but the form or structure.

Of course, like any structure of motivations, a constitution contains within its unified form the possibility for conflict and contradiction (349). These arise as the general form of motivations is applied to particular circumstances. Contradictions are unavoidable as one moves from constitution to particular laws or particular cases: "The law that frustrates one wish in the Constitution will, by the same token, gratify another" (378). The U.S. Constitution as a formal statement seems not to be contradictory, until its application in particular historical circumstances brings two or more of its components into conflict with each other.

Thinking homologically, we might understand this paradox of constitutions if we return to the argument in *Counter-Statement* that fundamental forms are reindividuated in ways that express the particular historical situations and the "ideology" of those experiencing the reindividuation. In moving down a level of abstraction from homology into particular experiences and texts, conflicts and contradictions may arise. For instance, the Christ myth that I identified earlier contains few or no conflicts or contradictions at the purely formal, abstract level: a stranger comes among us with strange powers, is persecuted, is changed, and in changing likewise changes us. It is when that form is reindividuated in a particular text in which the Christ persona is embodied in a European body that people of, say, Asian descent may wonder what their connection is to this person or how this person can change them. That contradiction is "contained" within the resources of the form, since the form identifies the element of a "stranger," who must, when embodied (reindividuated) be of one ethnic background or another. Each text or experience that embodies a homology thus entails its own ideological struggles and contradictions that arise from that embodiment in history.

As noted from the start, Burke does not use the term *homology* in his work, certainly not in the way I use it here. Yet I believe that we can see many of his ideas as expressing that concept and as enriching our understanding of it. Burke is far from alone in using ideas that are, explicitly or implicitly, homological. Having shown that many of his ideas can be seen from a perspective of homology, I will now pull together the discussion so far and attempt to outline some general principles and methods for homology as an instrument of critique. What follows is a perspective centrally informed by but not limited to Burke's method and philosophy.

Some Methodological Principles
for Rhetorical Homologies

In sum:

Innate within human nature is the necessity to transform each momentary sensation into sensation of a particular sort, in other words, into perceptions. Perceptions are then the basis for even more abstract sortings in cognition, emotion, aesthetics, and all our other thought processes. An innate necessity to sort, to abstract, does not mean that there is any innate necessity to abstract in any particular way. But neither do people abstract, or sort, willy-nilly or in largely idiosyncratic ways (although some may do so to some extent). Instead, people create perceptions and cognitions by processes of abstraction that are guided by socially shared mechanisms. Language and other sign systems are the material manifestations of these socially shared mechanisms, since language and other signs are rarely if ever individual—they are primarily socially shared. Language and society partially determine each other, as societies renew themselves on a foundation of existing discourses, altering and creating discourses in the process of renewal. So as we learn to use the signs held by our social groups, we learn to abstract and to sort in socially shared ways. And since we are enrolled in different, sometimes conflicting social groups—and since it is a technical characteristic of signs that they entail incomplete and contradictory signification— how we sort or abstract is always a site of struggle, partially determined by social structures, influenced by history and ideology.

This process of sorting and abstracting is the exercise of our capacity for *form*, which is innate in human nature. Form is how we turn sensation into a world of consciousness for ourselves in socially shared but not completely determinant ways. Since form is present from the inception of any cognition or perception in that it is entailed in abstraction or sorting, the distinction between form and content is relative though not trivial. Content or information is what we get in the historical, situated, less or least abstracted moment; form is what we get from the more or most abstracted patterns that cut across several historical, situated moments.

Homology is a formal linkage among two or more kinds of experience. It is a situation in which two or more kinds of experience appear or can be shown to be structured according to the same pattern in some important particulars of their material manifestations. In one sense, homology is always present wherever form is, since as in my argument presented earlier, every perception is already the result of more than one unique experience brought together cognitively as the same *sort* of experience. I recognize this thing falling past my window as a leaf because it is of the same sort as millions of other falling-leaf experiences I have had; in that sense they are homologous. This level of homology is important because it emphasizes the importance of form in basic cognition, but it is not necessarily interesting—it is not what the study of homologies is "for," it does not tell us interesting things about the world. For that we must consider more abstract levels of homology.

Any enrollment of particular sensations into a sort is a kind of linkage: it says that this experience and that experience are in important ways the same. To see two things as of the same type is to say that one may react to them in similar ways, that one might have the same motivations toward them. For purposes of understanding how people act and react, experiences of the same sort are more or less interchangeable. If I want to know how you will react to a black and red spider three inches across, nearly any spider of that sort will do to tell me how you construct and react to this particular sort of experience. If I understand a category, a sorting, of experiences that underlies your actions and reactions, I can not only explain why you do as you do in the past and present, I can to some extent predict how you will react to members of that sort in the future. We must be cautious here not to generalize too easily; history enters in and may alter how you react to large red and black spiders in the future, or in particular instances. Sorting is an ongoing process that is connected to the world, and is thus always a site of struggle over how individuals deal with their particular circumstances and how socially held instruments of sorting (form, language) influence our sorting. But taking history into consideration, knowledge of the patterns that you use in linking together experiences into the category of "large, dangerous, red and black spiders" helps me to understand something of how you act and how you will act.

Sometimes the categories, the forms, with which people make sense of the world are far-flung in the sense that they order together rather disparate experiences. This is the kind of homology that is theoretically interesting, and this is the focus of this study. As an example, in one previous study I showed that the content of haunted house movies, the experience of sitting in a movie theater, and certain "real life" experiences all manifested the same formal pattern of disjunction in time and space ("Electric"). Such a claim asserts a formal linkage among disparate experiences: texts, experiences of a medium of communication, social and work experiences, and so forth. To what end? What "good" did it do to identify a formal pattern that sorted together such far-flung elements? In other words, what knowledge is revealed by identifying a homology?

I want to answer that question by proposing a principle of *vulnerability*. To link experiences together formally is to make them vulnerable to one another. What "happens" with one kind of experience can thus affect the other experiences because they are vulnerable to influence from one another. The "affect" is precisely in the heads of the people who do the experiencing; if one experience is "affected" by another we are really saying that how I think about, how I formally construct one experience affects how I think about and formally order another experience. Vulnerability means that elements ordered together in homology have to do with one another, even if out of our awareness. I am then proposing that in rhetorical homologies, the experience of discourse is the key experience, for the form(s) manifested by a discourse anchor the ways in which people organize other, extradiscursive experiences.

I propose that the "payoff" to identifying a homology is the assertion of a relationship of vulnerability among the disparate experiences that are arrayed according to the homology. Vulnerability is but another way of saying that one experience may have *rhetorical* effects on how people perceive and order another experience or group of experiences if they are formally linked. Homology among widely, interestingly different experiences, grounded in discursive structures, is thus rhetorical homology. When we think of homology rhetorically, we are thinking of how the vulnerabilities among the experiences within a formal pattern channel rhetorical effect in the dimension of how people create, order, and understand the experiences. Since a rhetorical homology presumes a discursive mechanism of formal linkage, it must also presume that discursive manipulation (which is rhetoric) may alter how the elements in the homology are understood (which is a rhetorical effect).

Think of a homology then as *Star Trek*'s "Borg," in which whatever happens to one member of the group will affect the knowledge and per-spectives of every other member. All members of a rhetorical homology are linked together by the guiding intelligence (structure) of the discur-sive form that organizes them. Think of the formal pattern of the Christ myth as the grounding of such a "Borg," yet the ways in which any par-ticular iteration of the form is crafted, how it is received, the historical circumstances within which it is perceived to be received, all shift (even if minutely) the way in which the whole form and its other iterations are understood. At one level, this vulnerability is always happening in the sense that each new experience that fits a formal pattern alters the pat-tern, even if only slightly. In this way our views of the world grow; if I have a prejudice against donkeys, but gradually each new donkey I en-counter is more pleasant and agreeable to me, then the form by which I used to manifest donkeys as disagreeable animals begins to shift. Our donkey discourses shift so as to both reflect and regenerate this shifting homology.

Vulnerability, or the construction of a homology linking disparate experiences and texts, is a rhetorical construction and thus a site of struggle. For instance, at this writing there has for years been a string of news stories about mysterious, deadly illnesses that come from the third world and other similar locations: monkeypox, West Nile virus, and Ebola virus from Africa; SARS from China; hantavirus from the Navajo Southwest. The principle of rhetorical homology that I am proposing here insists that we do not simply "have" these illnesses but that news reports will be an ongoing site of struggle as to which sort of discourse is or can be homologous with these illnesses. Our choice of discourse is a choice of how to see other experiences, with political, social, *rhetorical* consequences. Among numerous possibilities, for instance, I can imag-ine that the illnesses might be talked about, portrayed, as homologous with histories (history here understood as an amalgam of what hap-pens and how we talk about what happens) of dangerous, exotic Oth-ers coming to a "pure" (White) American land—or—I can imagine that the illnesses might be portrayed as a just retribution against a rapa-cious (White) American land that has plundered and enslaved Others all over the world. Are the illnesses discursively bent toward imperialism or toward guilt? That is a question of "vulnerability." There is rhetori-cal struggle then over, literally, what to *make* of these illnesses at the same stroke that we struggle over which *sort* of discourses to array them within.

Explanation of the rhetorical results of homological linkage, enabled by vulnerability, must always be specific and local, in the time-honored tradition of rhetorical analysis. But also in the same tradition, one might propose certain principles for how the critical analysis of the rhetoric of homology proceeds. I propose to offer some principles that are not intended to be exhaustive or exclusive, and that are here presented as simply as possible so as to enable wide, flexible, and creative application. I take the key question to be, how is the discovery of a homology also the discovery of a mechanism of rhetorical influence by way of vulnerability? Or, what should one look for as the workings of the vulnerability principle within a homology so as to change how people see and manifest the world?

First, the critic looks for disparate experiences that appear to be ordered together by discursive structures. A given action, object, or event may fall into more than one, but probably not an infinite number, of such structures. The homology is an achieved or asserted formal structure enrolling both discourse and nondiscursive experiences. This multiplicity of homology is not a scandal given a multiplicity of discursive structures in the world. So the critic's assertion of a homology is understood not to exhaust the alternative formal resonances of which any given part of the homology is capable.

The critic takes care to identify the broad outline of the homology. Since a rhetorical homology is always grounded in a discursive structure, the homological pattern will often be in narrative form, albeit at an abstract level. Other forms the homology might take would include tropes, patterns of exigence and response, structures of alliance, opposition, domination and subordination, or transformation and the like. A study might identify recent outer space films and Western movies as formally linked because of structures of characters, place, and tension rather than because of plot developments, for instance. Or a homology might be identified based on the mechanisms of a particular rhetorical device. For example, a study might find the ironic stance played out in many texts and experiences in today's culture. We shall see that the later chapters in this book illustrate different kinds of rhetorical homologies.

Second, the critic looks for significant inclusions and exclusions within the formal set defined by the homology. Such inclusions and exclusions might happen systematically as the result of rhetorical interventions or they might happen as the byproduct of unintentional historical developments. Once an inclusion or exclusion begins to take hold formally, it begins to have its own rhetorical effects. As a very simple example, what new rhetorical structure is created if an office supervisor who has been acting "like a manager" begins to act "like a priest"? If the move "takes," what possibilities for rhetorical influence are created by the reorganized office homology?

Take the haunted house study I cited earlier as an example. For centuries, the content of haunted house stories (novels, plays) was homologous with disjunctions in time and space in material experience. A novel's depiction of a ghost from the past reappearing in the present would thus be homologous with the presence of an irremediable reactionary in an office, family, or social group; both experiences follow the pattern of the past appearing disconcertingly in the present. But the development of cinema changed the homology by excluding a significant new class of experiences into that pattern, into the sorting: the experiences of sitting in a movie theater. Stories and material experiences then became vulnerable to the influence of such experiences, which were linked by way of the homology. As my earlier study proposed, experiencing a haunted house story *and* the movie theater at the same time intensified the linkage to, the vulnerability of, and thus the rhetorical effects upon how people should act in those "real life" material experiences.

Third, the critic looks for the ways in which the "content" of specific experiences ordered by a homology is transferred by the vulnerability created through formal linkage to other members of the homology (this consideration is similar to Burke's discussion of "ramifications"). As noted earlier, suppose the content of a specific iteration of the Christ myth shows a dark-skinned "Christ" (e.g., *The Brother from Another Planet*). A linkage is suggested to other experiences of dark-skinned people by way of a new inclusion into the set. What might be the effect upon a hitherto racist audience member seeing a revered form (the Christ myth) including this particular iteration of a dark-skinned Christ, and how might that affect other experiences of dark-skinned people for our hypothetical racist, as those other experiences become now linked into the set? Content may have rhetorical effect in many different ways, so let me suggest another example without intending to exhaust the effects content may have. In my haunted house movie study, I argued that the content of different films varied in terms of the answers it gave to people who might be experiencing disjunctions of time and space in material experience. Some films cautioned the audience to avoid such disjunctions because they spelled certain doom (everyone in the house is destroyed). Some films encouraged the audience to confront such disjunctions because they can be overcome (the ghosts are vanquished). Some films warned the audience that disjunction cannot be overcome but can be avoided (the haunted escape the house successfully). Each film thus has rhetorical effect upon how people confront the material experiences of disjunction they are experiencing, and the connection between film and experience, intensified by the experience of the medium within the same homology, is enabled by the homology.

Fourth, the critic may consider ways in which the accretions of history as well as discursive structural changes alter the homology. Rhetorical changes can occur intentionally or as a byproduct of history in the homology itself, in the form or pattern and variations that are perceived to be still the "same" pattern. This is not the same thing as the content of a specific iteration having rhetorical effect, it is the accumulated effect of a long shifting of the whole homology. Haunted house stories have for centuries featured the spirits of dead humans so consistently that the "posthuman" ghost is part of the original homology. What happens as history begins to suggest the inclusion of technological ghosts? For instance, the many science fiction novels of William Gibson quite frequently use the term "ghost" or "spirit" to refer to cyber-entities (e.g., *Neuromancer, Count Zero, Mona Lisa Overdrive*). If the commercial success of his novels causes people to reorder the discursive pattern of ghost stories so as to include the nonhuman as permissible ghosts, what effect does that have on the patterns of vulnerability and influence created for any particular experience within the shifting homology?

These four principles are enough to get us started, and they are not intended to be the last word in rhetorical homologies, neither are they intended to be the sine qua non of homological criticism; if one of these principles seems not useful, one should not entertain it. Each principle is intended to encourage the critic to look both toward homology and toward the politics and history of specific iterations of form that break out in concrete material experiences. Such sites of real historical struggle have their own effects on other such experiences as well as on the homological structures within which other, perhaps future, experiences are understood—just as homological structures have effects on the ways in which the particular and historical is understood. With this intentionally loose set of guidelines in mind, let me now turn toward a series of studies in rhetorical homology that I hope will prove instructive as to the virtues of this way of thinking.

What follows are six chapters illustrating the use of rhetorical homology as a tool of rhetorical criticism. The next two chapters study homologies that order material experiences and discourses. Chapter two points to a particular kind of scene that one may find in a wide range of television and films, from old Laurel and Hardy films to today's professional wrestling: the ritual receiving of injury. The chapter identifies the rhetorical effects of episodes that manifest this enduring homology. Ritual injury expressed in these texts is homologous with, and thus rhetorically addresses, real injuries suffered in material experience. Chapter three argues that a venerable myth of the racial history of the United States, held and propagated largely by European Americans, is a homology underlying many discourses and experiences. The chapter identifies the myth at work in a film, *The Horse Whisperer*, that actually shows very few people of color. The chapter illustrates the importance of studying form over content if one wants to appreciate all the nuances of discourse.

Chapter four studies the rhetorical dynamics of a group of signs I call The Chair, dynamics in which signs from the tribe of Chair are used to signal power arrangements in experience as well as in discourse. The study examines ways in which the film *Get on the Bus* uses those discursive dynamics both within the film and in creating a physical experience for the audience. Going beyond the first two critical application chapters, this study of *Get on the Bus* includes experiences of a specific medium, film, as also structured by the homology at work.

Chapters five, six, and seven study tiers or levels of homology, in which patterns at different levels of abstraction interlock to structure rhetorical experiences. Chapter five argues that there are homologies between the dominant rhetorics of a period, in theory and in practice, and dominant weapons. The chapter pairs the Renaissance rhetorics of Castiglione and Machiavelli with the stiletto, the Enlightenment rhetorics of Locke and Campbell with the flintlock musket, and today's rhetorics of popular culture with the semi-automatic pistol. Fundamental structures of transformation are identified as the discursive grounding for these homologies that encompass material experience, theory about those experiences, and the different but related experiences of war, assassination, and murder.

Chapter six, written with Dr. Detine Bowers, identifies Oprah Winfrey and Sojourner Truth as embodying the mythic character of the Wise Woman. The chapter raises the question of how one can be a Wise Woman in an age of mass mediation, as Winfrey is certainly in that situation now and Truth emerged as a public figure early in the age of mass mediation. The rhetorical device of contradiction, we argue, is key to making that discursive structure work under those conditions. The chapter shows how discursive responses to similar exigencies are manifested in similar patterns of strategies even across time and place.

Chapter seven studies the discursive strategy of perfection as explained by Kenneth Burke, and argues that this linguistic mechanism provides a homological structure that emerges under certain conditions. Specifically, the chapter identifies presidential crises as periods in which anxiety over the head of state are expressed in discourses of perfection. The chapter studies the ways in which discursive responses to similar exigencies are understood in terms of the pattern of a single complex trope, that of teleological metaphors. A final chapter summarizes conclusions arrived at concerning homologies and explores some implications of those conclusions.

2

Stand and Receive
Ritual Injury in Media Martyrdoms

In the 2002 film *Drumline,* the student Devon, newly arrived from Harlem on the campus of "Atlanta A&T University," earns a place in the school's marching band. He is in the celebrated heart of the band, the *drumline.* These bands, significant social institutions at African American universities, engage in fierce competition with one another. These competitions involve the performance of intricate marching patterns and musical numbers on the football field. Sometimes the film depicts two bands or two drumlines on the field at the same time in head-to-head competition. In what is often the climax of the competition, two drumlines face each other like ranks of eighteenth-century soldiers on the field of battle. One drumline performs a high energy, complex pattern of drumming and movement while its enemy stands at attention. Then the other drumline attempts to top the first effort.

Twice in this film a remarkable scene is played out: one drumline, beating drums for all it's worth, comes closer and closer to the other line, which stands ramrod stiff at attention, eyes glaring at the approaching enemy. Then an invisible line between the two ranks is broken, and *the advancing drumline comes close enough to play upon its enemy's drums.* One would think that the drumline that has suffered this invasion would refuse it, push away the intruder, or move their drums aside to make this violation of space impossible. But it does not. Continuing to stand at stiff, stoic attention, the invaded drumline accepts this indignity un-moved, until the invaders finish with a mighty flourish and withdraw.

A similar scene is found in an earlier film, *The Longest Yard*. Actor Burt Reynolds portrays former professional football player Paul Crewe, in jail for auto theft and resisting arrest. Crewe's fame as a former Na-tional Football League player earns him the attention and sometimes the enmity of other inmates, some of whom test his strength and cour-age. In one scene, Crewe and a gang of inmates are up to their ankles in a swamp, shoveling mud and muck. One unfriendly inmate empties his shovel into Crewe's boot. The other inmates laugh and gather around to see the show. Crewe quietly looks down at his oozing boot, then silently picks up his own shovelful of mud and carefully puts the load into his antagonist's boot. The man can see it coming, but he does nothing to move out of the way, to fend off Crewe's shovel with his own, or to pre-vent this attack in any way. He nods imperceptibly as if to acknowledge the blow, then quietly and methodically proceeds to escalate the level of attack. Before long, each man is covered with mud and filth, their clothes are filled with the stuff, but each has taken his shovelsful with quiet dignity and returned the same to the other man with careful de-liberation. At no point does either man pull away, jump to one side, or run off. And at no point does either man shout, curse, or call out in pro-test. Each movement is slow and calculated, both the giving and the tak-ing of an injury done with a sense of occasion. For this brief moment, they have entered a space of exchanging and receiving blows with grace and gravity—with the methodical procedures of ritual.

The episodes in these two films portray an unworldly willingness to stand and receive offense. The offense is given and taken with cere-mony. Were someone to come at you or me in "real life" with a shovelful of swamp muck, we would run, protest, or fight back. The mannered taking and receiving of assaults, whether on one's person or on one's drum, happens largely in discourse, not material experience, as in the examples in these two films. Other examples that come to mind from the movies would be quite a few of the old Stan Laurel and Oliver Hardy movies, in which one or the other of "the boys," exasperated beyond all telling at the incompetence of his partner, steps into this separate space of slow, measured, gestured violence—running a paintbrush up a suit,

cutting off a tie, carefully placing a pie upon a face—and the victim receives this injury with quiet pomp and circumstance. What is going
on here?

This chapter develops the theme that discourses of ritual injury
provide audiences with discursive models of how to understand and
respond to real, everyday injury. The everyday slings and arrows that
people encounter at home and work are mirrored in and transformed by
discourses of ritual injury. Sometimes the mirroring moves the nature
of the injury "up" to depict it as a kind of saintly martyrdom, and sometimes the nature of the injury moves "down" into slapstick and burlesque. But all discourses of ritual injury provide audiences with different ways to transform the insults they received at the office or before the
hearth into a "sacred" space of ritual where the injury may be tran-
scended, absorbed, and overcome symbolically. Discourse of ritual injury is made homologous with material experiences of real injury so
that discourse may advise an audience rhetorically on how to handle the
contingencies of everyday trauma.

The homology studied here binds together a wide collection of discourse, stretching from stories of saints to televised professional wres-
tlers. This chapter illustrates the ways in which the ramifications of
content may have a rhetorical effect as they ride in on the back of form.
As the discursive form of ritual injury moves from real martyrdom to
slapstick through the inner city to the grotesque of the Worldwide Wrestling Association, we will find that the nature of each manifestation
of the form brings a different rhetorical emphasis to the experience of
the text. But we can also then see how the participation of these texts in
a homology influences the overall structure, each adding its own gravi-
tational weight to the form's ongoing push into the future.

I want to show how a wide range of discourses and material experiences are structured by a homology of receiving ritual injury. Beginning
with no received theory but instead working "outward" from examples, I
hope to show with disparate texts how a similar structure underlies different discourses as well as everyday experiences. I will trace the manifestations of the homology in texts depicting Christian martyrs, in Laurel
and Hardy films, in studies of "playing the dozens" or "signifying," and
in televised professional wrestling.

Christian Martyrs

Discourses of martyrdom are venerable and are likely found in every culture. Since the discourses we are examining are within Western culture, I will focus on the Christian tradition of martyr stories. In tales of Christian martyrs we find strong homologies with the other depictions of ritual injuries under investigation here. Understanding what is said about martyrdom can help us to understand the homology ordering several different kinds of texts. I will offer some examples from *Fox's Book of Martyrs*, (by Miles Stanford, which first appeared in the sixteenth century and has undergone several transformations and updating since then. This is a tale of martyrdom told from a Church of England perspective; Catholic martyr Sir Thomas More gets short shrift. A more recent volume is DC Talk's *Jesus Freaks*, a contemporary account of Christian martyrs of all persuasions throughout the centuries.

Both of these books support a reading of martyrdom, the calm reception of injury, as moral acts grounded in a long history of such sacrifices. *Jesus Freaks*, covering a wider range of history, intersperses recent with ancient martyrdoms, structurally conveying a sense of a form of injury that cuts across time. *Fox's Book* proceeds in chronological order, but in that way it still unifies the tales of 1,800 years of martyrs. Our interest of course is not with the actual injuries or martyrdoms themselves so much as with the telling of them. What we find in these stories illuminates our understanding of later, secular manifestations of the homologies.

The martyrdoms suffered by these saints grow out of ordinary, everyday contexts. The saints are going about their business, or they are quietly professing their faith, and they are taken up by civil or religious authorities. The ritual injury they suffer is interwoven with their real but ordinary sufferings. Of course, much of the intent of these stories is to urge readers to live saintly lives as well, so we must understand the martyr tales in the context of offering advice for everyday living. Showing how martyrdom grows out of the ordinary lives of plain people is a way of connecting ritual injury with everyday injury. It offers a discursive remedy for quotidian pain by moving it to the terrain of ritual.

Perhaps it goes without saying that all the martyrs depicted in these books lead blameless lives and are brought to their sufferings for that very reason, that they hold fast to a truth that is out of fashion with the religious, secular, or civil authorities of their day. As *Fox's Book* said of William Hunter, "he yielded up his life for the truth" (220). Someone has the power to do serious bodily harm to the martyr, and the martyr has the opportunity to appease that power by recanting truth. But the martyr refuses to do so, and is doomed in this world so as to triumph in the next. The acceptance of martyrdom is a subversion of established power so as to achieve a different kind of power by different means. Understanding this, most martyrs seem eager to receive the empowerment that comes with injury; scorning an offer of mercy, Mrs. Cicely Ormes "replied, (perhaps with more shrewdness than he expected,) that however great his desire might be to spare her sinful flesh, it could not equal her inclination to surrender it up in so great a quarrel" (Stanford, 264). Chinese martyr Gao Feng is clearly engaged in a struggle with power as his captors torment him, "but he didn't give up. They never broke his spirit" (Talk, 189).

Peter Ackerman and Jack DuVall's review of twentieth-century non-violent conflict, although it is not concerned exclusively with Christian martyrdom, affirms the idea that the ritualized, patient reception of injury is a move in a power struggle: "Those who used nonviolent action in our stories did not come to make peace. They came to fight" (5). The reception of blows in the struggles they analyze was not casual, it was calculated and performative. Civil rights activists in the American South, for instance, "In role-playing exercises . . . practiced taking physical and verbal abuse without striking back" (307). The power being struggled over is closely connected to the everyday hurts the martyrs suffer. Challenging power is a way of remedying their injuries.

Ritual injury is thus a sign of a guerrilla tactic whereby the weak overcome the strong discursively. The very acceptance of the injury with resignation and calm, even gladness, is key to the move around established power and the seizing of an alternative empowerment. Refusing injury, leaping out of the way, or fighting back meets power on its own terrain, acknowledging the grievousness of the injury. Injury is thus ritualized because it is part of a formula for calling down alternative forms of empowerment.

The one receiving an injury transcends the moment of insult by making the reception of attack a ritual. It is the unexpected response of quiet acceptance rather than the sudden reflex of defense, the performed showing of a stoic face, that makes the public presentation of a received injury into a different kind of gesture, into a ritual. Showing marks of the saint's patience, the victim ritualizes what would otherwise be an ordinary attack by moving the event onto the plain of martyrdom, which is a plain different from the mere suffering of everyday life. The "sacred space" (Eliade) into which the victim moves the attack empowers the victim even as it makes the reception of pain a ritual in sacred space. Thus, even the attacker, who is not the martyr and not really empowered, is pictured as engaging in a deliberate, gestured violence that mirrors the deliberate performance of ritual.

In their analysis of nonviolent action, Ackerman and DuVall assert that "it works by identifying an opponent's vulnerabilities and taking away his ability to maintain control" (494). The ritual acceptance of injury is closely connected to this logic, for in refusing to refuse the injury, the injured in these examples move an ordinary assault onto the space of a ritual that empowers them. One could argue that in examples such as Laurel and Hardy, where careful injuries are both accepted and as carefully returned, it is the mannered pace of the returned injury that reinforces the claim to a sacred ritual space established in the mannered pace of receiving injury in the first place.

Fox's Book describes the most exquisite tortures that bygone eras could produce, and the calm acceptance of them by martyrs. Constantia Bellione, an Italian martyr of the seventeenth century, refused to accept Catholicism. As a result, "the priest then ordered slices of her flesh to be cut off from several parts of her body"—and then we see the crucial move to a different, ritual plain—"which cruelty she bore with the most singular patience" (115). The story of the martyrdom of Dr. Rowland Taylor during the reign of Queen Mary I has one passage that is reminiscent of the ritual injuries in Laurel and Hardy films. The martyrdom begins in physically harmless, ritualistic fashion: "Bonner came to degrade him, bringing with him such ornaments as appertained to the massing mummery" (217). One can see Bonner carefully laying upon Taylor the vestments and insignia of Catholic ritual, and Taylor calmly standing and receiving them upon his body: an eighteenth-century Stan and Ollie. Worse trials are to follow of course, but "all the way Dr. Taylor was joyful and merry" (218). Arriving at the site of execution, "he went to the stake and kissed it." He suffers tortures and indignities before the flames engulf him, and all the while "he stood still without either crying or moving" (219). *Jesus Freaks* describes the trials of Private Moiseyev, who is made to stand outside in the Moscow winter: "How could he stand such cold?" (33). Worse injuries follow: "His commanders continued to interrogate him, trying to get him to deny Jesus. They put him in refrigerated cells. They clothed him in a special rubber suit, into which they pumped air until his chest was so compressed he scarcely could breathe" (34). But he patiently endures all. John Jue Han Ding must sustain one injury after another, being covered in "human waste," having to eat his food from the floor "through soiled lips," and so forth (271). The otherworldly endurance of such assaults makes martyrdoms into ritual performances rather than mere everyday sufferings.

The theme of stoic acceptance of injury pervades the martyrdoms in *Fox's Book*. Dr. Robert Farrar "most constantly sustained the torments of the fire" (221). The Reverend George Marsh "suffered great extremity, which notwithstanding he bore with Christian fortitude" and, at the end, "died gloriously patient" (224)—the incongruity of that last word in the face of torture capturing the essence of resignation that is key in ritual injury. Similarly, the Reverend John Bradford and an apprentice, John Leaf, endure the stake "like two lambs, without any alteration of their countenances, hoping to obtain that prize they had long run for" (229). Rose Munt suffers a "lighted candle under her hand, burning it crosswise on the back, until the tendons divided from the flesh" yet "she endured his rage unmoved" and invited further injury: "She asked him to begin at her feet or head" (260). Mrs. Cicely Ormes embraces the stake with, "Welcome, thou cross of Christ" and while burning "uttered no sigh of pain" (265).

Jesus Freaks describes the serial torments of Nikolai Khamara in Soviet Russia. Khamara's pastor will not betray his fellow Christians, so one of his parishioners, Khamara, is brought before him:

> The captain said, "We will gouge out Khamara's eyes." . . . The pastor could not bear it. He cried to Khamara, "How can I look at this? You will be blind!" Khamara replied, "when my eyes are taken away from me, I will see more beauty than I see with these eyes. I will see the Savior." . . .

When he had finished, seeing that the pastor had not yet given them the information they wanted, the captain turned to the pastor again and said, "If you do not betray your church, we will cut out Khamara's tongue." In despair, the pastor cried, "What should I do?" Khamara's last words were, "Praise the Lord Jesus Christ. I have said the highest words that can be said. Now, if you wish, you can cut out my tongue." Khamara died a martyr's death. (78)

Khamara is not only poised and accepting of terrible injury but is also able to compose affecting speeches on the brink of death. Likewise, Chieu-Chin-Hsiu and Ho-Hsiu-Tzu, during the Red Guard era, approach death "as pale but beautiful beyond belief; infinitely sad but sweet" (109). Pastor Kim and his congregation in North Korea endure first the hanging of all their children and then a slow death beneath a steamroller, during which torture they join in singing uplifting songs (124). Liuba Ganevskaya "patiently suffered" torture, starvation, and beatings in her Soviet jail cell (157). "Ten Christians" in China during the Red Guard era "were smiling" as they were "bound and beaten," and "their spirit and appearance were so lively and gracious that many were led to believe in Jesus by their example" (160). Missionary Jackie Hamill is "raped repeatedly" in prison, but "her face did not show panic, revulsion, or hatred, but glowed with the brightness of God's light" (226).

Most of the martyrdoms described are, of course, one way. There is no exchange of ritual injuries. But often a dialogue between martyr and persecutor is depicted that seems to follow the form of exchange in other discourses. *Fox's Book* depicts this tit for tat:

Before they proceeded to this extremity, the bishop proposed that prayer should be said for this conversion. "This," said White, "is like a godly bishop, and if your request be godly and right, and you pray as you ought, no doubt God will hear you; pray you, therefore to your God, and I will pray to my God." After the bishop and his party had done praying, he asked Rawlins if he would now revoke. "You find," said the latter, "your prayer is not granted, for I remain the same; and God will strengthen me in support of this truth." After this, the bishop tried what saying Mass would do; but Rawlins called all the people to witness that he did not bow down to the host. (221–22)

Rawlins eventually goes to the fire, "in which flame this good man bathed his hands so long, until such time as the sinews shrank, and the fat dropped away" (222), all the while without a murmur.

Stories of martyrdom reflect an unreal patience during torture that makes the injury into a moment of ritual. Where ordinary mortals might struggle or curse, saints go to their dooms with measured speech and deliberate gesture—the pious admonition to the crowd, the ostentatious kissing of the stake. These descriptions of unworldly, performative gestures are descriptions of ritual transformations of injury. The discourses do promise successful ritual resolution of every injury because they depict the saints completing their ultimate ritual injuries with demonstrations of peace and triumph. We turn now to twentieth-century depictions of ritual injury emerging from much more mundane trials in the films of Laurel and Hardy.

Two Laurel and Hardy Films

Stan Laurel and Oliver Hardy are not saints. More often than not they are pictured as ordinary, working-class stiffs with the same mixture of greed, kindness, diligence, laziness, and violence that one may find in anyone on the street. Audiences may have difficulty identifying with one who would cheerfully burn at the stake, but Laurel and Hardy's evergreen appeal has a lot to do with their performance of frustration at the conflict and incompetence that we ordinary mortals experience every day. Their enactment of ritual injury takes place squarely within the context of those everyday conflicts, frustrations, and misadventures, and thus invites the audience to symbolically transform their everyday trials on a ritual plain upon which resolution of difficulties may be accomplished.

This section examines two silent films from 1929, *Two Tars* and *Big Business*. The structure of the films is quite similar. Both of "the boys" are going about their ordinary lives of work (*Big Business*) or leisure (*Two Tars*), while hints and foreshadowings of ritual injury emerge. They fall into increasingly violent conflict with their fellow creatures, but within the real violence and real reactions to violence such as expressing pain, running away, or fending off blows we also see an escalation of ritual violence: of standing and receiving an injury with stoic acceptance. In a sense this strategy goes a step beyond the Christian martyrs, who never fought back. Stan and Ollie do fight back, sometimes with a right good will, but interspersed with this antagonism is a not-fighting-back, a patient reception of injury. This interweaving of ritual injury with real injury links the two levels of violence and invites the audience to encompass the day's injury on the symbolic terrain offered by ritual.

Big Business depicts Stan and Ollie selling Christmas trees door-to-door from the back of their truck in a markedly un-Christmas-like Los Angeles. Since this is a silent film, narrative appears on the screen from time to time, and the very first comment resonates completely with the ritual injury of Christian martyrdom: "The story of a man who turned the other cheek—and got punched in the nose."

Pulling up to the first house, we see intimations of ritual: Stan is extremely deliberate about putting on his gloves in order to pick up the tree and carry it to the front door. Ollie looks on in exasperation, and then looks at the camera with the same emotion as if to invite our empathy with one whose fellow-workers drive you nuts. But Stan is undeterred, his whole attention focused on putting on the gloves just so rather than on the task at hand. His engrossment in the process looks like the move into a different time and space found in ritual.

Carrying the tree to the front door to offer it for sale, Stan whacks Ollie with the tree twice, but Ollie reacts as any of us would, ducks out of the way and shoves the tree to one side. He is not yet in a mode of ritually receiving injury. Foiled in their attempt to make a sale, they return the tree to the truck. Stan begins to remove his gloves with as much ceremony and deliberation as he put them on with, and Ollie can take it no more. He grabs the gloves and throws them to the side. Here we see the first intimations of ritual injury, for Stan looks placidly in the direction of the discarded gloves but does nothing to prevent their loss and does not retrieve them.

The next ritual injury befalls Ollie. Our heroes knock on a door that clearly has a "no solicitors" sign posted. Surrealistically, a bare arm holding a hammer comes out through the door and knocks Ollie on the head. He faces the camera, winces, and rubs his head, but he doesn't move or protest. Indeed, he knocks once more, receiving the same treatment and making the same response toward the camera, for the audience's benefit. Ollie's response to the frustration of legal notices and superior physical force is to turn his injury into a ritual injury by treating it differently, accepting it with forbearance, and refusing self-defense.

The next house the boys arrive at is the site of their undoing. Dragging the tree to the door, Stan whacks Ollie with it again. Ollie's response is once more not one of ritual injury, for he pushes the tree away, slapping and dodging. The man of the house comes to the door but politely refuses their offer and closes the door—on the tree. They must ring the doorbell to summon him so that he can open the door and allow them to remove the tree. He does so, with a bit of pique. But then he closes the door a little too quickly, the tree remains stuck, and they must ring the bell again. The scene repeats itself as all characters become increasingly wrathful. The one time they do manage to extricate the tree in time, Stan gets his coat caught in the door and must ring the bell yet again. The situation is a nightmare; it is a frustration dream for all characters involved but also surely for the audience. From this scene of everyday frustration and failure, both real violence and ritual injury emerge.

Summoned to the door once too often, the man of the house emerges with enormous clippers, which he uses to cut the tree into pieces. Stan and Ollie watch with expressions of surprise and alarm, but they do nothing to stop it—it is the first enactment of ritual injury. Ritual and real injury will intertwine throughout this sequence, showing to the audience how the former is connected to the latter. Incensed at the destruction of their tree, Stan and Ollie remove the house numbers and part of the frame from the door. When the homeowner comes out to protest, Stan uses his knife to cut off some of his hair, an injury that he ritualizes by standing still to receive it, albeit with a shocked expression on his face. The homeowner yanks Ollie's watch from out of his pocket and crushes it on the ground; Stan and Ollie destroy his doorbell, and then his telephone as he calls for the police. He pulls out Ollie's shirttail and then his tie, cutting both of them off as Stan and Ollie stand perfectly still to receive the injuries. The homeowner walks out to their truck and pulls a headlight off; they do nothing to stop him. Stan and Ollie take their coats off as if for a fight, but the escalation of the conflict will be as an exchange of blows to property, not people. They watch as the homeowner breaks a fender off of their truck. He watches as they destroy his tree, door, and windows. The homeowner breaks Stan and Ollie's steering wheel as they begin throwing his furniture out of the broken window onto his lawn. All three men are in a perfect frenzy of destruction—blowing up the truck, digging holes in the lawn at random, enacting complete mayhem—when a police officer pulls up to observe.

Observing is about all he does for a while. He takes notes but does nothing to stop the carnage. He is enacting a kind of ritual injury at one remove, observing injury without taking the natural course of rushing to prevent it. Eventually he breaks up the fight, the men make peace, and everyone departs, weeping with emotion. The peace offering of a cigar that Stan and Ollie give to the homeowner is the final blow, however, for it explodes as he sits amidst the rubble of his home. As Stan and Ollie drive off, we see that they are laughing in victory at their trick and at having avoided arrest. This depiction of tricksters triumphant creates a sense of the efficacy of ritualizing injury, for no matter how grievous the real hurts they have suffered, they accept their situation at the end.

Two Tars is very similar in form to *Big Business;* no doubt the interweaving of ritual with real injury and the apocalyptic escalation of violence was an attractive formula for audiences. Stan and Ollie are two sailors on leave, driving down the street in a rented car. Stan, behind the wheel, nearly wrecks the car and almost hits a pedestrian—almost a real injury that is met with real protest from the pedestrian and with Ollie's frantic slapping at Stan. Ollie takes the wheel and runs the car into more violence, actually hitting a lamppost and knocking the glass globe from it onto his head. Ollie winces at this injury but does not jump from the car or react to fend off more blows—it is a first intimation of moving injury into a space of ritual.

The boys stop to flirt with two women (Ruby and Thelma, but it's never clear which is which) who are wrestling with a gumball machine in front of a store. Minor violence accompanies incompetence in their attempts to help. Stan looks at the machine but Ollie slaps him out of the way. Ollie gets his finger jammed in the machine, which breaks as he extricates his finger. Gumballs roll all over the sidewalk. Ollie looks at the camera in pain, inviting us to identify with this everyday failure and frustration.

Stan and the women prepare to flee, but Ollie goes to his knees, abandoning all dignity, and begins gathering gumballs to stuff into his pockets and shirt. The storeowner comes out and surveys the damage in dismay. Seeing Ollie with gumballs in his hands and bulging out of his clothes, the businessman begins slapping Ollie's hands and pulling out his shirt and pockets to release the incriminating gumballs. Caught in the acts of destruction and theft, Ollie stands and receives these indignities, transforming the assault into a ritual injury.

The episode is linked to further experiences of everyday injury when the women make the owner's assault a matter of manhood. One woman says of Ollie to Stan, "He don't wanna hit a little fella [the storekeeper]—you crash him!" As Ollie continues to accept the owner's assaults without fighting back or fleeing, Stan walks up and says, "You're flirtin' with death, son!" The owner punches Stan as well and down he goes onto the gumballs, which prevent him from regaining his feet to fight back. The women enter the fray and attack the owner; now it is his turn to transform injury into ritual as he patiently receives their blows and then simply stands there glaring at them. The women, Stan, and Ollie enter the car once again and zoom off for the climax of the film.

We next see this merry party stopped in a long line of cars waiting to move through a construction zone on a country highway. The men and women have exchanged hats, thus pulling forward the injurious issues of manhood raised earlier in the film. Shortly after they stop, they are bumped from behind by another car. One woman says to Ollie, "Are you gonna let that bozo bump our car?"—and the game is on. Ollie throws his car into reverse, initiating a fruitless exchange of blows in which each car bumps the other, but of course equally bumps itself in doing so. This model of pointless but real injury escalates, as the man in the car behind comes up and kicks Stan and Ollie's car. Stan goes back to pull off the man's headlight and throws it through his windshield. The man breaks a festive balloon that the party has tied to their car. At this point the attacks shift to a ritual footing occasionally interspersed amidst real injury. Stan picks up a trowel of cement from the construction site, removes the man's hat, dumps the cement on his head, and replaces the hat. All the while the man stands stock-still, hand on hip, receiving the injury with ritual deliberation. Recovering from this attack and reentering the world of real violence, he slashes Stan and Ollie's tire, then kicks Stan and pulls Ollie's hair. Stan pulls the radiator off of his car, then a door; the man pulls off a fender; Stan and Ollie pull off his convertible top; and then the violence spreads to the other cars. General mayhem erupts as picnic lunches provide ammunition for real violence. But moments of ritual violence continue to punctuate even this frantic free-for-all, as one man smashes a tomato in the face of another man who stands still to receive the injury. The women cheer on the general combat, but they also stand still to receive assaults such as the squirting of ink from a pen all over one woman's face.

As in *Big Business,* a police officer pulls up to watch a general battle scene but he does nothing. His role here, as in the first film, is as a sort of passive observer and thus reminder of ritual injury. Eventually he walks into the melee and demands to know who started it all (as did the officer in the first film). "They did," everyone cries, pointing at Stan and Ollie. The boys look contrite, but giggles escape as they watch the long line of wrecked cars go by them. As in *Big Business,* they have a sense of triumph and success despite the material losses to their car, a victory that may be credited symbolically to the assuagement of those injuries in ritual. Preparing to take them to jail, the officer's motorcycle is flattened by one of these vehicles and the boys gleefully escape.

In both of these films we see modeled the moments of patient, calm reception of injury, and the deliberate infliction of it, that we find hinted at in the stories of Christian martyrs. We also find a much clearer grounding of ritual injury in the midst of real injury, humiliation, and frustration. Thus, the ritual injury is clearly linked to real injury in these films in ways that invite the audience to see the ritual as a way to respond to and transcend the reality. Stan, Ollie, and their ritual victims stand like martyrs at the stake performing the reception of injury, allowing their flesh and property to become canvases upon which the careful enactment of harm is painted. We now consider a somewhat more recent form of discourse in which ritual injury predominates, amidst scenes of real injury and deprivation.

Playing the Dozens

Playing the dozens is a discursive form grounded in the African American community and, ultimately, in Africa. This discourse is known by a variety of other names such as signifying, sounding, woofing, chopping, and so forth (Labov, 306–07). The general form of the practice involves the trading of insults within the structure of "highly ritualized speech acts" (Baugh, 24). It is worth quoting from Geneva Smitherman's enlightening definition of "the dozens":

> A verbal ritual of talking negatively about someone's mother (or occasionally grandmothers and other female relatives) by coming up with outlandish, highly exaggerated, often sexually loaded, humorous "insults"; played among friends, associates, and those HIP to the game. The objective is to outtalk one's competitor, get the most laughs from the group, and not lose emotional control. A fundamental rule is that the "slander" must not be literally true because truth takes the group out of the realm of play into reality. (99–100)

Within the first six words of this definition, Smitherman merges ritual with the negative, or injury, later more specifically defined as insults. Playing the dozens is, as the end of this passage notes, on a ritual terrain out of the everyday world. William Labov helps us to understand how ritualized and structured an activity is the dozens through his extensive explanation of "rules for ritual insults" (297–353). Smitherman describes this terrain that is set apart as play, but we may with justification retain the word she used in the first line and call it ritual.

Henry Louis Gates Jr. defines "the dozens" as "the best-known mode of Signification, both because it depends so heavily on humor and because the success of its exchanges turns on insults of one's family members, especially one's mother" (99). Labov seconds this definition, describing the dozens as "any ritualized insult directed against a relative (307). Gates describes the dozens pithily as "verbal insult rituals" (69). Etymologically, Gates explains, the practice derives from injury, from "an eighteenth-century meaning of the verb *dozen*, 'to stun, stupefy, daze' . . . through language" (71). He gives several examples from H. Rap Brown, including,

> I fucked your mama
> Till she went blind.
> Her breath smells bad,
> But she sure can grind. (72)

In these definitions, Gates echoes Smitherman's perspective in combining ritual with injury and insult. John Baugh emphasizes the way in which the dozens parodies real injury with this combative wording: "Males, and occasionally females, hurl ritual insults at one another, involving their mothers as the target of the verbal assault" (26). Michael L. Hecht and his colleagues likewise describe playing the dozens in violent terms as "an aggressive contest often using obscene language in which the goal is to ridicule and demean the opponent's family members, notably the mother" (100). The dozens are transformed from being actual assault to a discourse that is played on a terrain set apart as ritual; the discourse fails if someone takes it as real insult, actual injury. Labov notes that "when ritual insult changes into personal insult, the difference between the two becomes quite clear" as the participants act as if the exchange were serious and real, as indeed it has become (330–31). And the key to this move to the real is that "an invariant rule" of the dozens is broken, the rule that insults "are not denied" (335). To not deny the insult is to suffer it ritually, to stand and receive it, even if one is preparing a rejoinder as good as the one received.

Richard Majors and Janet Mancini Billson place the dozens into a rhetorical context similar to that of the other discourses examined here (91–102). Playing the dozens is a ritualized insult that equips its audience and participants to confront the actual insults and injuries encountered in everyday life. This is especially true for African American youth who encounter the real injuries of oppression almost daily.

Majors and Billson see the ritual injury of the dozens as a rhetorical response to life's injuries:

> Playing the dozens helps adolescent black males maintain control and keep cool under adverse conditions. It prepares them for the socioeconomic problems they may later face and facilitates their search for masculinity, pride, status, social competence, and expressive sexuality. (91)

This preparation is explicitly described as a "ritualized verbal contest" (91), as "ritualistic insults" (98). The ritual is also clearly one of injury, for (they are quoting another source) "mothers are subject to vicious slander; fathers are 'queer, syphilitic'; 'sisters are whores, brothers are defective, cousins are "funny" and the opponent is himself diseased'" (92).

Yet it remains ritual, for failure is guaranteed if one steps out of the ritual and treats the injury as real. You win if "the taunting proceeds to draw the other into a fight, or reduce him to tears" (97); in other words, if the other treats the injury as real, the other loses. These ritual requirements also make the dozens a rhetorical response to real life adversity, for "the severely restrictive rituals of this game help young boys play out, in a highly controlled fashion, otherwise overpowering feelings of rage, hostility, and frustration" and help "blacks keep cool and think fast under pressure, without revealing their true feelings" (101). It is interesting to note Majors and Billson's observation that "playing the dozens helps the black male raise his threshold of tolerance for frustration" and to compare that function with the ways that frustrations are expressed and ritually transformed in the Laurel and Hardy films reviewed in the previous section (102). The parallel functions of each type of discourse suggest a structuring homology beneath both.

Labov notes that for the dozens, "the audience . . . is an essential ingredient" (339). This highlights a feature we have found in other manifestations of the homology of ritual injury, which is the showy performance of injury for the sake of those standing around, whether that audience is made of those who have gathered around the stake, those who have come to see Stan and Ollie battle it out with a homeowner, or the other young men gathered around to watch someone play the dozens. Ritual injury can scarcely be performed in private, for the translation of real injury into ritual is for the sake of the community, both the sufferer and her audience. This performance reaffirms the ability to receive and overcome injury for both the performer and his witnesses.

If studies of playing the dozens point us toward the importance of ritual injury for the audience, today's televised professional wrestling spectacles perfect the notion of the audience as key. Obviously theatrical, professional wrestling enacts ritual injury for millions of audience members today. Let us examine the manifestations of the homology in this televised spectacle.

Professional Wrestling

This section of the chapter examines three wrestling matches on the World Wrestling Entertainment television show *WWE Live*, televised in an episode titled "Raw." The actual matches are quite brief, and although they may be the focal point for the episode they do not contain a majority of the discourse and action. Professional wrestling, of course, purports to be a real sport with real contests in which the outcome is not predetermined. Many audience members persist in that belief despite the overwhelming evidence of staged theatricality presented to the senses with each broadcast. It is worth keeping in mind that the willing suspension of disbelief among many in the audience makes an especially strong connection between ritual injury in the shows and the real injuries of everyday life that the ritual assaults encompass. If the audience can persuade itself that they are watching real violence, insult, and degradation when it occurs, then the response to those "realities" in ritual becomes more efficacious.

The casual viewer of "Raw" may feel at a loss to understand the world that she has entered, since the program clearly follows many of the conventions of a soap opera. One is put immediately into the middle of an ongoing conversation, sort of a pugilistic Burkean parlor, with references to grudges, alliances, contests, and struggles occurring years into the past and anticipated for months into the future. The show opens with one Eric Bischoff in the parking garage of the arena in which the matches take place, coaching three thugs in the imminent destruction of Stone Cold Steve Austin. Why Mr. Bischoff is aggrieved at Mr. Austin must be clear to the long-time observer of this show, but not to the casual viewer. At any rate, the thugs (enormous, burly men wielding pipes, two-by-fours, and other weapons of focused destruction) are told, "You three are my Steve Austin welcoming committee. In fact, you're my very first line of defense." Bischoff tells them to "cave the rattlesnake's skull in" upon his arrival. This story line is not resolved during the three matches observed here, but reappears as intermezzos between other segments of the broadcast.

The camera shifts to very fast-paced, hectic images of rock-and-roll musicians, fireworks, lasers, and a little bit of wrestling. The announcers scream out the coming attractions as the crowd in the arena goes wild, displaying signs, waving arms, and dancing about. A large screen displays the words, "Can you dig it sucka," which is evidently the slogan of the wrestler Booker T, who enters the arena and steps into the ring to the approving cheers of the crowd.

It becomes clear quickly that each professional wrestler is a type, a representative of a genre of humanity with special relevance for the show's audience. Booker T enacts the prototype of the hard-working, deserving African American, no doubt as constructed within some sort of mainstream American Eurocentric mythology. Booker T has recently won the right to enter "Wrestlemania," which is to be broadcast later in the month. He is here to receive the cheers and adoration of the crowd. "Yeah, that's right, everybody know who I am. It's me, Booker T!" He explains why he is there: "You know, last week I won the twenty-man Battle Royal, but I didn't get no trip to Disneyland!" He is referring to the trip to Wrestlemania that he has earned instead.

But lo! His celebration is interrupted by the entrance into the arena of the heavyweight champion of the world, Triple X. Triple X is large, white, and blonde, dressed in a suit and carrying his championship gold belt over his shoulder, accompanied by his slick, blonde, white manager likewise dressed in a suit. Entering the arena with Booker T, Triple X and his manager commence an all-but-explicitly racist denigration of Booker T. Triple X, fully clothed, walks slowly around Booker T, smirking, his eyes mainly focused intently on the crotch of the African American who is clad only in tight shorts. His brown-skinned body oiled and on display, it is an uncomfortable inspection by an empowered white man. The announcers break in saying, "He's sizing up the competition," clearly referencing myths of genital size among African Americans.

Triple X offensively puts Booker T into his mythic place: "Booker, I think you're a little bit confused about your role in life here." He continues in this insulting, superior vein with obvious racial overtones. For instance: "You see, Booker T, somebody like you doesn't get to be a world champion. . . . You see, people like you don't deserve it, that's reserved for people like me. . . . You see, you're not here to be a competitor, you're here to be an entertainer. Hell, you entertain me all the time. . . . Go ahead, Book, why don't you entertain. Go ahead, Book, why don't you do a little dance for me." He will refer denigratingly to Booker T's "nappy hair." He will claim that Booker T was "lucky to make it to Wrestlemania." All the while his manager smirks and guffaws intolerably.

The patently racist nature of these affronts is not lost on the crowd, still on Booker T's side, which by now is chanting "asshole, asshole" in unison and loudly. Despite the obviously staged nature of the program, the insults hurled by Triple X are so provocative in today's social context that it is difficult not to feel them as real. During the whole course of Triple X's rant, however, Booker T enacts the form of ritual injury. He stands stock still, glaring fiercely at his tormentor, but does not refuse the slurs, nor break into physical violence, nor leave the ring in disgust during several minutes of Triple X's fulminations. It is a discursively powerful moment, since Triple X's insults are of such a sensitive nature that the audience is strongly moved to take them as real even if one knows the event is rigged. In an important sense, racial slurs *cannot* be faked in today's America, no matter what the circumstances. So Booker T's stoic reception of the insults clearly connects his ritualizing performance with the kind of real, everyday injury that the audience experiences and witnesses themselves.

Booker T's eventual response to this is so mild it might be seen as part of his performance of ritual injury. Playing off of Triple X's "somebody like you" repetitions, Booker T says, "Somebody like *me* is gonna ragtag your ass and beat you for the world heavyweight championship." He is angry but never angry enough to give Triple X the kind of verbal or physical response that might realistically occur in everyday life. His words are spoken with the slow, measured cadences of ritual. The announcers break in to connect this ritualized performance of injury with words that reference the kind of hard-knock life of real injury and difficult struggle that is familiar to the audience: "Booker T's gotta believe and he does believe. He's paid his dues. He's done everything asked of him. And Booker T's opportunity of a lifetime comes on March 30 on Wrestlemania."

After another brief episode of Eric Bischoff's recruitment of more thugs to beat up Steve Austin should he appear, the first match of the evening begins. If Booker T is the cold, hard-working, suffering African American, the competitor who now enters the ring is the prototype of the good, well-meaning, but emotionally unstable and ultimately ineffectual young person: Jeff Hardy. The announcers make this typecasting clear: "A great ovation for the very complex Jeff Hardy, who last week tried to do the right thing" by interfering in a match in which women were being cruelly used by male competitors in the ring. Hardy is to wrestle Christian, another young blonde bad guy.

It is not clear that Hardy's fragile mental state will survive the evening. He immediately attacks Christian once the latter has entered the ring, a surprising display of resolve, for as the announcers say, "Jeff Hardy not wasting any time . . . trying to gain some retribution here on Christian. Certainly Jeff Hardy, you saw what I thought was a very aggressive side of a young man that we have termed to be somewhat conflicted in recent weeks, Jeff Hardy." He is described in trendy psychospeak repeatedly as "frustrated," "conflicted," "confused," as "a bundle of emotions." He is clearly the young slacker, known to every member of the audience, who won't move out of his parents' basement, won't finish school, and won't get a job. These terms describe him as a born victim and habitual recipient of real injury.

This match follows a pattern we will see in all three of tonight's struggles. Although of course the blows are staged to inflict no real punishment, the violence in the early stages of the match looks authentic. It *appears* to be a kind of real-life injury fest. But then gradually one or both of the combatants shift into a stance of ritual injury. Their movements slow a bit, their stances take on a more performative and showy aspect. Christian begins to administer the "abdominal stretch" to Hardy, and the fact that each move has its proper name helps to move real, flailing violence to the terrain of measured ritual. But Hardy's arm actually moves in place around Christian's shoulder to facilitate this move; he is assisting in his own injury. Hardy regains his footing and strikes Christian, who stands still to receive the blows. Christian picks up Hardy by the armpits and Hardy allows it, spreading his arms out a bit so that Christian can get a grip underneath them. Christian walks around behind Hardy and pulls him backward by the face. Hardy certainly has time to realize what is happening and to move, but he does not. The announcers urge him on: "Jeff Hardy, don't get conflicted right here in the middle of the match," a comment that links his embodiment of young-man-angst with violence that is represented as real and with violence that is performed as ritual. Alas! Jeff Hardy is soundly trounced by Christian.

We have another brief interlude of Eric Bischoff's arraying of his thugs to catch Steve Austin, and then we move to the next match. Chief of Staff Morley, another large white man with an aggressive attitude, enters the arena. He is not a popular figure for the crowd, and no wonder, for he is enacting the prototype of the sinister power-behind-the-throne of business or government. He is the "boss man" for a high-tech, corporate era, and in this capacity he is a reminder of the real injuries and insults endured by many members of the audience in their work lives. The announcers join in the crowd's disapproval of this character, noting of his shorts (which display "Chief Morley" across the seat), "What an appropriate place for his title, right across his posterior."

Morley struts around the ring antagonizing the crowd, announcing, "I can make a match as interesting as I want," and in general reminding the crowd of one who expects to wield power over others. This portrayal of the corporate or governmental heavyweight is described as a "jerk" by the announcers. A representative of the kind of ordinary person who is injured in everyday experience by this kind of overseer is about to appear, for Spike Dudley comes running into the arena at top speed. He obviously weighs at least one hundred pounds less than Morley, but he never breaks stride as he charges up into the ring and slides under the ropes to attack the Chief. "Spike Dudley's got so much heart," the announcers say, and it is clear from their repetition of such pronouncements as "he's got a great heart" that Dudley stands in for the audience and their own courageous suffering at the hands of administrators.

This match follows the pattern of the Jeff Hardy–Christian match almost exactly. The violence is staged so as to appear authentic at the start, but shortly Spike Dudley begins to stand and receive the blows administered by Chief Morley. Barely perceptible movements place Dudley's arms in positions to allow him to be thrown about. At one point Dudley seems to forget to put his arm in place on Morley's shoulder; Morley places it for him and Dudley does not resist. He stands still to receive blows that he must know are coming. He moves his body into convenient positions for throws. The conclusion is foregone, and "Little Spike," as the announcer calls him, is defeated.

One more interlude with the thugs awaiting Steve Austin is followed by a match among four female competitors: Trish, Jackie, Jazz, and Victoria. The first two enter and exit together but it is not clear whether they are a team, and the match itself appears to be a free-for-all. Jazz and Victoria will be the villains in this contest, and are portrayed in stereotypically sexist insults. Jazz enters the arena to the announcement, "The bitch is back." The announcer describes Victoria as "one bipolar Jezebel, if you ask me," echoing the psychotherapeutic language applied earlier to Jeff Hardy. There is less posturing in the ring than there has been for the men. This "divas' tag team matchup" follows the same pattern for violence that we have seen in male contests. What is enacted as real injury early in the match gradually transposes into the taking of careful stances and poses as the injury becomes ritualized. Late in the match, Jackie is propped up in a corner of the ring. She obligingly spreads her arms and stands there to receive blows. Trish bends over, grabs the lower ropes of the ring, and waits patiently for Victoria to leap on her back. Some sort of decision is reached, although to those who are not aficionados of the game it is not apparent who won or lost. Trish and Jackie leave the arena as Jazz and Victoria shout threats at them from within the ring.

The final scene appears to be part of an ongoing narrative that, as with the "welcoming committee" for Steve Austin, stretches beyond the immediate episode. Another wrestler, The Rock, answers a knock on the door to his dressing room. It is a journalist who wants to interview him. He is insufferably rude to the man, shouting in his face dismissals such as "I can't be dealin' with that. The Rock has a big night." The journalist enacts some amount of ritual injury as he stands quietly to receive this rudeness. The Rock withdraws inside his room and pulls aside a curtain only to discover a masked wrestler, Hurricane, hiding in his closet. Hurricane leaps out and the two launch into an exchange that appears to follow very closely the patterns of playing the dozens—and in doing so becomes a form of ritual injury. Hurricane ridicules The Rock for losing to Booker T as The Rock stands still, with an open-mouthed expression of disbelief, to receive these taunts. Hurricane likewise stands and receives descriptions of himself as a "Hamburglar green monkey ass" and "you ain't nothin', what are you, president of student council?" Hurricane's taunts come even closer to playing the dozens, as he rhymes his attacks, accusing The Rock's partner Scorpion King of "having a tiny ding-a-ling." The insertion of a discourse that is so clearly parallel to playing the dozens emphasizes the centrality of ritual injury throughout this broadcast of professional wrestling.

Conclusion

In ritual, we move into a place set apart in which the practices and expectations of everyday life no longer apply. Yet ritual can be a powerful answer to the problems of everyday life. Ritual injury is a form manifested in many discourses, and thus is structured by a homology shared among the discourses. Ritual injury is always linked in some way to real injury; sometimes it is depicted in the midst of real injury, sometimes real injury is mentioned in connection to the ritual, sometimes movements performed in ritual injury are echoes of actions suffered in reality. In many of the instances examined, real injury in a text gradually gives way to its reflection and transformation in ritual.

Injury is ritualistically transformed by marked differences in how the reception of the injury is portrayed. Realistic evasion, protests, refusals, and counterattacks give way to a relatively calm demeanor, passive physical stance, patient words, and nondefensive gestures. Movement slows perceptibly and the usual rules of engagement in conflict seem to alter. Blows become gestures. The acceptance of injury becomes performed, with what seems to be a clear sense of an audience to observe the ritual. Expressions of triumph and joy are signs of the efficacy of the ritual encompassing of injury.

The remarkably consistent recurrence of ritual injury across a wide range of discourses spanning a wide range of years reveals a homological structure. It appears as if the transformation of real injury into mannered, ritualized, discursive injury is a venerable way of addressing life's problems. That bare fact may not seem terribly surprising. What this chapter may have contributed is an invitation to think about the diversity of discourses that enact ritual injury, and the ways in which discourses and practices may participate unexpectedly in that homology. In this way we see how ritual breaks into the everyday at many levels so as to address the ongoing injuries of everyday life. The method of rhetorical homologies may help us to see more of the ritual discourses by which that process occurs.

This study may also suggest that the content of discourses of ritual injury is moving from the serious slaughter in venerable tales of saints to the light entertainment of slapstick or the frankly cynical posturing of professional wrestling. At the same time, is it possible that for most people who would consume such discourse, life's real injuries are moving in a "softer" direction? As life expectancy expands, religious and cultural tolerance spreads, and the social welfare safety net settles into entitlement, are the real injuries that are assuaged by ritual injury likewise becoming less dire over the long span of centuries? Forms underlying homologies do change over time, although as form they are relatively stable and slow to change. But the content of discourse and experience ordered by homology changes in history, and if it changes in similar ways (here, from death and damnation to social gaffes and contretemps) then homologies may be affected by, and as they emerge in, history. And homology may affect how we see that history itself: is the move from stories of saints' martyrdoms to *The Longest Yard* a force that has contributed to our increasingly ironic culture?

In the next chapter we continue a theme of examining a homology that orders discourse and experience together. We will examine a mythic form, the discursive structure that underlies white liberal history of race relations in the United States, a form that has emerged repeatedly in our history in several discourses. It is a discursive form with powerful rhetorical impact, as it orders social relations. We examine one film, *The Horse Whisperer,* that participates in this homology almost entirely at the level of form rather than content, and is thus an interesting example of how rhetorical impact may be created at the formal level.

3

Whispers of a Racial Past

Forms of White Liberal History in
The Horse Whisperer

Synopsis

The 1998 film *The Horse Whisperer* is a long, splendidly visual tour de
force by director and star Robert Redford. The film opens on a snowy,
beautiful rural scene outside New York City. Thirteen-year-old Grace
MacLean rises early on her country estate, saddles up her horse Pilgrim,
and goes riding with her friend Judith. The two teenagers ride through
beautiful Currier and Ives scenes wearing proper, traditional attire and
gossiping about boys—until they attempt to climb a snow-slick hill. The
horses lose their footing and slip down the hill and onto a country road,
with Judith falling from her mount yet still connected to it by a foot
caught in a stirrup. As the girls attempt to control the horses and to free
Judith, a massive truck rounds the corner of the road and cannot stop
in time. Judith is killed, Pilgrim horribly injured, and Grace herself
loses a leg.

Summoned to the hospital, Grace's parents—her father, attorney
Robert MacLean, and mother, magazine editor Annie MacLean—learn
the terrible truth of Grace's injuries. They are consumed by Grace's recovery and their own busy careers over the coming days and weeks. Yet
a decision they are asked to face quickly is put off, with terrible cost:
the veterinarian asks to destroy the injured Pilgrim. Grace and Annie
struggle over the decision, and Annie, unable to devote her attention to

the matter fully in the press of her daughter's crisis and her editorial duties, refuses to allow the horse to be put down. The veterinarian does what she can to heal Pilgrim, but he is badly scarred, wild, and unmanageable.

The same may be said for Grace, who sinks into sullenness and depression. Her unwillingness or inability to recover is linked to that of Pilgrim. "We're losing her," Annie says to Robert, and so she seeks a cure. She discovers that Tom Booker, a "cowboy vet" in Montana, is a successful "horse whisperer," able to heal broken animals through empathic methods. She calls him and offers to fly him to New York, but he is unwilling to leave his work and dismisses the offer. Undaunted, Annie loads up the horse, the unwilling Grace, and herself in a car and trailer and drives to Montana.

This is not a decision gladly accepted by Grace or Robert, and it increases some evident strains that already exist in the MacLeans' marriage. The friction between Annie and Robert is an ongoing subtext of the film. It is evident in strained looks and conversations between the two and in Grace's manifest anxiety over that tension.

Toiling across the vast distances, Annie and her cargo finally reach Montana. With some difficulty she finds Tom Booker on his family ranch, which he works with his brother, Frank, and Frank's wife, Diane, and their sons. An astonished Tom realizes that Annie is the woman he spoke to some days earlier, and reluctantly agrees to work with Pilgrim.

There follows a long period of time in which Grace and Annie move into a guesthouse on the property and begin to share in the ranch work, while Tom begins the slow process of healing for Pilgrim, which is ultimately successful. Grace's hostility slowly gives way to acceptance and finally she is able to ride Pilgrim again. In the meantime, Tom and Annie begin to fall in love. She is faced with the choice of whether to give up her New York world of sophistication for the utterly alien life of a rancher's wife in Montana—a decision that is brought to a head by her firing as editor due to her long absence.

Robert MacLean arrives unexpectedly for a visit in the midst of this drama. Annie's attraction to Tom becomes clear to him. He expresses his love for her and urges her to make a decision as to where she will live. Robert returns to New York with Grace. Sadly, Annie decides that although she loves Tom she could not live the life of a rancher, and so she follows her family to New York with Pilgrim in tow.

White Folks

The real star of *The Horse Whisperer* is Montana. Beautiful, lush scenes of vast prairies and grand mountains captivate the viewer. The people of Montana are also depicted as quite attractive. They are strong, virtuous, polite, sociable—and White. In scene after scene of cowboys and their families at work, at barn dances, relaxing on the front porch at the end of the day, we see no people of color whatsoever. Tom has an affecting story about an Indian he knew years ago as a youngster, and Grace and Annie stop at the Little Big Horn battlefield memorial on their way to Montana, but no actual Indians ever appear on screen, much less Hispanics, African Americans, or Asians.

And yet, if one looks not for the literal presence of color but for the form or pattern of color as a narrative element in American cultural myth, then black, brown, and yellow faces begin to emerge from beneath the white skin tones. For the people of color in this film are the Mac-Leans, exotic sufferers moving west to seek healing and redemption—but in whose story? In this chapter I argue that there is a liberal, White, mainstream American myth (hereafter, The Myth) of the racial history of this country, a discursive form that generates myriad explanations that this empowered demographic tells itself in films, television, around the dinner table, and in school curricula. The Myth is a form creating a homology underlying many texts of popular culture and of White, liberal constructions of history. As new texts (such as *The Horse Whisperer*) emerge, they reindividuate the form and push the homology along in time, perpetuating a hegemonic ideology that props up the well-mannered dominance of White liberalism in mainstream American thought, politics, and culture. The Myth thus also orders the behaviors and the perceptions of those who share it. History itself, as lived experience, as story, as perceptions of others, becomes part of the homology grounded in The Myth.

I will show the homological bones of the film as I read it according to that mythic discursive form. In this way, I hope that a reading of the film can reveal some characteristics and nuances of The Myth at the same time that The Myth can be used to open up interpretive possibilities in the film—thus modeling the same possibilities in other critical efforts. Let me begin by considering the overall structure of the mythic homology, and then returning to this unhappy family, the MacLeans, stripping off the content of the masks they wear and revealing the roles they enact as people of color within this great White liberal American myth of racial history.

What's the Story?

Although it is alive and well in pockets here and there, outright racial bigotry has gone out of fashion in the United States. In the way of all successful tools of empowerment, racism dropped the tiring strong-arm practices of Jim Crow and standing in the schoolhouse door in favor of the more genteel masks of *hegemony*. If an empowered group perpetuates the idea that their empowerment is natural, acceptable, and preferable—especially if such ideas are accepted by the disempowered— we would say that such a group has hegemony. Hegemony is created and perpetuated by a rhetoric of common sense, a rhetoric of the natural. Of course, hegemony is often refused, struggled over, and subverted by those unwilling to accept it. The idea may be traced in the twentieth century to Louis Althusser and to a later, more sophisticated treatment by Antonio Gramsci.

Systems of empowerment based on constructions of race have employed a myth, a discursive structure, that underlies many texts and practices in Western culture. This myth has enough narrative cohesion and plausibility (I do *not* say that it is *true*) to find adherents and collaborators among all races (although we must acknowledge the many struggles that emerge in refusal of The Myth). The homology it creates links seemingly disparate texts and practices in creating a hegemonic understanding of how the West, and specifically the United States, came to be the way it is in terms of racial politics.

Expressed as a "representative anecdote," at a general level of abstraction, The Myth is told from the standpoint of White, Western culture in the United States, and it sounds like this:

There is a race of people (them) who have had a horrible, violent, and injurious past. They have been overcome in the past through superior Western technology and social organization. These injuries may well have been inflicted by people *like us,* but it was not *us.* At any rate, the victims in the past (and/or their compatriots) were complicit with their injuries and are thus partially responsible. Pain, anger, and a capacity for violence are the legacies of these injuries. As a result of injury and as a possible ground for healing, *they* have come to *us,* making cultural, psychological, and physical journeys. We offer healing and wholeness (we can do it, we have the "technology"), but through *integration* with us on our terms, in our space, literally on our grounds. Of course, we mean a guarded integration: They will always be exotic and different, but we'll take them in—they can sleep *over there.* This is a totally free choice we offer; there are no constraints on either side. But sadly, so many of *them* refuse the bargain. They return—sometimes physically, sometimes culturally, sometimes psychologically—to the less than idyllic historical/cultural/psychological/geographical places from which they came. They leave *us* sad but blameless, for we had extended our hand.

This is "history" told about Africans who came west in slavery, Indians who were pushed west to clear the land, Hispanics who came north to pick the crops, Asians who came east to build the railroads—and the descendants of these people. That every American of European descent made the same journey (west) is usually forgotten as White, homogenized, mainstream culture becomes the discursive center, the default, the culture always already in place. *We* have *always* lived in the castle.

The Myth provides a homology ordering and generating many discourses as well as behaviors. It is essentially the form beneath the film *The Green Mile,* for instance. In that film the viewer is given to understand that the tormented but angelic, exotic African American character is the way he is because of a racist society—and we see the cautious, arms-length efforts of the White power structure in the prison to help him—but ultimately such efforts fail and the prisoner goes gently, even eagerly, into that good night. It is the form beneath news stories of families of color that succumb in successive generations to crime or to poverty despite the best efforts of White-dominated power structures to help them.

As we saw in the first chapter, every retelling of the discursive structure underlying a homology is a reindividuation that introduces new elements, with rhetorical effect. *The Horse Whisperer* embodies The Myth, and in doing so helps us to see some dimensions of The Myth—but also carries its own freight of rhetorical impact. To understand how such a long (160 minutes), rich film reindividuates The Myth, I will first turn the discussion to the main characters and their experiences, up to the point at which they encounter the West.

Dark Folks

Of course it is outrageous to claim that the MacLeans are reindividuations of The Myth's construction of people of color. But perhaps it is no more outrageous than were the frequent humorous comments that Bill Clinton was the "first Black president." Both attributions depend upon a discounting of information and an attention to patterns of experience, style, and conduct. I trust that my analysis here will show that the MacLeans embody The Myth in that manner consistently. To offer up one example by way of appetizer before the complete analysis: The central character in the family, Annie MacLean, although White is in fact an exotic foreigner, being British by nationality but having lived all over the world. She has come West as a stranger, to a Western culture already in place (in New York), and we are constantly reminded of her strangeness in the text of the film and in her British accent every time she speaks. She is not the British-regal *Anne* that her heritage and high-powered job would seem to demand, she is the folksier, working-class, more American *Annie*.

The rest of the family, in their own ways, rings to the frequency of this strong central character who is enacting the strangeness and movement toward the West attributed by The Myth to people of color. The fact that the actual racial identities of the characters, on the level of content or information, are White suggests an interesting reversal—and the rhetorical effects of that reversal will be discussed later as well.

The Myth depends upon constructing people of color in certain ways. The MacLeans and their horse, Pilgrim, represent not only reindividuations of particular types of people in The Myth, but also dimensions attributed to the characters of people of color. Although I will not attempt to articulate these dimensions with the Freudian constructs of id, ego, and superego, I do want to make a parallel argument. The Myth constructs an image of Otherness in people of color, based on certain recurring attributed dimensions of those people. As The Myth is reindividuated in particular texts, stock characters may be created to embody those stereotypical dimensions. Later in the film Tom Booker will affirm the status of each character as but a dimension of a complex mythic character when he claims that the horse's recovery is integral with Grace's healing, and by extension with Annie's and Robert's as well. The relationships among these characters/dimensions is complex, and the ways in which a network of relationship in *The Horse Whisperer* emerges to express third-world character will take some unpacking.

However, to preview that structure: One recurring dimension of The Myth is the emasculation of people of color. Strong males and, more importantly, male principles of control, law, and dominance are understood by The Myth to be recessive if not downright absent. These absent male principles are metaphors for the homeland fathers long ago who lost control, who let their people go, but who in some sense remain to keep open the door for a return. So it is with Robert MacLean, who is clearly less "high powered" than is Annie and who is in fact absent for much of the film as he remains in New York while his family travels to Montana. He is an echo in the collective memory of his family. In the absence of the male principle, The Myth posits the rise of a strong, controlling female presence—in this film, clearly the mother, Annie MacLean. Yet in The Myth this female principle is ultimately ineffective and weak, emerging elsewhere in tales of single parent households and welfare mothers unable to control their unruly children. The Myth thus imagines a waspish but ultimately ineffectual Sapphire, an imposing but fundamentally impotent mammy.

In The Myth, people of color bear the scars of a lost innocence, an original Edenic happiness that was destroyed in horrible injury and violence. People of color are thus understood to be sullen, resentful, and hurting—as is Grace MacLean, the once innocent thirteen year old who is torn in mind, body, and spirit. She is unreasonable and unreachable in her pain, as is the enduring sense of injury in The Myth. Finally, The

Myth maintains the image of a lurking potential for violence among people of color. The more liberal The Myth, the more it is understood that this violence, this power waiting to erupt, has good reason to be so because of injuries and oppression suffered in history. But violence is nevertheless deplored, and the inability of people of color themselves to do anything about that lurking violent proclivity is likewise deplored—and here we see, obviously, the powerful, wounded horse, Pilgrim.

These mythic forms used again and again to construct people of color emerge clearly in the discursive construction of these exotics, the MacLeans, from the start of the film. Let us turn now in detail to the personae of the MacLean family to see how they express these attributions of The Myth in the first part of the film, in their "homeland" of New York and during the "middle passage" to Montana. We begin with the father, Robert MacLean.

As the film opens, Grace awakens in her room on the MacLeans' country estate outside the city. She peeks in at her sleeping father on her way to her fateful ride. Her mother is at the family's apartment in Manhattan, finishing the week's work. Robert MacLean is thus pictured as master of the homeland, the original ground on which Grace lives out her life of idyllic innocence. Yet he is a sleeping lord of all he surveys, not awake to warn Grace of the slick conditions that might exist in the snowy world outside as she slips off to go riding.

After the accident, it is Robert who is positioned as the centering influence at home. He is first at the hospital to be with Grace, and breaks the news of the disaster to his breathless wife. As Annie rushes around managing affairs, bossing nurses and fussing over IV bags, Robert is the one nursing the stricken Grace, stroking her head and apologizing to the hospital staff for his wife. The same solicitous care for humanity continues at home. Grace slips and nearly falls rising from the dinner table, yet spurns Robert's quick rush to her side to help her. Later, Annie scolds him for this caring sensibility: "You've got to stop doing that . . . helping her all the time, running to her every time she trips, anticipating her." It is Robert who promotes familial togetherness by suggesting a vacation: "Why don't we go someplace warm, the three of us . . . Bermuda, or the Bahamas"—a trip to third-world warmth that Annie rejects on the practical grounds that Grace could not wear a swimsuit or sun dress in such tropical places. It is Robert who maintains the social unit even outside of the family, as he goes by himself to a dinner with people because, after all, "we're still friends" with them, as he explains to Annie.

All this social nurturing is one of several reversals in the film, in which Robert the father figure is emasculated and cast into more traditional (under patriarchy) female roles. He is the nurse, the homebody, the keeper of the flame in the family hearth. Although he is allegedly a high-powered lawyer in Manhattan, we never see him at work (as we do Annie). Although he tries to assert his voice in family decisions, it is Annie who decides to take horse and daughter into the great West to see the mysterious horse whisperer, and Robert's initial objections turn to capitulation. As his family heads off to strange lands (Grace and Pilgrim most unwillingly and in virtual captivity), Robert remains behind to keep the home places going on a skeleton crew. In this way he enacts The Myth's construction of the spirit of the original homeland for people of color (whether that be Africa, China, the forest primeval of Pocahontas, or some other scene): a present but emasculated masculinity, a fatherland that in some sense is intact and waiting but no longer where the action is in terms of the "family" unit. In The Myth, the "spirit" of the original scene is barely active as its people journey to the unfamiliar and distant West.

Annie MacLean is clearly positioned as the center of control in this family, although that will evaporate as the family moves west. We first see her running (not "jogging," as she will later correct Tom Booker) near the family's Manhattan apartment. She goes to her work as editor-in-chief of a large, glitzy magazine, with assistants and functionaries running here and there at her bidding. From that seat of power she calls Robert at their country home and is clearly "in charge" of the situation, telling him when she expects to arrive and refusing his offer of a ride, saying she will take a taxi from the train station.

Annie's scene of power is another of the film's interesting reversals, for although it is culturally of the West it is functionally of The Myth: the production of a magazine like Annie is running, requires furious energy that results in ultimately ephemeral, even futile, real outcome—an attribution frequently made about third-world economic prowess. Positioned in a seat of power, but in the world of entertainment, Annie is placed in as de-Westernized a place of control as can be. But in that site she is queen, and tough as nails. Scolding her boss on the telephone for his timid reaction to a lawsuit, she says, "You're not going soft on me, are you?" Later she will order her staff to bring her information on horse healers that she needs for her personal life, and will do so imperiously: "I want it *now*." With her staff around her she ticks off the merits of the latest cover's photography, layout, cropping, and so forth, but then says, "and I am so bloody bored," and orders them to do it over again.

Arriving breathless at the hospital, Annie is task oriented and domineering. Told that "Judith is dead" by Robert, she pauses, considering, then gets to the point: "What about Grace?" When informed that a leg has been removed, she objectively assesses the situation while keeping emotions in check. "Which leg?" she asks, as if it mattered. She orders the hospital staff around while her husband comforts their child. "I'm gonna get to know all the nurses' names; it's good to know that," she declares. Annie directs her husband to remain with Grace while she runs errands. She is just as no-nonsense with the veterinarian, who asks that the horse be "put down." "You mean *shoot* him," Annie replies. When Grace refuses to return to school because she is gawked at her first day back on crutches, Annie reads her the riot act: "Well you're not going to stay home all day feeling sorry for yourself, you're going to get up and figure this thing out." Rebuffed by her initial attempt to fly Tom Booker to New York, she imposes her desire to drive Grace and Pilgrim to Montana on the rest of the unwilling family.

Yet this Iron Lady shows signs of weakness and ineffectuality, which grow as she travels toward the West. Asked to give permission for Pilgrim to be destroyed, she cannot make the decision: "I cannot deal with this now, Liz, if you need a yes or a no then don't do it, OK?" Visiting Pilgrim for the first time with Grace, Annie stares at the broken, wild horse with an expression of despair on her face. The task of going west is daunting, and she knows it. Once the thrashing, flailing horse is put into the trailer the veterinarian asks Annie, "You got a gun just in case?" "Of course not," she replies. To which the vet returns a prophetic warning: "You may want to shoot *yourself* halfway through Ohio."

During the journey huge trucks on a rainy highway frighten her. Battling a sullen Grace the whole way, Annie's imperious office manner gives way to weak, mocking impersonations of her daughter behind her back. During one of their many fights, Grace accuses Annie of having imposed her will on others: "It's all about you, about you being right."

To which a confused Annie replies, "I don't have all the answers." She runs off into the night to collapse weeping by a park monument. What power there is in this community is thus shown to be more bark than bite, and much of it evaporates as these strangers approach the golden West. In this pattern we see The Myth's construction of non-White society as matriarchies governed by dragon ladies, big mommas, and other paper goddesses who prove to be unequal to the task of maintaining true power.

Grace herself is the site of injury, pain, and loss; she is damage personified. Pain constructed as a child, she thus raises questions of *guilt*: What more could we have done, who is responsible, who was watching out? Her loss is nicely (from the perspective of how The Myth works) balanced between complicity and fate: on the one hand she could have done things differently, but on the other hand this just simply happened (in the past). The Myth thus neutralizes the pain and loss suffered by people of color in the past, and blunts connections to ongoing structures and processes that sustain that pain.

On the morning of the accident Grace awakens in a scene of Edenic innocence, a quilt-covered bed in a child's room filled with statues and images of horses. She meets her friend Judith as snow slowly coats the countryside with purity, and they gossip about boys as they ride along. In this state of [g]race, she controls the power and violence represented easily by the horse. In the first of what will be a recurring image, once she has taken Pilgrim from the stall she shuts its door with a decisive clang of a black iron clasp. That mark of physical control over the powerful horse, the clasp, is matched by the gentleness of her mastery through love, as she sweet-talks the horse in echoes of the boy-gossip she shares with Judith. Grace will maintain this control until the injury; it is Judith, not Grace, whose horse loses its footing and who tangles her own foot in the stirrups. Grace is injured as she comes to Judith's aid.

The accident scene is horrifying but also surreal. It is shot in quickly alternating segments that show the panic and fear of the girls and their animals as the White man behind the wheel of an enormous truck slides his overwhelming technology inexorably toward them. The moment of loss, the accident, the source of pain, is thus remembered as in a mirror darkly; it is a confused image from the past. The Myth preserves the horror of the original loss at the same time that it refuses to remember historically specific events that might raise uncomfortable questions of responsibility (how fast was the truck going? Who owned the slave ships? Was the driver sober? Who profited from the cheap labor? Who eats all that fruit? and so forth).

The loss is terrible. The living envy the dead. The pain shared by Grace and by the embodiment of power, Pilgrim, is explicitly equated. After seeing Pilgrim for the first time after the accident, wildly in pain, Grace says, "I've decided about Pilgrim. I think we should put him down. It's not fair for him to suffer." As Annie begins to applaud Grace's calm maturity in such a decision, Grace drops the other shoe: "Maybe we should put me down, too. I'm not much use anymore," a statement that stuns Annie in its pain and grief and prompts the trip to the West. The lost innocence of Grace represents the theme in The Myth of people of color as damaged, torn beyond repair, with parts removed. The loss suffered by those who come to the West, in The Myth, is so great that accommodation and prostheses are all that can be hoped for; there will never be wholeness.

The broken, fallen, former innocents who arrive in the West are also problematic, for their loss has emerged in an uncontrollable rage and violence. The bad things that happened to them have created terrible resentments, perhaps understandable under the circumstances but now wholly out of control. These resentments, this enraged power, must be managed in some way if social accommodation is ever to be achieved. This dimension of The Myth is clearly enacted in Grace's loss of control over Pilgrim. It is foreshadowed by her inability to control Pilgrim entirely, as she and Judith slide into the road. Recuperating in bed, Grace watches videotapes of herself riding Pilgrim in steeplechase competition, gracefully mastering his power. But that control is gone. She wants to see Pilgrim, and so goes to the veterinarian's barn. "Hey, hello beautiful boy," she coos to him in tones of old, and is shocked by the eruption of violence and power that is Pilgrim's reply. She is horrified by the sight of his still raw flesh, red and oozing on muzzle and flank. Backing away in a panic, she understands that the ability to control power has vanished with her innocence.

Grace's ability to control anything at all has vanished. She becomes a social outcast. One wonders where her friends are in all of this; at any rate, nobody is seen visiting her, nobody is kind to her at school, she cannot manage to keep up her social connections. "I don't want to come back, that's all," she tells her mother. Taken unwillingly on the trip to the West, she fights Annie all the way. When an exasperated Annie asks if she wants to return, Grace expresses her powerlessness: "What are you asking me for? You didn't ask if I wanted to come in the first place. Now *I* get to decide?"

As for Pilgrim: Twilight scenes of horses running open the movie, bringing the animals' power to the foreground. The original unity between this power and innocence is established in camera shots that alternate back and forth between Grace and Pilgrim as she saddles him up and as they ride toward their shared doom. Embodied power is "all right" as long as innocence is unharmed. With pain and loss comes an unappeasable drive to violence. Uncontrolled, angry power bursts forth from the wound left in the body of innocence.

The anger and violence represented by the horse is an important part of The Myth, which sees that violence as inherent in the complex of character that it attributes to people of color, and sees it as always in danger of eruption. Pilgrim is full of fire and spirit even before the accident, but he is mastered by Grace. Faced with the oncoming truck, he rises up to strike at it with his hooves, futilely opposing physical force to unopposable technology (as spears and arrows were once opposed to musket and cannon). When Pilgrim's body is broken, so is the hold that Grace has over his power. That hold was fragile to begin with. Reading about horses after the accident, Annie learns this: "A million years before man they grazed the vast and empty plains. They first came to know man as the hunter, not the hunted . . . the alliance with man would forever be fragile, for the fear he struck in their hearts would never be dislodged." And the first pictures shown to accompany this narrative are of American Indians and what would appear to be Assyrians. This "fragile" balance is destroyed by the historical disaster that befell Africans, Asians, Indians, and so forth, and the potential for violence is thus on the loose. As the wild, eruptive stallion is locked into the trailer for the ride into the West, we see another close-up of an iron latch being clanged shut, emphasizing the strength that must be contained within the aluminum walls.

It is important in The Myth that violence is made to emerge from this afflicted people because of the pain they have suffered. The connection to injury provides a justification, although the violence is nevertheless regrettable. This connection to pain is what makes this a liberal myth rather than one of simpler racist attributions of violence; The Myth is a more complicated racist attribution of violence. In the film, the hideous injuries suffered by the horse are clearly marked as the cause of its newly emerged violent behavior. We see the horse first after the accident taking refuge under a bridge. The condition of his injuries, in which flesh hangs from him in strips, takes the veterinarian's (and the audience's) breath away. "Oh, Jesus!" exclaims the veterinarian. The horse overpowers her efforts to control it, overwhelmingly violent even in its injured state. It is eventually subdued, but even under tranquilizers in the hospital it is violent, kicking out with its legs against the stall. The change wrought by injury is made clear by the veterinarian: "Well Grace, you see, Pilgrim just isn't the same horse he used to be." She is more blunt with Annie: "This animal's beyond help."

The stage is thus set for these dimensions attributed to people of color, these complex interlocking parts of The Myth's racial theory, to reenact the historic journey to the West. With an unwilling Grace and a drugged Pilgrim, an uncertain Annie weighs anchor on her SUV and makes way for a distant land. We have had early indications that they will be strangers in that strange land. When Annie first called Tom Booker to solicit his help, she confidently announced, "This is Annie MacLean, from Cover . . . you know, the magazine." Tom stares impatiently into the middle distance, completely unimpressed by this meaningless declaration of her tribal affiliation. "Is there something I can do for you, ma'am?" he queries. The strangeness that the MacLeans will represent as they move into the West becomes clearer the farther they go. Hip-hop and oldies radio begins to give way to the sounds of farm reports, country-western, and evangelists even as the land flattens while mountains rise in the distance. The strangeness that people must have felt arriving from Africa, Asia, and other parts of the Americas is echoed as these New Yorkers enter the West, and their own strangeness will be made plain to them once they get there. A significant break in the narrative of the film occurs as Annie, Grace, and Pilgrim arrive in Montana and declare themselves to the man of the West, Tom Booker.

The Man of the West

Tom Booker is a stereotypical cowboy, that mythical personification of White, patriarchal America. His rugged, weather-beaten face exudes strength and confidence. As noted, we first see him in a telephone conversation with Annie as she tries to impress him with her magazine credentials and woo him to visit darkest New York. He stares into the horizon, mastering impatience to be on the trail, refusing to leave his grounded place in Montana. He is who The Myth would like to imagine the benign patriarchs of the West to be, there to suffer the entreaties of the matriarchal societies that fate has brought to his shores.

Tom Booker will also enact The Myth's conviction that people of color, represented often in female form, are attracted (physically and spiritually) to the men of the West. The sexual attraction Annie will come to feel stands in for the social attraction imagined by The Myth. "They" want "us," says The Myth, even as the men of the West make the fulfillment of that desire a perfectly "free" choice for "them." Tom Booker does very little to woo Annie, other than to be himself; she falls head over heels giggling in love. This attraction is also expressed in other ways. Reading about horse whisperers in general, Annie learns that, "since that Neolithic moment when a horse was first haltered, there were those among men . . . who could see into the creature's soul and soothe the wounds they found there." All of the whisperers pictured in the film at that moment are White. The men of the West are thus pictured as sources of healing and love, waiting for wounded people of color to come to them.

Moving ahead of the approaching MacLeans, the camera first shows us Tom in Montana tending an animal as his brother, Frank, and Frank's adolescent son look on. Tom's nephew is relating a story he heard in school about how geese can "imprint" on an airplane and follow it around, and he recommends that the family try to get a foal, newly born on the ranch, to imprint on them. Tom smiles and says, "Might be all right for geese to grow up thinking they're an airplane. A horse, far as I can tell, can't fly." This is precisely the kind of parable that an older generation of racists might have used to explain why birds of different feathers ought not flock together—a version of racism that The Myth updates and replaces. At that precise moment, the car and trailer from

New York pull into their yard with its freight of strange, exotic birds from distant lands.

Assuming her best managerial style, Annie extends her hand to Tom: "Annie MacLean, from New York. We talked on the phone. I had a little trouble finding the place, there are *nooooo* signs." Annie natters on in her British/New York urban sophisticated way while Tom regards her as if she were a Martian newly dropped from the skies. "Oh, there are plenty of signs, just not many that are printed," he replies, thus laying claim to a knowledge of how to negotiate *this* place that is denied to this exotic. She implores him again to examine Pilgrim, and when he begins to demur she snaps at him, "Look, please don't do the 'shucks, ma'am' thing again," a rather grating thing to say under the circumstances. Tom never answers, staring at her all the while. His is a communicative strategy that Annie and Grace will both encounter and engage in often during their stay in Montana: questions go unanswered, remarks go unremarked. The film thus enacts The Myth's assertion of a lack of connection and communication among people of diverse backgrounds, and suggests that the snippy social manner of the matriarchal Others may be largely to blame for the disjunction.

Annie and Grace appear as Other to Tom when he goes to their refugee camp, disguised as a motel, to examine Pilgrim. There he sees for the first time Grace's artificial leg. Annie is in another room doing her magazine business by phone. Grace is watching the television show *Friends,* about as un-Montana as you can get. "This your first time in Montana?" Tom asks, and Grace makes no reply. "Is she gonna be long?" he asks of Annie, still on the phone. "Probably, she's on the phone twenty-three hours a day," says Grace. Then she offers up this gracious observation: "Just in case she hasn't told you, which she probably hasn't, I don't want to be a part of this, OK?" Difference, separation, lack of connection mark the interaction from the start.

I have mentioned before the extent to which locks and clasps appear regularly in the film. Entering Pilgrim's stall, Tom undoes a heavy metal chain. He uses a coiled rope, an instrument of constraint and control, to wave at Pilgrim in an attempt to subdue the horse, as if the rope were a talisman. Pilgrim has not been led around in months, much less ridden, but he still wears a bridle. The film features close-ups of these instruments of mastery. In the context of the racial history of America, they are also reminders of the physical bondage of people in slavery, incarceration, and other situations of oppression, and they emphasize the position of Tom as the White man of the West, and of the MacLeans and their horse as the exotic third world.

However, the film embodies The Myth by granting the man of the West his instruments of physical (if need be, brutal) control but locating the real source of his power in his spiritual purity, social dominance, and strength of character. In the corral we see the first of many episodes in which Tom will look deeply and intently at the horse, as if divining the secrets of his soul. Annie remarks at the immediate effect: "Well, you're the closest anyone's come" to Pilgrim. Tom's plan for healing emphasizes the connection between Grace and Pilgrim, between damaged innocence and unruly violence in the third world: "I need to know something right now. It's a question for Grace. You see, when I work with a horse, it's no good just me doing it, the owner's got to be involved, too." When she objects that she cannot be involved since she cannot physically ride, he dismisses the argument: "Either you want to or you don't." In doing so he shifts the problem with Grace (and with these people) from a physical one to a moral one: her disability is restated as one of will, not of historical fact. It is a way in which The Myth urges "moving on" beyond the fact of historical injury, to overcome that history by an act of will and moral transcendence. Of course, the man of the West is thus placed in a position of moral superiority and judgment. When Annie also objects, Tom overrules her: "This is her decision, not yours," thus speaking for and directing this social group that has come to his place, and empowering the man of the West over these exotic strangers.

Back home with his brother Frank and family, Frank's wife Diane has all kinds of objections to Tom's working with the MacLeans. "Well, I just think she's got a lot of nerve showing up here and that, you know, poor animal and that child." She all but wonders why they don't go back where they came from. The strangeness of the MacLeans is emphasized gastronomically. Frank hypothesizes that Annie eats "big salads . . . I believe women from New York eat big salads," which prompts another assertion of difference and strangeness from Diane: "Well that's just what we need, a vegetarian from New York on our cattle ranch." In this episode the characters reenact The Myth's attribution of legitimate grievance for Whites, at the same time it notes their patient acceptance and assistance of people of color.

Themes in The Myth that have been established so far are continued and elaborated upon as the film progresses. In his first sessions with Pilgrim on Tom's own ranch, we see more close-ups of coiled rope, which Tom has in his hands often and waves at the horse so as to control his movements. Ropes are used to lead Pilgrim through water. Annie's attempts to exercise her own poor power in this context are shown to be useless, especially as she questions these attempts to control the horse's power. "What's he doing? Is this some kind of physical therapy?" she asks, and is ignored. Many of the scenes in which the MacLeans' questions are ignored are situations in which force is being used to subdue the violent horse. In this way The Myth shows people of color the futility of questioning the "legitimate" use of state power in controlling expressions of rage. During this episode Annie's cell phone goes off, sending the horse into a flailing panic. Officiously, she chides Tom: "Mr. Booker, I'm really not comfortable with you taking these kinds of risks." She clearly has no idea of what she is talking about, nor any standing to make such a comment. The Myth uses the film to position the West as exercising a necessary control over the unruly power of people of color, a control that is questioned by the ignorant, ineffectual sites of matriarchal power. The Myth thus legitimizes means of coercive control as serving a higher, even spiritual purpose that will not be understood by those being controlled.

The spiritual grounding of ropes and chains in The Myth is made clear by what follows this scene. Pilgrim is allowed to run off, with Tom following. The horse stops in a meadow, and Tom simply stops as well, some yards from him, and sits, staring intently at the horse. Annie, not understanding the higher purposes that are being served, querulously asks, "Are we in the way? Should we leave?" And when she is completely ignored, as she is so often, she says, "I guess we'll go then." Tom waits in the meadow the entire day, until toward dusk the horse gives up the spiritual struggle and comes to him, bowing his head. Capitulation of angry power and a move toward the ground of, the site of, the man of the West is regarded as a great spiritual victory. Tom's only comment is to chide Annie for her major link to the homeland: "From now on, leave your phone somewhere else."

Once anger has bowed its head, even if only for the moment, the exotic MacLeans are deemed civilized enough to be invited in for dinner, which Diane does. Their utter difference from this centered Montanan family is clear: They scarcely know what to do as the family prays before dinner, and their conversation is about restaurants in New York as the family attempts to discuss different breeds of cattle. Frank, in a moment of generosity, offers Annie and Grace the use of a spare house on the ranch while they are there. From the amazed expression of Tom and the appalled expression of Diane, it is clear that he has committed a faux pas in actually inviting these people into the neighborhood, but the deed has been done. Diane's subtle objections are hardly noticed, and Annie seems not to pick up on the cues that she might not be welcome. Grace pipes up that the house would be a good place to receive Robert when he comes to visit, prompting Diane to ask, "Where *is* your dad, sweetie?" "He's at home, working," she replies, but her embarrassment at her disunified family is clear.

This episode expresses the discomfort inherent in The Myth with meaningful integration—a conviction that integration must be done on the ground of the West (*they* must come to *us*)—and a sense that the brokenness asserted for people of color is an embarrassment to them, a looming scandal of which they are always aware. That embarrassment continues *en famille* as later that evening Robert asks Annie, on the telephone, "So when are you coming home?" Annie replies evasively, "You know, I asked him that tonight, he doesn't know"—a reply that places decision making for this family with the man of the West, Tom Booker. Once she hangs up Grace asks her, "Did you ask him to come visit?" to which Annie replies, again evasively, "You already did." The dysfunction of the family is clear, as it is in The Myth.

The next day, Tom is again in the corral with Pilgrim. He throws a rope over the neck of the horse and wraps the other end around himself, using his own body as a lever with which to control the horse's wild running and rearing. Questioning *this* use of force by the man of the West to control violence, Annie asks, "How is it going?" of a ranch hand—and is again ignored. Pulling the loop (the noose?) around the horse's neck tighter and tighter, in what can surely be read as an echo of lynching, Tom finally brings the horse to a standstill. Pilgrim walks calmly to Tom, as he did the day before, and *again bows his head* before the man of the West, allowing the rope to be removed. At this point Tom and the ranch hand exchange knowing looks and brief nods, a confirmation of Tom's success in controlling violence and restoring order, but also an exchange that completely excludes Annie, making success an achievement of these two White men as they exercise their secret and powerful knowledge.

If the point about control over violence were not yet clear, there follows a long passage of scenes showing the branding of cattle. Rambunctious calves are shown on the ground, irons becoming white-hot in the fire, the scorching of flesh as the brands are pressed to hide. A major component of The Myth is the complicity of people of color with their own misfortunes, the idea that Africans sold Africans to the West, Asians and South Americans willingly came here to work, and so forth. Into these scenes of branding, of violent control, come Annie and Grace to observe. Tom asks each of them to "make yourself useful," and they are quickly put to task helping willingly with this work of mastery and marking. Annie is laughed at good-naturedly as she falls in the corral, landing in Tom's arms at one point to her embarrassment. Grace learns to brand, and presses a hot iron onto live flesh with a smile on her face. Annie wears her difference like a signboard, asking an incredulous Tom, "Is it cocktail hour yet?" Tom recruits Grace even further into the project of control and mastery, saying, "You handled that pretty well. I think it's time you started earning your keep around here," and suggests that she groom and feed the horses. "Think you can handle it?" he asks. "That's not a question, is it?" Grace replies, to which he says, "No." She does not object, and thus damaged innocence is willingly recruited in the project of mastery and control.

The Myth understands that strangers came here with history, but that history is usually understood as one of pain and suffering. The West is positioned as the site of a rich, positive history that is the center to which other, less privileged cultures come. In *The Horse Whisperer*, the Booker family is pictured as such a center, having lived for generations on their ranch laying down a sedimented history and family tradition. This point is made in the evening of the branding day, when a picnic supper shows real cowboys who could well be straight out of Western movies, playing guitars and singing around campfires. In this site of venerable grounded (if imaginary) history, Tom and Frank's aged mother tells stories of the family. She asks Annie, "Where do you call home?" Answering for her from a position of dominance, Tom replies, "She's from New York, Mom." But Annie explains that her strangeness is even stranger: "I'm from all over, really, my father was a diplomat, we moved all over." And although Mrs. Booker praises Annie for such an exotic life, Annie mournfully replies, "It's not like *knowing* a place, like this." She remarks as she views pictures in the old-fashioned parlor, "This family has quite a history." Diane says, "Yup, it's a story all right." Diane relates stories of Tom and Frank's Western boyhoods as Annie sees a picture of a close family life unfold.

Annie's lack of centeredness continues to be made clear as she wanders onto the front porch and finds Tom demonstrating a string game to the children. He offers her his jacket as she sits and fidgets. "Don't you ever sit still?" he asks. "Well, you sit still too long in New York and you get renovated," she replies, marking herself as Other. She also marks herself as disempowered:

> "Why is it, Mr. Booker, that sometimes I get the feeling that you're laughing at me?"
> "I don't know, why?"
> "No; you're supposed to say you're not laughing at me."
> "Oh I see, you take care of both sides of the conversation."
> "It's a man's world, Mr. Booker, most women have to."

She is the wanderer, a visitor from a foreign place but also the disempowered woman, come to a patriarchal society that seems always to have been here, that seems naturally grounded in the land. "It's beautiful country, and I can see having some kind of vacation place or retreat, but don't you miss the rest of the world?" Annie asks. "What's to miss?" Tom asks in return. Annie lists museums and opera and so forth, to which Tom replies that he enjoyed those things when he lived in Chicago, a revelation that surprises Annie. The man of the West thus lacks nothing; his groundedness does not come at the expense of sophistication. He knows which fork to use as much as the next gent. But he also belongs somewhere, a groundedness denied this vagabond, exotic female.

Annie's Otherness is also apparent the next morning, when she confronts Tom out early; he is riding, she is running. "Oh, a jogger, eh?" he asks her. "I don't jog, Mr. Booker, I run," she replies. "Oh, that's lucky for you, the grizzlies around here mostly go for joggers," he returns. It is clear that her seeking exercise for its own sake is a mark of difference on this hard-working ranch, but she is also marked with naiveté in her ignorance of the danger from bears in that country.

This man of the West introduces his exotic visitors to his customs. It is revealed that Annie used to ride in her youth, although, "I've never ridden Western before," she demurs, emphasizing her sojourner's status. Tom shows up with a horse for her to ride and gradually teaches her the ways of riding on his own grounds. Likewise, he later shows up at the guesthouse with a pickup truck (a novel technology for a Manhattanite, surely) and insists that Grace drive it, even with her artificial leg. She is reluctant, claiming her disability, but he insists, and she eventually proves capable of mastering this new machine. Tom thus enacts The Myth's claims that the exotic visitors to this land need training and exposure to new practices and technology that will improve their lives.

The learning is not reciprocal; The Myth makes little room for the visitors to bring anything with them worth sharing. Annie's urban, even global sophistication has little or no value in the West. She envies old Mrs. Booker because, "It must be great to be her age and to be at that point in life where you have no more guesswork, no more impossible decisions to make." Tom replies by asserting the currency of that certitude among the men of the West generally: "I don't think you have to wait to be her age to find that kind of peace." He gets it by "waking up on the ranch, knowing what I'm supposed to do that day, knowing I'm home." Annie replies that she wakes up full of doubt, and she surely wakes up in a strange place, whether Montana or back home in one of her two dwellings. "The more I try to fix things the more they fall apart," she says, displaying her ineffectuality. Tom invites her to let them do so, thus encouraging her weakness, although it is pretty clear that he does not do so himself in mastering the land and cattle of his home. Her place in the West is uncertain even to her: "Do you think I was right to come?" Although The Myth is happy to raise that issue, it puts the man of the West in the position of granting at least the appearance of perfect freedom to make a decision about whether to stay or not, for Tom replies, "I can't answer that, Annie." His own wife, from whom he is divorced, made the wrong decision in coming, however—"Too much space, she said"—and thus returned to where she came from. Tom makes clear his groundedness in where he is and his unwillingness to be on anyone else's turf.

The pain and ineffectuality of these exotics continues to be displayed. Cooking a meal for the Bookers, Annie clumsily drops pans and curses audibly from the kitchen. She wails despairingly to Tom, "It's been so long since I've done this." When he buttons her undone dress in the back, she simpers and frisks like a schoolgirl; gone is the strong leader of the New York magazine. As the Bookers take their leave, a fight erupts between Annie and Grace; Tom takes it upon himself to tell her how to manage her family: "Don't let her turn you away." In the ensuing conversation, these exotic women expose their own pain and ineffectuality. Annie complains, "Whatever I do, it's wrong, whatever I say, it's wrong." When Grace accuses her of *pushing,* she replies "I don't push for me, I push for you so you don't spend half your life not knowing where you belong," as, clearly, Annie has done. Grace reveals her own pain by breaking down in grief and crying, "Who's ever going to want me like this?"

The ability of the man of the West to manage power is compared to the inability of these strange visitors to do so. One short scene shows Tom sitting in a corral with his back to Pilgrim, working on a complicated harness that may well be used on Pilgrim. Pilgrim observes and walks around the corral but does not trouble Tom, a serenely confident center of power. However, the next scene shows Grace summoning the courage to enter Pilgrim's stall. But it is clear that he is unwilling to be approached and mastered by her; scenes of the accident flash by and he displays the old signs of violence and unmanageability, leaving Grace in tears. Hope for taming the angry violence brought by people of color to these shores is thus invested in the man of the West, according to The Myth.

Tom will be a source of healing for Grace as well, as The Myth puts very little stock in the ability of those who are injured to help themselves. Grace tells Tom that she is ready to talk about the accident, which she does in tears, showing her pain. Tom absolves Grace by saying, "You didn't do anything wrong." He then tells the story of (pointedly, from the perspective of The Myth) an *Indian* boy who used to work on the Booker ranch (of course). "He and I were really good friends," Tom says, but this person of color suffered a violent injury (of course) and became a (helpless) quadriplegic. Tom went to visit him a few times after the accident, but "his mind, his spirit, whatever you want to call it, just disappeared. The only thing left was his anger." Grace reinscribes her equivalence to people of color generally by saying, "I know where he goes." Tom says, "I know you do. Don't *you* disappear." She begins to respond to this call from the man of the West in ways that she never did among her own people.

Tom and Annie become increasingly close, spending time together, laughing and talking. A cattle drive takes the whole party out camping for a few days, where the relationship strengthens. The growing closeness is observed with concern by Grace and by Diane. Differences in communication styles between Annie and Diane enact The Myth's stereotypical attributions, for Annie is indirect and stylized in her expressions (the signifying African, the inscrutable Asian) while Diane is plainspoken and gets to the point. Annie beats around the bush but eventually admits, after an initial denial, that "fired" is exactly the right word to describe what has happened to her in terms of her magazine job. Diane replies, "I guess you don't have to figure it out until you get home," which of course raises anxiety for Annie since she does not know whether "home" is where she wants to be. "Did you always know this was the life you wanted?" she asks Diane, who responds with a certainty equal to Tom's, "Well, I was a rancher's daughter, it wasn't too far to go to be a rancher's wife." Annie hems and haws in asking about Tom's wife, at which point Diane goes to the point directly and comments on their different styles: "Hey look, Annie, I'm no good at this sort of talk, goes round and round something and never gets to it so let's just say what it is. . . . Don't you go looking here for whatever it is you're looking for," she warns. Sisterhood clearly only goes so far, and the woman of the West is not willing for this exotic stranger to get too close to the family.

Later that evening, Tom and Annie, on walks away from the others (Tom walks out first, Annie goes to *him*), share a first kiss. Love seems to be in the air, but lo! upon their return to the ranch they find that Robert has arrived, having arranged a last minute surprise visit. Robert, Annie, and Grace enact the happy family for the Bookers, but it is clear that they are strange and exotic. Tom looks at Annie with appraising eyes as Grace and Robert repeat family stories of how the parents met: Annie was a journalist for an English magazine who stumbled upon Robert, a Peace Corps worker on a hiking holiday, in farthest India. The longer the story goes the stranger (and more third world) do the MacLeans appear in the context of centered Montana.

Later that night, Annie's face is a picture of confusion as she and Robert prepare for bed. It is clear that she does not welcome physical closeness. She says, "You have every right to be here," but her arm is shaking and it is clear she feels ambivalence in her utterance. Thus The Myth expresses its ambivalence as to whether the spirit of the fatherland really belongs in the West, really has a place with its separated and dis-empowered relics that it has sent here and whether the displaced people who are *in* the West really feel a connection to their home.

Tom maintains a careful neutrality since Robert's arrival, enacting The Myth's depiction of the third world wanting and needing the West more than the West wants and needs the third world. Annie confronts Tom over his sudden distance. He is putting the decision entirely in her hands: "You've got to figure out what you want." Annie replies, "Do you know what *you* want?" He says, "I do know what I want. . . . Annie this is where I belong, this is who I am. Is *this* what you want?" He thus expresses his chief priority as groundedness in the West rather than in terms of social bonding with the Other. When she says yes to his question, Tom replies, "Can you tell that to your family? To Robert, to Grace? If you had a chance to go home and change things, would you?" Annie replies, "You can't ask me that, it's not that simple." Tom responds: "It *is.*" Annie's inability to act prompts Tom to take things in hand. In the very next scene we see him in Pilgrim's stall saying, "There's something you've got to do tomorrow, boy." Tom is going to "change things" for the family by finally healing Grace and Pilgrim.

This exchange between Annie and Tom is a key expression of The Myth in this film. It positions the West as desiring integration with people of color, but it removes the West entirely from any position of *need* for such a thing; it's Annie's decision, after all, and she had come to the man of the West seeking healing in the first place. The Myth in this film expresses the belief that one alternative for the third world is that things can be "changed" and the alleged brokenness of people of color can be healed, but not by remaining as whole, authentic people in the

West. On the one hand, people can change and become Western. On the other hand, the promise of a return, whether physical or spiritual, to the place of origins is offered as an alternative to the preferred option of forsaking that origin and one's roots, giving up one's wandering and becoming one with the West, on the West's own terms and on its ground. In the end, the West is to take pity and do what must be done to heal people of color, since they cannot do it themselves.

In the corral the next day Pilgrim is bridled and saddled; we see lots of close-ups of metal buckles, ropes, and other instruments of mastery. Grace tries to mount the horse conventionally, but he refuses her. Frank assures her, "Tom'll get him all right." Tom and a ranch hand prepare a complicated rig of roping and hook it around Pilgrim's leg. As in the past, the impending use of forceful control over power is questioned; Grace says, "It's not gonna hurt him, right?" For once she is answered, but obliquely, for Tom says, "Nothing we've done has hurt him. Grace, this is Pilgrim's chance, and it's yours, too." The atmosphere is sinister; we know that something akin to punishment, some act of control and restraint, is about to occur.

Sure enough, Tom uses the rope system to hobble the horse, raising one leg off the ground. Pilgrim fights it, but in the end Tom drops him to the ground as the family watches in fear. Considered in terms of The Myth, parallels to lynching seem unavoidable. Grace cries out, "That's enough, stop!" Tom and the horse eye each other in a contest of wills, but in the end rope, control, technique, and the man of the West win out. It is then that Tom, sitting on Pilgrim's side, strokes him lovingly (once he's down!). He invites Grace to do the same: "Grace, this is where you come in. . . . He's OK, and you never did anything to let him down. Grace you've got to do this. Trust me one more time." Grace does so, weeping. Pilgrim relaxes, and makes sounds that the film presents in ways that resemble weeping as well. Tom says, "Now we're gonna show Pilgrim here how to help you get on him. Because you see there's a point where neither one of you's gonna need me any more. And we're there . . . I'm *not* asking." Tom wraps caring inside a position of mastery and control: the man of the West is going to heal these folks whether they like it or not. Grace sits on the saddle, Pilgrim rolls to his feet and stands upright with Grace astride him. It is an epiphany for all. They begin to ride while everyone looks on, transfixed. Robert and Annie hold hands. The family seems reunited. Tom helps Grace to dismount, they hug and then Grace runs to her parents to embrace them.

The family prepares to return to New York, Robert and Grace by airplane, Annie to follow with Pilgrim in the trailer. Robert confronts Annie and tells her to "take your time" in returning: "I sat there looking at that horse and I swear I felt the same thing was happening to me. . . . I can either fight the way things are or accept them." He says he knows what is going on and depicts himself as always having loved Annie more than she loves him. He articulates Annie's indecisiveness: "You don't know how you feel about me. You don't know if you want a life with me any more." He gives her a free and open choice to "come home" or not, but not until she knows how she feels. He and Grace drive away.

Annie is left by herself to finish packing. She wanders Tom's house seeing all the Western decorations and seems to come to a decision as to where she belongs. We see a final close-up of the latch on the trailer being lifted as Annie walks in to see Pilgrim, who is now perfectly tame. Tom arrives on the scene. Annie says, "I don't want to leave you." Tom replies, "I don't want you to." But she knows she must go. Indirect to the end, she asks him to prepare horses for one last ride. As he does so, she drives off, thus avoiding the last goodbye.

Conclusion

I have observed before that *The Horse Whisperer* has a number of interesting reversals. A myth about people of color is manifested in a movie about White people. The father figure, or male principal, for third-world people is represented as having more traditionally female characteristics of nurturing than his domineering wife. In enacting a form that also underlies many other texts, the film thus introduces content or information that is the reverse of what one might expect. As we noted in the first chapter, such information often piggybacks on form, and is thus one of the sites of rhetorical appeal in texts.

The underlying claim that the film is homologous with The Myth is supported if one considers a trajectory of homology among related texts. The "original" idea of horse whispering was introduced to a mass audience in Monty Roberts's book about his own experience with horses, *The Man Who Listens to Horses*. This book is less well known, less widely distributed, than are the film and the book upon which the film is based, Nicholas Evans's *The Horse Whisperer*. Horse whispering as described by Roberts has little or nothing to do with domination and control. The link between horse and whisperer is spiritual and equal, one of respect and cooperation. Domination and empowerment of the whisperer over the horse is emphasized in the more popular Evans book. That antagonistic position between human and horse ends differently in that book than it does in the film, for in the book Tom Booker is killed by a herd of still "angry" and defiant horses in the end. The film, as we have seen, is an unambiguous celebration of domination and control, and its triumph over the horse—and the film is the most popular of these texts. As a text increases in popularity and distribution in American culture, then, it aligns more closely with themes of power over "lesser beings" that is central to The Myth.

Given the nature of the reversals in this film, an important rhetorical effect is that The Myth is affirmed, perpetuated, and reindividuated in disguise. Since it is about White people on the level of content, it seems not to be saying anything about people of color. Since everyone displays the same pigmentation on the level of information, the film seems not to be about the history of race in America. It can therefore deliver its message without the accuracy of the message being questioned. The Myth comes in under the critical radar. The film reinscribes a way of thinking that has often been used to think about race, but it does so without being about race on a content level. Nevertheless, it exercises a formal muscle, a formal potential, in the minds of specifically American (especially White) audiences, a formal faculty that has been used to perpetuate what is obviously an instrument of racist hegemony and domination.

The film thus calls our attention to the importance of form over content. Especially for critics who want to intervene in social conflict by advising readers and students about the ways in which inequities are perpetuated rhetorically, attention to form rather than to the literal level of content or information is a vital strategy and an important task of vigilance. We must likewise teach our students and readers to see political work at a formal level in addition to the more easily detectable work of claims, assertions, propositions, and accusations at the level of information.

If it is possible for a film that shows no literal people of color to be about color, *The Horse Whisperer* also suggests that race in America is not *only* based on physical features. In other words, race itself is not really about color, nor are the rhetorics that maintain race and racism. Race as a concept and racially based domination is based upon certain symbolic strategies that are fundamental, that cut across many times and places, and that can transcend the historical specificities of particular constructions of race. Patterns based on emasculation, assertions of terrible loss and injury, Otherness and exoticism, and so forth are always already *available* in American thinking. If domination over people of one socially constructed racial group someday no longer serves hegemonic interests, the formal pattern is there to extend The Myth homologically into new situations so as to underlie the construction of new historical specificities of race, group, and identity. This study thus illustrates the importance of thinking about rhetorical homologies as highly adaptive engines for ordering social consciousness in the service of power.

In the next chapter we expand our understanding of homology. Our focus remains on the study of a homology that orders a wide range of experiences and texts, but instead of homology as a narrative structure we will think of homology as the form uniting a whole family of signs, specifically the family of chairs, stools, benches, thrones, and other experiences that I shall call "The Chair." We will also include within the net of homology another element, the experience of a medium that is conveying the homologous texts and experiences. What difference does it make if one apprehends a text by experiencing a medium that is ordered by the homology? We also add to the study of homology a consideration of homologous structures beneath signs, and a consideration of media.

4

Some Rhetorical Implications of The Chair, Illustrated in *Get on the Bus*

On December 1, 1955, Rosa Parks refused to give up her seat on a bus to a White man in Montgomery, Alabama. Her subsequent arrest sparked a 381-day boycott of the bus system and made of Parks a mythic figure in the civil rights movement (Albin). In a parallel pair of incidents ninety years earlier (1865), another human rights pioneer, Sojourner Truth, successfully brought suit against two streetcar conductors in Washington, D.C., for their forcible opposition to her taking a seat in their cars; in both cases she got the conductors dismissed, and in one case, convicted of assault and battery (Painter, 210–11). For both Parks and Truth, claims of empowerment and resistance to those claims were made *in terms of* a place to *sit.*

Where there is so much repetition of a key fact, there must be something in kilter. In this chapter I argue that chairs, seats, thrones, benches, pews, and others of their tribe, sitting, reclining, standing or moving in relation to sitting—plus talk and images *about* these things—constitute a sign with widespread rhetorical applications, yet a sign that is insufficiently studied. That complex sign I shall call The Chair. The homology studied in this chapter may be understood as anchored in a key, recurring sign, but more than that, a family or a structure of signs. There is a homology uniting the different manifestations of The Chair, I shall argue, and that homology likewise grounds discourses, experiences, and media that feature The Chair.

This chapter is based on some earlier research (Brummett, "Homology;" *Rhetorical*; Jameson) that suggested that when the content of a mediated text, the experience of the medium, and certain rhetorical situations faced by the audience are *homologous,* the rhetorical effect of the text is enhanced. A key component of the experience of the movies is that one sits in a chair and then rises at the end to go out into the world. That obvious but insufficiently considered fact is linked homologically to the rhetorical effect of some films that make heavy use of signs keyed to sitting or standing; in other words, to films that use The Chair. One such film is Spike Lee's *Get on the Bus.* The rhetoric of this film depends in large part on its use of signs of sitting and rising at the same time that it moves its audience through a cycle of sitting and standing. The content of the film studied and the audience's experience of the film in a theater are homological with the discursive structure making The Chair a family of signs. Previous chapters of this book have treated homology as a kind of narrative structure, moving in time, in a sense. This chapter treats homology as a more spatial structure, which is the form underlying a family of signs, a structure that may then also be caught up in the narrative, linear sequences of discourse and experience.

We cannot understand how a sign works in any particular film without considering the network of meanings the sign brings with it from general cultural usage. In this chapter I first explain a range of complicated meanings connected to The Chair. I then briefly discuss some issues in homology theory to explain why The Chair may be especially important in understanding certain kinds of films. Finally, I argue that Lee's use of The Chair was an especially powerful rhetorical tactic for cinematic audiences of *Get on the Bus.* The contributions made by this chapter are thus (a) greater understanding of a widely occurring but seldom studied sign, The Chair, (b) further development of homology theory as applied to the study of film through, and (c) a critical analysis of *Get on the Bus* that reveals an important dimension of its rhetorical power.

I focus my analysis here on the meanings facilitated by The Chair in recent Western culture. However, we shall see some evidence that The Chair is a sign with stable, widespread, and ancient meanings. Although Witold Rybczynski argues that the modern chair and the development of our social uses for it began to take shape only as recently as the fifteenth century (26), we shall consider some evidence further on in this chapter that its meanings may be more far-flung. Certainly the dominance of The Chair in the Victorian novels of Henry James and Charles Dickens that we examine here and in *Get on the Bus,* a film created by the highly Afrocentric director Lee, points to the possibility that The Chair may be a widely understood sign. Indeed, to understand the symbolic dimensions of The Chair is to understand a homological structure uniting this intricate family of signs as well as texts and experiences keyed to the sign.

The Chair is used in complex ways to signify power relations through status, hierarchy, belonging, action, and identity. In support of this claim I review ways in which The Chair is a locus of power and control, ways in which it reciprocally signifies subordination, ways in which The Chair is a site of belonging and acceptance, and ways in which The Chair is a site of personal centeredness, empowerment, and identity.

A Row of Chairs: Four Dimensions of Meaning and Effect

The Chair manages claims of power through four dimensions of meaning facilitated by that sign, four dimensions to be examined here. To support my claims I will use well-known examples from contemporary and historical cultural practice and discourse. The Chair is a sign that manages resources of power in two ways, through *being* and *action* (the former is more common). When it is the locus of control or a site of belonging, The Chair is not a reflection of action or of meritorious deeds so much as it is a sign of *empowerment through being.* That is because that iteration of The Chair refuses action, although it may command action in others and may be linked to certain actions. To sit in, to be called, or to be assigned The Chair is to claim power not through action but through being, with the status, power, belonging, and hierarchy that being implies. The Chair thus reciprocally indicates subordination or deference through the obligation to rise (or sometimes, not rise) from a chair as a signal of subordination. Sometimes the polarities of The Chair reverse and subordinates are required to sit. In those cases,

The Chair creates *empowerment through action* in relation to those who must sit.

The Chair as a Locus of Power and Control

When we refer metaphorically to someone who is "in the driver's seat" or "in the director's chair," we mean that she is in control of events. The empowerment is expressed through the sign of The Chair. A chair is what an empowered person need *not* rise up out of during interactions with others. To rise is an acknowledgment of equality or deference, even if only temporary. So one rises from a chair at a table or desk to greet a visitor with deference, but remains seated as a signal that such deference need not be displayed. What it means to remain seated then is not necessarily disrespect so much as an acknowledgment of status that is agreed upon, or an offer of status for a newcomer. Thus, business executives may sit to witness the presentation of one who is courting a decision from them; the sitting of the executives denotes their relative power in the situation. Rybczynski traces this meaning of The Chair back to at least the Middle Ages, during which "chairs . . . were not intended to be comfortable; they were symbols of authority. You had to be important to sit down in a chair—unimportant people sat on benches" (26). The power of The Chair is familiar even in children's games: The winner of Musical Chairs is the last one to find a Chair, the loser is left standing.

Academics, of course, are familiar with the idea of a named or endowed Chair as a site of power and control in the academy. This usage metonymically contains the image of a learned sage occupying a site to which students and pilgrims come for favors, benefit, and wisdom. The professor is reduced to The Chair, which retains the power. Academics are also familiar with speaking of the Chair or Chairperson of a department as a person of power and control. One may encounter such an officer more often on the hoof than in an actual chair. Furthermore, there may not be any single material chair in which this officer sits. Nevertheless, one signals her power in calling her not the Desk, the Carpet, or the Office, but the Chair.

Such usage resonates with more widespread references to the Chair, Chairman, or Chairperson of a meeting. That being is also a locus of control, and the location of the image in furniture is important.

Rybczynski notes that in centuries past, "the man who sat down was important—whence the term 'chairman'—and his upright, dignified posture reflected his social stature. This association of the seat itself with authority has remained an integral part of European and American culture" (81). Someone else in the meeting may "take the Chair" if the incumbent must step out of it for some reason. Power and control remain with The Chair itself, not the one who occupied it.

My use of the familiar term *incumbent* calls to mind the widely attributed advantage or power of being an incumbent in public office. An "incumbent President" is also described as a "sitting President," and both are presumed to have some advantage in future elections or in the use of power today. The *American Heritage Dictionary of the English Language* defines *incumbent* as the adjective, "lying, leaning, or resting upon something else," or as the noun, "a person who holds an office or ecclesiastical benefice." The root of the word is given as the Latin *incumbens,* to lean upon. The noun and the adjectival forms put together give a sense of that which the office holder leans or reclines upon as the source of the power of the office. An incumbent is powerful because of The Chair in which he sits.

A related and widespread usage of The Chair lies in references to chairs or seats on "the bench" of courts, or on the Supreme Court of a state or the nation, a seat on the County Board or on a planning commission, and so forth. One issue in presidential elections may be the number of "seats on the Supreme Court" that are likely to need filling in the next term. Attorneys arguing before a judge will not ask to come near the judge herself if a confidential matter must be discussed, but will instead ask to "approach the bench," validating The Chair as the site of power in the room.

We are but one step from judges to thrones. When The Chair takes the form of a throne, we see especially that it is the sign itself that is the locus of power, as when one refers to "the throne of England" as a synecdoche for the whole power of the monarch, or when we read in history of struggles to succeed to the "throne of France." The *American Heritage Dictionary* connects thrones to The Chair in defining them as "the chair occupied by a sovereign, bishop, or other exalted personage on state or ceremonial occasions," such occasions of course observing the location of power in that place. The power of a throne is ironically reflected in the colloquial, vulgar use of that term to mean a toilet seat. To say of someone who is sitting on a toilet that "she is on the throne" does precisely the work of exposing their temporary discomfiture and disempowerment to ridicule.

From Chairs to thrones to the seat of God is a natural entelechy. People have long expressed the power of God through The Chair's synecdoche of the throne of God. Early in *The Revelation to St. John* the apostle sees that "a throne stood in heaven, with one seated on the throne!" (4:2). It is clearly the site of power: "From the throne issue flashes of lightning, and voices and peals of thunder" (4:5). Acknowledgment of that power is ongoing: "And whenever the living creatures give glory and honor and thanks to him who is seated on the throne, who lives for ever and ever, the twenty-four elders fall down before him who is seated on the throne and worship him who lives for ever and ever; they cast their crowns before the throne" (4:9–10).

Although my concern, for reasons of limited space, is to explain how The Chair works as a sign in Western cultures, there is intriguing evidence that it facilitates similar meanings in other cultures. One thinks of Persia's Peacock Throne, or of the importance of the chief's stool in Africa. Monica Sjöö and Barbara Mor offer these fascinating glimpses of The Chair's connection to power in non-Western cultures:

> Images of the pregnant Goddess were also found in the excavations of Tell Haraf, dating from 5000 B.C. This Goddess is shown sitting on the earth, embodying the earth that belongs to her. In ritual and custom, to sit on something has the symbolic meaning of "taking possession." In later matriarchal times, *she was the throne*—the throne symbolized her lap. The Queen came to power by sitting on this lap or womb of the Goddess, so becoming one with her power. Among the Ashanti of West Africa there was a cult of the throne, and giant throne-replicas have been found in the Ashanti graves. . . . All the great mountains were seen as the Goddess "sitting" on the earth. (72–73)

The Chair as a Reciprocal Sign of Subordination and Deference

If one speaks of The Chair as a site of power and control, one must also speak of ways in which it is reciprocally an index of subordination. The clearest sense in which this is true is that if one acquires power by sitting in The Chair, then having to stand or rise out of a chair is a mark of subordination and deference. In the most perfect democracy, everyone sits or everyone stands; the leveling of entitlements to The Chair levels empowerment. For instance, Robert Farrar Capon suggests that when giving parties there should be a minimum of chairs so as to ensure equality of empowerment. Lack of chairs "guarantees constant rising and mixing on the part of all the guests," he notes (*Party*, 42–43).

The obligation to give up a chair signals subordination. Most law courts open sessions with everyone standing for the entrance of the judge, and in some jurisdictions everyone rises in the same way for the jury. This happens as both judge and jury make their way to where they will be seated. The defendant must usually rise to hear a verdict of the empowered jury. Military personnel typically rise in the presence of, or at the entrance of, a superior officer, and resume their chairs only at the bidding of the commander.

The kind or design of The Chair may also be a way of managing power and of reciprocally asserting that even those sitting, or especially those sitting, are subordinates. In a courtroom or office, the relative size or height of chairs denotes status. Judges are almost always higher than anyone else, and juries may be higher than common spectators or litigants. In powerful trucks and SUVs, drivers sit higher than do people in "lesser" vehicles. The Chair in this regard may be a special case of what George Lakoff and Mark Johnson call "orientational metaphors," in which up, or height, is good, and down, or low, is undesirable (14–19). Likewise, Peter Stallybrass and Allon White note the wide recurrence of "hierarchies of high and low" in managing social power throughout history (2–3).

The size, design, and opulence of the chair behind a desk may signal the power of the one who sits in it. Rybczynski notes that "the medieval diner was less concerned with how she or he sat than with *where* he or she sat. To be placed 'above the salt' was an honor reserved only for a distinguished few. To sit in the wrong place, or next to the wrong person, was a serious gaffe" (32). Today, he notes, "in a modern office the size of an executive's chair is an indication of status and influence" (82).

The Dire Chair may signal the ultimate subordination of a person, specifically, the electric chair—and we also note that gas chambers required the convict to sit. The more brutal method of hanging requires standing. Lethal injections are widely held to be a more humane means of execution. In addition to the specific means of killing—the medically sanctioned injection rather than the brutal shock of electricity, rope, or gas—would it be too far-fetched to suggest that the placement of the condemned on a cot or gurney, lying down rather than standing or sitting, is felt as less dehumanizing and insulting? that the removal of the convict from the logic of The Chair is preferred in part because it removes her from a site whose longstanding cultural meanings are those of power management?

Although the empowered usually sit and the subordinate usually stand, the polarities of the sign may be reversed. The choice between sitting or rising may have ambivalent, complicated social uses, and whether standing or sitting is a claim to power may vary with how we call it. Over the last hundred years of Western culture, women have become relatively more empowered and equal with men. It was not always so. The older practice of a "gentleman" rising as a "lady" enters the room, with the corollary expectation that a "lady" may continue to sit as a "gentleman" enters, may well have been a way to manage a deeper social inequality. The practice may have masked the absence of basic human rights for women, in other words, and one indication of that function is that as real empowerment has begun to level, the practice has receded. Rising or sitting marks gender less and less, while it still marks other forms of status and prestige. In particular, rising marks a shift in the polarities of the sign: it empowers *action* even as it gives a nod to what seems to be the empowerment of sitting.

Another example of the ambivalence of empowerment in The Chair has to do with benches. We have seen *both* Rybczynski's comment that the empowered sat on chairs while the poor people sat on benches *and* references to empowered judges as sitting on the bench. To further complicate this particular iteration of the bench, we note that the bench in sports usage is the site of the disempowered, less able players, and that one's disgrace as an athlete is signaled by "being benched." To make an athlete sit is to empower action on the field and to disempower her mere being or status as a sitting athlete.

The academy shows us more ambivalence in The Chair's connection with power. We noted earlier that The Chair has ancient academic antecedents, and that "sitting at the feet" of a teacher or sage is a common phrase denoting the deference of the student. Note that the phrase refers to the sitting of the subordinate, although perhaps on the ground and not in an empowered chair. Many teachers from kindergarten through college do in fact stand while their students sit in chairs. The act of sitting by one privileged to stand may be a move toward an expression of more equality on the part of the empowered teacher, as in the more typical arrangement of a graduate seminar where everyone sits around a table together.

The relative weighting of standing or sitting may also *change* dramatically, but predictably. In very traditional, preparatory school, or "Old World" educational contexts, the students may be required to rise upon the entrance of the professor (as the courtroom would for a judge or jury), but then in an instant they are required to sit while the professor stands. The professor stands so as to be the center of action in the conduct of the class. The right to stand and the obligation to sit reflect a power structure; a student who refuses such an arrangement clearly threatens that structure and is likely to be considered rude and unruly. Think of the effect of a student rising to his feet during a college lecture and remaining there while the discomfited professor tries to continue. In earlier times, such a student's subordinate status might be forcibly expressed by requiring him to sit in the corner on a stool, a truncated Chair, and to wear a dunce cap. The power assigned to standing in the classroom is a power through action. A similar example is the power of the dentist, who often stands while acting upon the teeth of a powerless, seated patient.

That empowerment can be signaled *both* by the sitting of a judge *and* by the standing of a lecturer is neither contradictory nor arbitrary. In either case, The Chair has definite and predictable consequences for the management of power in a specific context, and those consequences are widely if tacitly understood by everyone involved. Specifically, the reversal of polarities in The Chair's meaning carries meanings of empowerment through action rather than being or status. The Chair is an important instrument for the signaling or the refusing of power and reciprocal subordination.

The Chair as a Site of Social Belonging and Acceptance

The Chair is often taken to be not the assertion of superior power or subordinated deference but of belonging and acceptance. It is used to say that someone belongs here, in this group, with these people, in this place. In that sense The Chair is a domesticating device; it makes a space homelike and welcoming, as in this example from Henry James's *Portrait of a Lady,* in which "Madame Merle and the Countess had chairs brought out, and as the afternoon was lovely, the Countess proposed they should take their tea in the open air," which thus becomes domestic through The Chair's good influence (214–15). The Chair in this sense is a sign of equality and inclusion, which is still a function of power management but also is an assertion of equal power. In describing the "sit-down dinner" as "the most elegant and considerable of all forms of entertaining," Capon identifies a grand form of socializing that is both inclusive and empowering for all who participate (*Supper,* 168).

We are familiar with domestic examples of The Chair's meaning. Many families order much of their interaction around whose chair is whose: the recliner is father's, this chair is mother's, family members have specific places where they sit around the dinner table, and even the dog may claim that end of the sofa. The Chair defines a place to belong. In Charles Dickens's *A Christmas Carol,* the Second Ghost lets Scrooge know through The Chair that Tiny Tim's place within the family circle is imperiled: "'I see a vacant seat,'" replied the Ghost, "'in the poor chimney corner'" (53). The bond between where one sits and belonging extends throughout many social practices; for example, students and churchgoers alike are apt to gravitate toward specific places to sit in classroom and sanctuary. Such personal identification with The Chair is not merely a matter of convenience but is also a way to assert belonging and identity within the social group of the family, class, or congregation. Capon reminds us of the inclusive nature of bidding people to sit and dine, for when the host "sits down at his table, he declares himself willing to let me into his own life. He puts me into my place" in the most accepting sense (*Supper,* 170). Christians extend this use of The Chair in the celebration of "The Lord's Supper." Although rarely observed around an actual table, the taking of bread and wine follows a metaphor of sitting in chairs around a table, and its inclusive, unifying nature is signaled by the common usage of "taking communion."

To bid a visitor to "come in and sit a spell" is to offer affiliation and acceptance beyond the family, if only for a while. The old-fashioned "sitting room" as a site of either family gatherings or reception of friendly visitors denotes The Chair's role as offering inclusion and belonging. Henry James calls our attention to the kind of claim one makes in inviting guests to sit by noting the importance of the quality of The Chair upon which the sitting is done. His character Isabel is in her "office," which is "a chamber of disgrace for old pieces of furniture. . . . There was an old haircloth sofa in especial, to which she had confided a hundred childish sorrows" (25). In this site of Bad Chairs Isabel receives an unexpected visitor: "'Oh,' she began, 'is that where you usually sit?' She looked about at the heterogeneous chairs and tables. 'Not when I have visitors,' said Isabel, getting up to receive the intruder" (26). In *A Christmas Carol*, Dickens humorously acknowledges the inclusive dimensions of The Chair as Scrooge decides that he will let Marley's ghost remain in his lodgings: "'Can you—can you sit down?' asked Scrooge, looking doubtfully at him. 'I can.' 'Do it, then.' Scrooge asked the question, because he didn't know whether a ghost so transparent might find himself in a condition to take a chair; and felt that in the event of its being impossible, it might involve the necessity of an embarrassing explanation" (16). And we might note that the ghost signals a remaining vestige of humanity and connection with Scrooge in accepting his offer to sit.

Martin Luther King Jr. poignantly used The Chair in this inclusive sense by dreaming "that one day on the red hills of Georgia the sons of former slaves and the sons of former slave owners will be able to sit down together at the table of brotherhood" in his "I Have a Dream" address. His dream was one of inclusion and belonging within the human family for African Americans. King's use of The Chair came within the context of the civil rights struggles and demonstrations of the 1960s, in which one of the most visible signs of resistance to Jim Crow laws was sitting down at segregated lunch counters, restaurants, waiting rooms, and so forth. To sit in a chair and silently suffer the taunts and outrages of segregationists was to assert a claim of being, belonging, and status in defiance of laws that attempted to assign second-class personhood to African Americans. To combat that situation, thousands of people of different cultures took their seats on buses to travel to the South in support of civil rights demonstrations. It is telling that King uses the Chair-connected metaphor of dining, for as Capon reminds us, "Persons matter at table. We sit in real and estimable places" (*Supper*, 170). M. F. K. Fisher expresses the friendly acceptance of a shared meal in terms of the ability to sit: "And above all, friends should possess the rare gift of sitting. They should be able, no, eager to sit for hours—three, four, six—over a meal of soup and wine and cheese, as well as one of twenty fabulous courses" (44).

One somewhat ambivalent example of this usage is the assignment of numbered chairs at sports events and concerts. One pays money and thus "belongs" in a certain seat; it is yours, and is the place you are to be for this time. A similar use of The Chair is found in the old and now largely outdated practice of the family pew, in which specific seats within a church belonged to certain families. The ambivalence arises from the fact that superiority and subordination, of course, sneak back in to the arrangement. The Chairs in these cases are where one belongs, but they may also well designate differences in status, as more money earns one a cushier pew or a seat closer to ringside. Likewise, both our opening examples of Sojourner Truth and Rosa Parks describe cases in which The Chair was bought and should have been theirs by right, but instead racism intruded and turned The Chair into an instrument of domination and control.

The Chair as a Site of Personal Empowerment, Identity, and Centeredness

This final dimension of meaning facilitated by The Chair is not quite as widespread as the others, but is nevertheless significant. One sits in a chair to recuperate one's powers and centeredness. The act of refusing busy-ness is an act of restoration of strength, of focus and concentration, centered on one's being.

Yoga and other meditative practices incorporate sitting (although not always in an actual chair) as a key element of personal empowerment and centeredness. Different positions of sitting are thought to facilitate the restoration of different powers. The more conventional practice of sitting in a pew in church, synagogue, confessional, or chapel is, in addition to being a claim of inclusion and belonging, also an act of recruiting one's strength and peace. There one might hear a spirit call, "Be still and know that I am God," bidding one to remain in The Chair for enlightenment. In such circumstances, to move to one's knees, out of The Chair, is an admission of guilt, of lack of wholeness and centeredness, of a need for restoration.

These four dimensions of meaning explain some of the rhetorical potential contained with The Chair. It is a complex sign, incorporating actions, objects, events, and discourse about them. But signs' rhetorical potential reaches fruition in the actual texts in which they enter history. Spike Lee's film *Get on the Bus*, like all his films, was made with the intention of shaping audience attitudes and motives for reacting to and acting in history. The Chair is a central sign in that film, and the four dimensions of meaning it facilitates are among the most important vehicles for its rhetorical message. What potentiates the power of those meanings is the homology obtaining between uses of The Chair in the film and the chairs in which real audiences sit. To understand how that may be, let us turn to a brief review of homology theory.

Homologies and Media

Homology theory is based on the idea, as discussed in the first chapter, that people respond naturally and powerfully to *form*. We find formal patterns attractive and compelling. This simple truth may be realized by considering that people would rather hear their favorite song (which like most music is highly formal) over and over again than to hear a random directory of telephone-book listings (which is full of information but not very formal) read to them even once.

A homology is a formal resemblance between some aspect of a discourse and some other dimension of experience, whether that be another discourse, a real life experience, a way of using technology, and so forth. Little Red Riding Hood is homologous with real-life experiences of dangerous strangers or deceptive appearances. The link is formal, and makes the story relevant to life at a formal level.

A text and an experience may be made to link homologically through the intentional design of a rhetor or through a serendipitous formal conjunction for a particular auditor. In either case, I would claim, we may see a dimension of the rhetorical power of a text at work. J. K. Rowling's *Harry Potter* series of books, for instance, must connect powerfully with real-life experience for at least some of its millions of readers. But it must do so at the level of form, since I suppose few readers are really enrolled in a wizard's school. That rhetorical connection occurs whether Rowling set out to speak to her audience's experience of being strange and different in real life or whether audiences make that connection themselves.

A formal resemblance among A, B, and C not only links those three but calls attention to what the three have to do with one another. When the orders of experience that are formally linked are *discourse, media, and real experience,* the formal linkage explains how a medium can amplify the ability of a discourse to speak to and thus rhetorically alter experience. A homology between text and real experience suggests a strong rhetorical link, but when experience of the medium that carries the text participates in the same homology, the rhetorical effect is even stronger. Earlier research (Brummett, "Homology") noted that the characteristic of ownership that is key to possession of videotaped pornography amplifies the assumption of male ownership of female bodies in pornographic texts, and that such a formal link further amplifies the ability of those texts to rhetorically create an assumption in a male audience that the real women they encounter are like ownable objects.

We have reviewed some of the rhetorical potential of The Chair, and let me note that our review has been at a formal level, for we have been considering patterns of sitting and standing, of belonging, inclusion, and the exercise of power, instead of any particular act or experience. When texts use The Chair in ways that parallel an audience's real experience formally, then that sign has rhetorical effect not just at the level of explicit appeal but also at the level of form. For instance, the reference to Tiny Tim's chair as a sign of family inclusion reminds us that reading about his empty chair might affect an audience that in real life is experiencing, not the actual loss of Tiny Tim, but rather a familial loss that parallels the pattern in *A Christmas Carol.*

But suppose one consumes such a text using a medium in a way that enacts the formal pattern linking text with experience? As a matter of fact, *A Christmas Carol* in the medium of the book is probably going to be consumed while sitting in a chair in a domestic context; that is how we use the medium of books and specifically of books of great literature. What extra work does the experience of the medium do when it participates in the homology linking text and reality? In terms of Dickens, that question must be answered in another study. This present study now uses homology theory to suggest ways in which experience of the film *Get on the Bus* energized the text's ability to speak rhetorically to certain real-life experiences of the audience. Here we consider ways in which the symbolic dimensions of The Chair as a powerful, recurring sign underlie not only texts and experiences but also the experience of the *medium* used to convey a text.

Get on the Bus

This film, created in 1996 by acclaimed director Spike Lee, follows the journey of about twenty African American men as they take a charter bus from Los Angeles to Washington, D.C., to join the 1995 Million Man March. The characters reflect the diversity among African American men: young and old, gay and straight, Christian and Moslem, radical, liberal, and conservative. As they travel, tensions and conflicts arise that mirror those facing African American men in society: violence, family responsibilities, color awareness among African Americans, racism, and so forth. At the end of the journey the elder, Jeremiah, is stricken with a fatal heart attack. The men gather round him and miss the March, but create for themselves a new awareness of their strength and possibilities.

Let me make three observations in general about this film. First, the film is about a journey toward confrontation with serious issues faced by African Americans. In some ways it is a journey back in time so as to be able to face the future, as the bus journeys from the new golden land of California through the racist South to Washington, in the heart of the ancient slave-holding region; the bus is in some sense a modern ship taking its African cargo to and through scenes of painful memory. That sense of confronting a troubling history is made clear; the opening credits roll over images of old slave shackles binding the hands and feet of a man of African heritage as well as modern handcuffs and chains. The final scene is of discarded chains left on the floor of the Lincoln Memorial. How the past binds and how African Americans can become unbound is a central theme in the film.

Consider one ongoing example of a social issue confronted by the characters in the film. The first people we see enter the bus are Evan Thomas Sr. and his son, Evan Jr. ("Call me Smoooooth"), who are literally shackled together. Evan Jr. is under court order to be chained to his father for seventy-two hours as punishment for stealing money. George, the tour manager, immediately remarks on the "plantation" references called up by this shocking sight, and the complaint is raised repeatedly by other members of the tour throughout the film. The image condenses many issues: Evan Sr. justifies the chaining of his son by showing people the court order, thus accepting complicity with a White power structure. His compliance chains him fully as much as his son. He and his son are chained by bonds of blood relationship, yet their personal relationship is more complicated and less solid. The ability of either father or son to act independently as men is hampered by their acceptance of chains. As George remarks when Evan offers to drive the bus for a while, "It's gonna be hard for you to take the wheel [sit in the driver's seat] with them shackles"; the comment is about who to be and how to act in life, not just in a bus. But the comment is expressed in terms of The Chair, and so I shall inquire into how The Chair is a sign through which they journey into confrontation with a troubling history.

Second, the movie is reflexive; it is about itself in significant ways. We see much of the film through the camera of Xavier, the nineteen-year-old film student who videotapes the stories of the men on the bus. He is jokingly referred to as "Spike Lee Jr." by George; of course, the real Spike Lee is directing the action. In short, much of what the audience sees is a film within a film, or a film about the film Xavier is making, which brings to the foreground an awareness for the audience of what they are witnessing.

Why is the film reflexive in that way? I believe that one reason has directly to do with my purposes here, and that is that the film presents a story of people who are taking a journey in seats for which they have paid—to people who likewise are invited to take a journey in seats for which they have paid. In other words, text and audience are made homologous. The audience is "on the bus" in an important sense, invited to come along and confront its own troubling pasts. That is especially likely to be true for African American men, who may be the primary intended audience for the film, although audiences of many backgrounds will find some connection to it. Most of the film is of people sitting in seats, for the benefit of an audience sitting in seats. The reflexivity of the film as film invites a reflexivity of The Chair, and I believe that this not only justifies but also demands attention to the role played by The Chair as the film carries its passengers, both celluloid and flesh, into a confrontation with history. A film in reflexive form thus invites its audience (especially African American men) to confront the same issues faced by the passengers in the film.

Third, there are two major structural oppositions within the film between standing and sitting, and the trajectory of the film moves from one opposition to the other. One opposition is between empowered sitting and disempowered standing. This is the dominant opposition, and is front-loaded in the sense of dominating the first two-thirds or so of the film. As the film begins, those who are empowered are those who are privileged to sit on the bus; standing becomes a sign of disengagement or even expulsion from the community. Being, empowerment, and belonging as the right of male African Americans marks The Chair in this first opposition.

The second opposition is between empowered standing and disempowered sitting. There is less of this structure in the film, but it is backloaded and is the opposition toward which the film moves. This opposition marks the choice of the men on the bus to leave the empowerment of The Chair and seek instead the empowerment of action, responsibility, and movement. The audience is invited to do the same through the reflexive structure of their relation to The Chair and to the film. As the film moves to this second opposition, the polarities of The Chair reverse. We noted that such a switch signals a change of empowerment, from being and status to action. *To urge the audience to act out precisely that reversal is the rhetorical message of the film.* The film seems to emphasize specific admonitions (care for your children and women, be tolerant of differences within the community) less than it calls for action itself—in large part through reversing the polarities of The Chair.

Empowered Sitting—Disempowered Standing

The film begins with expression of joy and eagerness among most of the men as they board the bus and take their seats. It is empowering for them to have seats on the bus. Evan Jr. is the exception; he is sullenly resisting the journey. But his father is insistent: "Yo, I'm getting *on* that bus!" George, the tour manager announces, "Anyone else going to the Million Man March, it's time to get on the bus." He tells the seated passengers, "If you want to go to the Slawson Swap Meet, the Brentwood Mansion, the L.A. Zoo, or the LaBrea Tar Pits, then your Black ass is on the *wrong* bus. This bad boy is going to Washington D.C., for the Million

Man March." The "ass" reference highlights The Chair, for it is their location in seats for which they have paid that marks the start of their journey and their right to have a seat. When the obnoxious Flip arrives late and loud, George challenges his right to be there in terms of that bought seat: "You got a ticket? *You* better have a ticket." And George expresses his hesitation in allowing the car salesman Wendell to enter the bus at Memphis by noting, "Everybody paid *money* to get on this bus."

The empowerment granted by a purchased ticket is limited to male African Americans, however. As is true for The Chair generally, it is an empowerment of being, status, identity, and belonging. Several categories of being besides race are invoked, as when Evan Sr. lays down the law to his son on the basis of familial ties: "I'm your father; you're my son; so let's get on that bus together." And the empowerment obtaining to gender is invoked by complaints received by two women at a rest stop and by the traveler Gary's girlfriend, who objects to his going at the start: "This whole thing is sexist and exclusionary." The predominant characteristic of being that leads to the empowerment of being seated is to be male and African American. Jamal says excitedly, "Looks like the brothers are getting ready to board this bus!" "Black power, brothers!" shouts Jeremiah as he boards, giving the clenched fist salute, and "Black power!" is returned to him. Jeremiah will later urge George to let Wendell board the bus in Memphis by saying, "We're talking about a *brother* here." Empowerment through status and being begins early as the men chant a "roll call" by which, through clever rhymes, they announce who they are—an exercise in which *every* passenger is seated in his place.

The Chairs on the bus are thus reserved to empower those of a particular racial and gender background; those not sharing that background are suspect. Flip grills the biracial Gary about where he is from: "Where're you from?" Gary: "Uh, I live in Pasadena." Flip: "No, not where you live, where're you from?" Gary: "Uh, I'm from Monterey originally," which Flip immediately seizes on as a sign that Gary's background is not entirely African American. And when the original bus driver must be replaced by Rick, a Jew, Flip complains, "George, we can't roll to the Million Man March with a White boy at the wheel," expressing in the sign of the driver's seat the kind of empowerment that The Chair marks on this bus. Rick the driver eventually abdicates his claim to empowered seating by telling George, "No way am I getting my White ass back in that bus"; the "ass" would or would not find empowerment specifically in a Chair.

As I noted earlier, a central issue for the film is the working out of issues from the past. These are momentous, for the men are "pilgrims on a bus that's bound for glory" according to Jeremiah. As they travel, issues from the past that confront African Americans are first identified and then worked out in terms of The Chair. The film's audience is invited to confront the same issues while in *their* seats.

Some of the problems the men are to confront are marked through seating patterns. Kyle and Randall are a gay couple, and they begin the journey sitting together. But their relationship is on the rocks, and as they begin to quarrel Kyle remarks in a loud voice, "Good! Then you won't mind if I change my seat," and his movement to a different Chair is one sign (followed by loud, revealing remarks from Randall) of the nature of their relationship. They are outed, in part, by The Chair. Evan Sr. and Evan Jr. *must* sit together, and the issues represented by their chains are reinforced by their contiguous Chairs.

More often, we see problems confronted as the men move into different seating arrangements. There is plenty of room on the bus for each rider to have his own solitary seat, but different pairings or groups form in adjacent seating. It is usually while in The Chair that they face issues from history. Evan Sr. and Jr. work out what to call each other, which is a working out of how a father and son are to relate in a context of racism and broken families, while sitting together; Sr. hates being called "dog," while Jr. objects to "Junior." Flip (actually Phillip) and X (actually Xavier) work out the complexities of names and what forms of address to use while seated next to each other. Randall and the White driver Rick argue about racial issues specifically within the historical context of whether African Americans or Jews have suffered more, until George intervenes to stop the dispute—all while the three are seated close together at the front. Jeremiah brings the African past into the present when at a rest stop he sits on the bus steps and plays his drum: "I am gonna use this drum to take all you brothers back to the Motherland." While seated at a rest stop lunch counter in Memphis, Evan Jr. and Evan Sr. amicably work out an understanding with two inquiring rednecks as to whether the March is racist. Kyle and Randall return to sitting together later in the film as they resolve their differences. And Gary, Jamal, and Flip sit together playing cards, which leads to Jamal's revelation of his criminal past and Gary's revelation that his police officer father was murdered by just such a gang member as Jamal used to be; issues of violence among African Americans is thus played out while in Chairs.

If sitting is a site of empowerment and of confrontation with problems from the past, standing is often a marker (in the first two-thirds of the film) of a failure of communication, an inability to work constructively through past problems, or of outright hostility. A refusal of the Chair, within this opposition, leads to estrangement and disempowerment. Reflexively, the audience member will "miss something" if he must leave his seat for any reason during the film.

The dialog between Gary and Jamal, for instance, over Jamal's gang past collapses as Flip, sensing powerful emotions, abruptly leaves his seat among the trio. Standing is even a mark of forcible expulsion and disempowerment. New rider Wendell becomes more and more offensive, using the word "nigger" at least three times in each sentence, and reveals that his only intention in going to the March is to sell cars. He is summarily removed from his seat of empowerment and thrown from the bus onto the roadside.

An extended example illustrates well the tension between empowered sitting and disempowered standing. Gary and Flip are seated together and Flip begins goading Gary as to whether he, being biracial, empathizes with Rick, the White driver. Their ability to work out that issue fails as Gary becomes angry. Jeremiah tells Flip to leave Gary alone. Flip marks the rupture by rising to walk up and down the aisle complaining angrily about slavery and the privileges historically given to light-skinned African Americans. He ends his speech and resumes his seat in a different part of the bus, where Randall attempts to challenge his views. Flip will not work through issues calmly with Randall either, and so he rises again and while standing trades barbs with Kyle and Evan Sr. Kyle becomes so incensed that he also rises and while standing the two engage in a fistfight. The bus stops to let them fight, which of course does not resolve the issue and empowers neither of them. While fighting, however, the temporarily unchained Evan Jr. runs away. His father runs after him, but it is only when they both tumble to sitting positions in the nearby forest that they finally work through their familial issues and come to a tearful rapprochement. This series of sitting, standing, fighting, running, and sitting again marks the ways in which The Chair is a site of empowerment and constructive confrontation with the past, while standing is either disempowering or a refusal to engage history.

Disempowered Sitting—Empowered Standing

We have seen that The Chair is a form of empowerment based on status, being, and identity. Throughout most of the first two-thirds of *Get on the Bus,* the men claim power by sitting in Chairs reserved for them as men, as African Americans, and there they confront issues from the past that have troubled them. It is when they stand that they are disempowered, excluded, or stymied in their working-out of problems. We have seen that this opposition follows the dominant meanings of The Chair.

But we also noted earlier that The Chair may be used reciprocally to signal disempowerment through sitting and empowerment through standing. In this film, that potential for signification is exploited in the last third of the movie. Without denying the seated empowerment that comes with being, belonging, and identity, the film urges its characters (and its seated audience) to an empowerment of action and responsibility, through a reversal of the dominant polarities of The Chair.

There are early hints of the disempowerment of sitting. Jamal remarks to Jeremiah as both take their seats (at the *back* of the bus), "Not much leg room, is there?" to which Jeremiah responds, "No, I'm going to have to stretch these crackerjack bones every chance I get." Mike fears disempowerment through sitting as he voices a conspiracy theory: "We could be on our way to getting *done.*" He paints this image: "Think about all the trains, planes, and cars filled with Black men" on their way to Washington, a sure target for annihilation by a racist madman. George justifies the change to the White driver by describing the driver's seat as a position of servitude: "Oh come on, used to be, you know, we always had to chauffeur the White man, this time the White man is chauffeuring us." In these examples, to sit is to be discomfited, vulnerable, and disempowered.

In other examples, the injunction to sit or the act of sitting is disempowering. Flip stands to announce that he has learned by cell phone that he got a coveted acting role. But that news earns him no empowerment; in fact, George expresses his disdain through The Chair as he tells him, "Congratulations! Now why don't you sit down and shut up?" Later, Jeremiah is discovered to have suffered the heart attack that will prove fatal while sitting in his seat, and his friends sit to wait powerlessly in the hospital waiting room.

The most dramatic moment of disempowerment occurs as the bus is stopped in eastern Tennessee for reasons of racial profiling. Two White state troopers enter the bus and announce that they and their German shepherd dog will search the bus for drugs. Gary stands and confidently shows the officers his LAPD badge, but its authority has no weight here, and his disempowerment is made explicit in being told to "take a seat." As one standing trooper shines lights on sullen, worried faces, the other trooper and dog search the bus, following such calls as "look back there under that seat there." The troopers find nothing and leave the bus, but the passengers, who have been disempowered *because* of their being and identity, sit shaken, angry, and fearful. The men want to do something active, to rise out of their seats, to respond, but they cannot because of the police power the troopers represent.

The journey as well as the film moves toward Washington, where standing will mark empowerment. It is the *March*, after all, that will bring power and energy to the men who attend it, and one marches standing up. Images of standing abound. Jeremiah says of people back in Los Angeles, "I told 'em, I was gonna be first in line at the revolution." He asks to offer prayer at the start of the trip, and stands to do so while others remain seated. George acknowledges that form of empowerment: "The floor is yours, Pop." As Xavier goes around filming comments from the passengers, Jay says, "I think it's time for brothers to stand up and be responsible." Evan Jr. must ask to be unchained to go to the bathroom on the bus, and once he is unchained he is able to stand and act independently.

Once at the March, signs say "Stand Up Black Man" and "United We Stand." News footage from the actual march is interspersed into this film, featuring the calls of speakers for African American men to assume active control of their communities, to commit themselves to change, and to stand up for freedom. The passengers miss the March while waiting for Jeremiah in the hospital. Once he has died, they return dispirited to sit in the bus. But George, standing in the aisle, gives an inspiring speech: "At least we stood by a brother when he needed us," he says. "The real Million Man March won't start until we Black men take charge," he says. And so in the final scene they gather to stand in the Lincoln Memorial. There they hear the prayer read that Jeremiah had written for the journey's end. The end of the film calls for men to move from empowerment through sitting to empowerment through standing. The message is that although the empowerment of being, status, and identity, of belonging to a community, has been important in the past, the working through of those problems leads to a shift to empowerment of action. Men who began the journey empowered to sit as African Americans end the journey empowered through standing and acting. The credits roll, the screen darkens. And the audience itself stands to walk out of the theater—to what end, and with what mission? The homology of the film thus moves the audience as well from empowered sitting to empowered, inspired standing and action—and *that* is the message both of the film and of the March.

Conclusion

We have seen that The Chair is a complex sign. It may reverse its polarity, although it need not do so in every usage, and when it does it does so in predictable and regular ways. The Chair signals empowerment and disempowerment, being, identity, and belonging as compared to action. It is a widely known and widely used sign that may facilitate many different rhetorical messages. One such message is the film *Get on the Bus*. We have seen that it uses the potential meanings inherent within The Chair to urge its audience, which has been sutured into the film through its own immediate theatrical experience of The Chair, to accept action and responsibility as well.

Research into homology is part of the larger project, stretching across the humanities, of studying the ways in which form in discourse connects with experience outside of discourse. That project clearly has an important rhetorical dimension. Homologies in general need more study. One way to do that is to identify widely occurring signs or longer discursive units and to explain the range of meanings they facilitate. Such meanings provide a clue as to how texts speak to experience at a formal level. Here we have seen how patterns of inclusion, power, status, belonging, and so forth make use of The Chair both in texts and in experience, thus helping us to see how texts can rhetorically advise audiences in regard to experience.

The particular kind of homology presented in this chapter has been keyed not to a myth or to a narrative structure, as in earlier chapters, but to a structure uniting a large group of signs: The Chair. In this way The Chair is a key, recurring, even archetypal sign with recurring, complex symbolic dynamics. Meaning is structured in predictable ways by the signs participating in this homology—of—a—sign.

When we also ask about the effect that the form of the experience of mediation might add to the homology, we likewise consider an important media dimension. Homology research, in other words, calls our attention to the *form of mediated experience,* and thus opens an important front in the critical analysis of media. This chapter may be read, then, as an example of how homologies may be identified and studied in the context of mediated texts. Much work remains to be done in identifying the formal characteristics of mediation and the ways in which those forms may connect to both texts and experiences.

One kind of discourse that we have yet to consider closely is theory. Theory is discourse that comments upon experience and upon other discourses. Theory may also be homologous with experiences and discourses, and it may do so across history in recurring ways.

In the next chapter we include theoretical discourses into the mix of discourse and experience ordered by homology. We also include ways in which homology can unite discourse and experience in different moments of history without hampering, denying, or occluding the historical specificity of how discourse and experience emerge from moment to moment. This happens when homologies predictably recur, but *not the same* homology in each case. Such recurrence suggests a homology of homologies, a kind of super homology. We will see how rhetoric, theories of rhetoric, and dominant weapons may vary from era to era in history, yet they emerge homologously within a given historical moment. We will consider what might be the super homology uniting these disparate homologies.

5

Some Homologies between Rhetorics and Weapons

In *A Rhetoric of Motives,* Kenneth Burke surveys images of killing and of suicide in literature by John Milton, Matthew Arnold, and others. He concludes that "the so-called 'desire to kill' a certain person is much more properly analyzable as a desire to *transform the principle* which that person *represents*" (13). Such transformation is inherently rhetorical, Burke argues, for when we persuade we transform another. From this conceptual base Burke goes on to develop in the *Rhetoric* (252–66) and in later works an understanding of how many images of killing, blame, destruction, banishment, and so forth perform a scapegoating function.

Later in the *Rhetoric,* in what might seem to be a section unrelated to images of killing, Burke calls our attention to the ways in which the principles and practice of courtly rhetoric might be manifested in experiences that seem not strictly connected to the court. Burke's chief example in that argument is Baldassare Castiglione's *The Book of the Courtier,* a Renaissance text. Burke observes that "we can thus discern the presence of the same rhetorical, courtly motive in many varied transformations that on their face may seem disrelated" (224). He thus models our method of finding formal resemblances (homologies) among apparently disparate texts, practices, and contexts that speak to fundamental patterns of communicative behavior. Robert Hariman employs the same method in his admirable book *Political Style,* in which he traces the patterns of four political styles, among them the courtly style, across different contexts including those that may seem not to be "political" in the usual sense. "A political style can be understood as the artistic expression of a political theory," argues Hariman (71), asserting a homology between politics and art.

Let us put together the idea of formal linkage, or homology, with the idea of images of killing. If an *image* of killing can embody a rhetoric, might not an actual *means* of killing embody one of the dominant rhetorics of its time as well? We would look for such embodiment at the formal level, as we do when we find courtly rhetoric where there is no court. Similarly, does not Aristotle assert a formal link between violence and rhetoric in arguing that "it is absurd to hold that a man ought to be ashamed of being unable to defend himself with his limbs, but not of being unable to defend himself with speech and reason" (1355b)? One might also note Friedrich Kittler's suggestion that formal parallels between war and cinema made the latter an effective propaganda tool in the twentieth century (124).

In this chapter I claim that within any given social, historical era, some widely used weapons will parallel some widely used rhetorics; the principles and practices of the one may be seen in the other at a formal level. By principles and practices I mean both the enactment of rhetoric in moments of persuasion and theories of how that enactment works, written in the scholarly literature of each period. I shall offer three sets of examples: I believe that the rhetoric of the Renaissance is homologous with the stiletto; that seventeenth- and eighteenth-century Enlightenment rhetoric is homologous with the flintlock musket; and that today's postmodern, mediated rhetorics of popular culture are homologous with the semi-automatic pistol. After explaining the dimensions on which they are homologous, I will make some observations about the theoretical implications of identifying these parallels.

The homology linking Renaissance rhetorical theory and practice with the stiletto is not the same homology that links Enlightenment rhetoric with the musket, or rhetorics of popular culture with the semi-automatic pistol. In that sense, different historical circumstances support different homological patterns. But the recurrence of homologies of the same *sort* suggests a kind of *super homology* cutting across history—a homology ordering the ways in which more historically specific homologies are created. Rhetorics and weapons are homologous in patterns specific to their historical emergence, I argue, yet there is likewise a more fundamental homology that consistently links rhetorics and weapons across historical circumstances. This chapter adds to our consideration of homology then by introducing the idea of tiers of homology, by examining this new level, this homology of homologies, and studying the implications of that phenomenon. We will see how homologies can be transhistorical as well as situated in historical particularities.

Renaissance Rhetoric and the Stiletto

Rhetoric in everyday life is messy and slops out of the boxes into which the critics and historians of later eras put it. When we refer to Renaissance rhetoric, it is important to keep in mind that there were many rhetorical theories and practices of that era. It is also important to remember that any given theorist or practitioner may not, in his or her own time, have fit so neatly into the niche to which later eras have assigned him or her. For instance, Hariman's distinction between the political realism of Niccolò Machiavelli and the courtly style of Castiglione is largely just, but we might find elements of both rhetorics in each. One might see Machiavelli as the hidden realpolitik lying concealed beneath Castiglione's fine courtier's gown. As Christian Gauss put it in describing Machiavelli, "His book . . . is not an abstract treatise; it is a concise manual, a handbook for those who would acquire or increase their political power" (8), which may describe courtiers as well as princes. Consider Machiavelli's observation that "a prince being thus obliged to know well how to act as a beast must imitate the fox and the lion, for the lion cannot protect himself from traps, and the fox cannot defend himself from wolves" (92). Do we not see his own realism in the lion and Castiglione's sly courtier in the fox, both in the same prince? Surely Machiavelli, often treated as a proponent of realist power alone, had also to cultivate the art of dealing with "flatterers, of which the courts are full" (116). I use both Castiglione's *The Book of the Courtier* and some of Machiavelli's thought in *The Prince* to illustrate the same principles. To find this rhetoric homologous with the stiletto is almost not a formal argument, since the stiletto was so often used precisely at court. But perhaps it is best to begin with the more obvious and move toward the less.

Courtly rhetoric was practiced by courtiers: politicians, nobles, attendants, and other hangers-on in the courts of the Renaissance. By "courts" I mean the physical locations of central power of European governments, the sites of the chief bureaucracies of a principality but also, principally, the site of the prince himself. Decisions in these contexts were often centrally made by the prince or by powerful officials, but those decisions could be influenced by lesser officials, nobles, family members, and those in attendance: the courtiers.

A court was a site for both the political realism and the courtly style of the politically ambitious. Patricia Bizzell and Bruce Herzberg argue that "the power of the individual public man diminished, and political rhetoric increasingly became the province of the courtier or government functionary (474). Heinrich F. Plett describes the context in which a courtly rhetoric grounded in the halls of government arose:

> The Humanists were not only ardent lovers of classical rhetoric and excellent scholars but also practical-minded men whose professions were often those of a lawyer, notary or secretary, and as such they pursued public careers. . . . Rhetoricians, as a rule, had ambitions of entering a diplomatic career as ambassadors of their governments. A notorious example of a politician turned rhetorician is Niccolò Machiavelli (1469–1527) who in his treatise *Il principe* (*The Prince*, 1513) developed a theory of statesmanship recommending that the ruler imitate not the strong lion but the crafty fox in his speaking and acting. (680)

On a parallel track that I shall link to Renaissance rhetoric, the stiletto was a weapon that came into widespread use among privileged classes during the Renaissance, although it was originally developed as a battlefield weapon in the Middle Ages designed to pierce chain mail. It is a kind of dagger. The blade, usually eight to twelve inches in length, has no cutting edge. Instead, it is three-(sometimes four) sided, often with scalloped "blood" grooves running the full length of each side so as to allow for the easy escape of blood once inserted into the body. It is thus a kind of large ice pick in form. Crosspieces, or *quillons,* separate the blade from the handle, and are usually at right angles to the handle and blade. The handle is of a length to just fit a single hand. The quillons and handles are almost always carved, decorated, or inlaid in some way; many stilettos are works of art.

The stiletto was an early concealed weapon, being of such a size that it could be tucked away into the voluminous gowns and cloaks of the period. Its concealability and quietness (compared to, say, an early firearm) made it a favorite weapon of assassins. The lack of a cutting blade on a stiletto equips it for very few uses beyond homicide; one cannot peel an apple or sharpen a pencil with it.

It is an intimate weapon, even a parody of the male penetrative sexual act. It requires one to come close to the target and then to stab with a thrust that brings one, and one's hand, into close personal contact with the victim. The stiletto would typically be withdrawn and the victim left to bleed to death since the wound would be quite deep and, due to the thickness of the blade and the multiple sides it creates in the hole, unlikely to knit together quickly. Also, such decorated blades, if left behind, might be traced to specific owners. If we turn now to some principles of Renaissance rhetoric, we will find interesting homologies between those practices and theories and the stiletto.

Renaissance rhetoric is in several senses *personal*. Bizzell and Herzberg note that in the Renaissance, "the social situation of private discourse did enter the domain of rhetoric" in the form of "letter writing, private conversation, and courtly etiquette" that "placed rhetoric at the site of considerable political power in a society increasingly governed by monarchs and their advisers" (9). Renaissance rhetoric is usually not a form of *mass* address, although it may well be public address. Often it is manifested in the earnest entreaties of one person to another. Bizzell and Herzberg say that in courtly rhetoric, "Some scope for politically effective oral rhetoric was retained in the form of courtly conversation, which involved an audience of only a few people, or perhaps only one auditor, the ruler" (483). In this sense courtly rhetoric is focused, specific, and defined. The more personal is courtly rhetoric, the more it seeks to conceal itself from general view—it can be a secretive rhetoric.

Homologously, the stiletto is also intensely personal. Not mass-produced, each weapon would be individual and customized to the desires of its owner. It was meant for personal, one-on-one "application." One cannot, for example, imagine an advancing army with stilettos extended; it is a weapon kept on the individual person. Its field of use was in private settings, the merged public/domestic space of the Renaissance court.

Courtly rhetoric centers on the *body* of the prince, as Hariman argues: "The courtly style is centered on the body of the sovereign, displaces speech with gesture, and culminates in immobility" (4). It is focused on the corporeality of one in power. Hariman urges us to "recall the courtier's scramble for places in the emperor's traveling entourage: Their power depended on actual physical proximity to the king" (58); "consequently, questions of privilege and responsibility, and of prudence and principle, often will be understood and resolved with primary regard to the disposition of bodies" (61). The corporeality of those in attendance is likewise important. Castiglione advises the courtier, while speaking, to be mindful of "certain movements of the entire body, not affected or violent but tempered by an agreeable expression of the face and movement of the eyes" (77). Clearly, a stiletto centers on the body. It is a weapon that must bring one into close proximity with the body of another. One must get in close enough to see every mole and scar to be able to use the stiletto. One experiences its effects on the body of another in close proximity, for the blood and agony is not way over "there" but right here where your hand meets your victim's flesh.

Throughout Machiavelli, the prince is taken to be a metonymy of the state itself. Note the physicality, the intimacy, of Machiavelli's claim that "men must either be caressed or else annihilated" (37). The intimacy and sexual parody of the stiletto connects homologically here; one must push it physically so as to enter another's body, suggesting the gruesome conjuncture of Machiavelli's caressing and annihilating.

Of course, a rhetoric that celebrates the body of power is but a step away from the management of power through manipulation of the body, violently if necessary. The rhetoric of political realism that flourished in the Renaissance is also concerned with force, violence, and the body. As Bizzell and Herzberg note, "Machiavelli . . . says, the prince should do whatever the times require to preserve his state in a political world governed not by virtue but by force" (468). Gauss likewise identifies the forceful, violent nature of Machiavelli's view that "the state is . . . a dynamic, amoral entity, a force . . . the role of the prince is to direct this force. . . . There is no inherent purpose in the state. Any direction it may receive must be imposed upon it by the ruler" (16). Note the centrality of violence in Machiavelli's statement that, "The chief foundations of all states, whether new, old, or mixed, are good laws and good arms" (72), and note the pun between weapons and the body in that term "arms." But Castiglione agrees in saying, "I judge that the first and true profession of the courtier must be that of arms" (57), and "his first duty is to know how to handle expertly every kind of weapon" (61). Likewise, Machiavelli argues that, "A prince should therefore have no other aim or thought, nor take up any other thing for his study, but war and its organization and discipline" (81). The stiletto is then a manifestation of these larger violent struggles on the level of the individual prince or courtier.

William Covino and David Jolliffe note the links between magic and rhetoric in the Renaissance, being concerned with the transformation, even the physical transformation, of subjects: "The power of language to transform consciousness was a central occupation of those who associated rhetoric with magic. . . . The most famous Renaissance magician, Cornelius Agrippa, says . . . that properly uttered discourse can change not only the hearers but also other bodies and things that have no life" (79). This observation does not point us specifically to the stiletto, but it does suggest a strong Renaissance homology among those theories and practices that could affect bodies and influence matters of life or death; a discourse of transformation is thus structurally parallel to a practice of transformation.

Much Renaissance rhetoric is personal in the sense that it is a kind of *performance*. Hariman tells us that, "The courtier's sense of self is aesthetic because it is an achievement of theatricality confirmed by the act of pleasing others and rewarded in part by taking pleasure in one's own performances" (74). Castiglione advises the courtier to perform his exploits "if possible under the very eyes of the prince he is serving" (115) so as to be noticed—although he must not seem to want to be noticed. Later, he explicitly describes the ability to display talents previously unrevealed as "a redoubtable performance" (149). Bizzell and Herzberg note the increasing popularity of the concept of the self as performance during the Renaissance, and its influence on the understanding and practice of courtly rhetoric:

> Yet the notion of self as performance became increasingly important to humanists in their role as public servants because the city-states in the fifteenth century increasingly came under the control of single families, such as the Medici in Florence. Under these conditions, the Ciceronian public man, who exercised some political power openly in the state, was increasingly replaced by the figure of the courtier, who had to be deferential to the ruler in public and exercise political influence behind the scenes. (468)

Courtly rhetoric is, as Hariman reminds us, embodied in performative "techniques by which decorous presentation activates power and establishes selfhood" (76). Similarly, use of a stiletto is, like a performance, a highly personal presentation that must be delivered in the flesh before a (initially) live audience. It is neither a push-button nor a long-distance weapon. The integral connection of the stiletto to the courtier's presentation of self is echoed in the decorated nature of the weapon. Few such weapons are plain, even if they are rarely seen in public.

As performance, *stylistic* and *aesthetic* considerations are paramount in courtly rhetoric. Renaissance rhetoric in general emphasized the aesthetic dimension of linguistic style. As Bizzell and Herzberg note, "The emphasis on style [entailed] amplification of the names of figures and copious demonstrations of their use for the delectation of other experts" (9). Style came to be an important manifestation of courtly rhetoric: "[Late Renaissance writers] tended to emphasize the study of style and to treat rhetoric more as a courtly accomplishment than a powerful political tool" (474).

Renaissance rhetoric is aesthetic, depending upon ornament and display that nevertheless carry out political functions. Victoria Kahn argues that this emphasis on aesthetics was due to the shrinking role of political action in rhetoric; as rhetoric went underground with the courtier, it took aesthetic form (236–37). Hence, "The early humanist conception of rhetoric thus involves a precarious synthesis of aesthetic, political, and religious factors. Aesthetic decorum is seen to be inseparable from political effectiveness" (240). It is telling that L. A. Coutant describes the courtier's function in Castiglione as largely aesthetic: "The goal of the courtier . . . should be to practice an aesthetic contemplation of beauty" (97). Hariman notes, "Rather than merely ornamenting power, at court the rules of decorum serve as the primary means for accomplishing the essential task of any political system: regulating subordinate behavior without force" (54–55), and "Courtly hierarchy operates symbolically not only as a principle of order but also as a source of social invention and artistic creativity" (57). All these observations are homologous with the decorated nature of the stiletto; it is an ornamented, aesthetic object, although its aesthetic dimension is not necessary for its practical effectiveness. It embodies a rhetoric in which imperatives of ornament and practical political power run on parallel tracks.

That parallelism between ornament and practical outcome is also seen in manners. Performative rhetoric is a rhetoric of manners. Writing of Renaissance rhetoric, Michel Jeanneret explains, "In Erasmus's definition, civility, which is guaranteed by moral commitment and natural politeness, implies an authentic and integrated way of living. The aesthetic of manners therefore has an ethical basis; elegance is not just a show put on for others, it also begins to be propagated, contains the seeds of its own destruction. It is designed to be seen and admired, and so risks overdoing things. Whatever the pedagogues say, politeness and good conduct always presuppose an element of pretence and role playing" (45). The balance between aesthetics and practical outcomes is likewise found in the decorated, ornamented stiletto, which was designed for practical use.

Aesthetic display is paradoxically a kind of concealment, especially when it conceals power politics (here again we see the usefulness of merging Hariman's courtly and realist styles for the moment). The performative dimension of courtly rhetoric is the public side of a rhetorical practice that also has a secretive nature. Castiglione advises his courtier "above all to avoid ostentation" (59) and says of the courtier that "he should always be diffident and reserved rather than forward" (91). It is assumed that there is more going on than the courtier articulates openly; in Hariman's analysis, "in courtly rhetoric, motives are assumed to always be mixed" (75). Part of the courtier's concealment may lie in hiding true emotions behind a façade of pleasantness while serving the prince, for Castiglione "could have our courtier act in this manner, even if it is against his nature, in such a way that whenever his prince sees him he believes that the courtier will have something agreeable to say," (125) whether that is in the courtier's heart or not.

A concealed rhetoric is homologous with a concealed weapon. The

secret exercise of rhetorical influence moves underneath a display of ornament and pomp, just as the stiletto rode on the hip beneath gowns
of satin and brocade. Bizzell and Herzberg note that "the increasingly
covert character of the public servant's political power is symbolized in
part by the concept of *sprezzatura,* according to which the talented and
humanistically learned person should make his or her accomplishments
appear to be the outcome of unstudied nature, not art. This covert exercise of power fosters a rhetoric of dissimulation, not display" (468).
Sprezzatura is mentioned also in Coutant's comment, "The concept of
sprezzatura (nonchalance) . . . refers to the courtier's need to make his
studied accomplishments seem effortless" (97). When Castiglione advises the courtier that "true art is what does not seem to be art" (67), he
suggests hiding the truth about strategies and designs behind a show of
naturalness. The value of hiding the truth behind appearance is seen in
Machiavelli who remarks, after listing several princely virtues, "It is not,
therefore, necessary for a prince to have all the above-named qualities,
but it is very necessary to seem to have them" (93). All of these characteristics are homologous with a weapon meant to be kept hidden, a
stiletto that would serve the purposes of a courtier who, by outward appearance, was unarmed and merely dressed for show.

A hidden rhetoric is by its nature narrow in scope, to the point, focused, and oriented toward effect. It is individually practiced, based,
as Hariman tells us, in "social settings that are focused on a specific individual's decisions or performances and are relatively isolated from
democratic accountability" (78). We see an example in Castiglione's advice that, "I should wish our courtier to bolster up his inherent worth
with skill and cunning, and ensure that whenever he has to go where he
is a stranger and unknown that he is preceded by a good reputation"
(141); the courtier's rhetoric is focused upon himself and his own reception. Charles Sears Baldwin observes the focus of a hidden rhetoric as
well when he says of the rhetorical style favored by Machiavelli, "Fused
also is the style, . . . never decorated, never diffused, so ascetically con-
formed to its message as never to obtrude. This is not negatively the art
that knows how to conceal itself, but positively the art that is devoted
singly. True in the choice of words, it is expert in the telling emphasis of
sentences. Its reasoned balances suffice without the empty iteration of
English euphuism. They are played never for display, always for point"
(222). Baldwin's remarks are in every particular homologous with the

stiletto, which was designed not to "obtrude" from its concealing gowns, which was decorated but never *seen* to be so, publicly. It has a "single" use and single method of application (by stabbing); it creates a telling emphasis, causing a wound just there rather than in the broad swathe of a cutting edge; it is nicely "balanced" in the hand; and it relies entirely on its "point"!

Comparing Machiavelli's style to Castiglione's, Baldwin presents them as the decorated and the hidden sides of Renaissance rhetoric: "Machiavelli's style is stripped and so fused with the message as to be inseparable; Castiglione's is ample, manipulating the decorative diffuseness of its time and its setting to elegance. Machiavelli's economy is insistent, urgent; Castiglione's is gracious, deliberate, suggestive, rising to oratory" (223). The two together parallel the decorated, hidden stiletto.

The secretiveness of courtly rhetoric opened it up for practice by women, who had previously been excluded from widespread public speaking: Margaret L. King reminds us, "Since a woman had no role outside of household or convent, the art of oratory would be for her useless" (194). But "female courtiers, too, could practice the politically significant courtly conversation," note Bizzell and Herzberg (483), and they comment that "Christine's [de Pisan] female ruler, like the courtier, works behind the scenes; her public actions are performed by surrogates, by the men she has moved" (487). Homologously, the stiletto, unlike a heavy sword, is a weapon well suited to the smaller physical frame and, at least at that time, strength of women. Its effectiveness may be obtained not just from sheer muscular strength but from physically leaning into the thrust, which women would be well able to do.

In sum, the stiletto is formally parallel with many characteristics of Renaissance rhetorical theory and practice. If we look for the intersections between the political realism and the courtly performance of the time, we find patterns of discourse that match patterns of homicide. Let us look for a similar match between rhetoric and weapons in a somewhat later era of history, the Enlightenment.

Enlightenment Rhetoric and the Flintlock Musket

The Enlightenment, roughly 1600–1800, was a period of profound scientific development, with an emphasis on reason and rational methods for the advancement of knowledge. The rationalization of procedure and scientific advancement made the Enlightenment also the dawn of the Industrial Age, as the inspiring models of the machine, the clock, and the automaton came to invigorate development of manufacturing processes that would flower in the nineteenth and twentieth centuries. Rhetorical theory and practice were heavily influenced by John Locke's critique of the inadequacies of ordinary language in reflecting accurately the thoughts of the speaker (see Peaden, 398–99, for a good list of some studies of this rhetoric). Values such as clarity thus came to the fore in rhetoric. Locke's and others' critiques of the understanding also led to the development of new psychologies, principally faculty psychologies, in which the mind was conceived of in terms of certain basic, universal capacities such as understanding, imagination, reason, or will (see Golden and Corbett, 9–10). George Campbell and others developed rhetorics designed to appeal to the faculties in the minds of an audience. Indeed, Douglas Ehninger sums up the entire era by saying that "the rhetoric of the [eighteenth century] is best described as 'psychological'" (330).

As the size and fortunes of nation-states and empires grew during the Enlightenment, so did the armies that maintained them. Absolutely central to the development of these early modern armies was the development of the firearms that were the standard weapon of every foot soldier. And in the Enlightenment, the specific weapon that no effective army could afford to be without was the flintlock musket. As Christopher Chant explains, "It was only from about 1625 that the flintlock began to gain universal acceptance, and it rapidly became the classic action for muzzle-loading small arms during the second half of the 17th century" (20).

The musket is the ancestor of the rifle. As Jeff Cooper notes, "The rifle has not been with us long—something on the order of 200 years— and it has been available to us in its modern form for just one short century" (1). The musket shooter rammed gunpowder and padding down the musket barrel, followed by a lead ball, using a thin metal rod. The bore of this barrel was in the beginning smooth, to facilitate this loading process. Later rifles would have "rifled" barrels, grooves cut lengthwise into the barrel, and the shooter would have a harder job to push the lead ball down the barrel as it engaged these grooves. Rifled barrels were

more accurate than muskets, but until the development of breech loading, they were more difficult to operate.

One put a small amount of powder in the musket's pan, a tiny recep-
tacle by the side of the base of the barrel, which communicated with the
inside of the barrel by way of a small channel. The idea was to pull
the trigger so as to activate a mechanism that would instantly ignite the
powder in the pan, which would then burn explosively through the
channel into the base of the barrel, thus igniting the much larger charge
of powder placed there, which would propel the ball out of the barrel at
ballistic speed.

The trick was to avoid being only a "flash in the pan"; reliable and
convenient ways of delivering fire to the charge in the pan proved to be
a technological challenge. Earlier technologies such as the wheelock,
snaphaunce, or matchlock proved unreliable, especially in battle (Ezell,
20). The flintlock musket was a breakthrough, first appearing around
1595–1620 (20). The trigger released a hammer (which some thought re-
sembled a cock's head; hence, one cocked the hammer first); the hammer held a piece of flint that was brought down with force upon a piece
of steel just above the pan. The resulting spark was far and away a more
reliable means of igniting one's charge than previous technologies had
been, and was universally adopted. We will see that several homologies
obtain between the flintlock and Enlightenment thinking about effective discourse.

Enlightenment rhetoric was built on the emerging psychological and
epistemological theories of Locke and others; as Ehninger puts it, "Locke
and his successors among the British empiricists began to develop more
sophisticated systems of psychology and epistemology" (331). Locke argues that words are "external sensible signs" of the "invisible ideas which
[a person's] thoughts are made up of" (323). Thus, "the use, then, of
words is to be sensible marks of ideas" (323). Locke insists that language does not represent reality directly, but only "those ideas we have
in our own minds" about reality (325). The two purposes of language in
Locke's view, then, are: "One for the recording of our own thoughts.
Secondly, the Other for the communicating of our thoughts to others"
(385). Although everyone, including scientists, uses language as if they
were referring to the world, the actual grounding of language in the
mind, in human psychology, introduces problems of accuracy. Locke

expresses that goal of language in saying that "the chief end of language in communication being to be understood, words serve not well for that end . . . when any word does not excite in the hearer the same idea which it stands for in the mind of the speaker" (386). Yet he explains many reasons why language, especially in everyday usage, might fail in that task (385–412).

Building a theory of discourse upon the vagaries of human thought and perception means that there is a poignancy at the heart of Enlightenment thinking about language and rhetoric: The purpose of language is understood to be the representation of thoughts in one mind to another mind, or the representation of our ideas of reality to the minds of others, yet completely accurate representation may be impossible. Locke expresses this poignancy in realizing "the imperfections of language" at the same time that he assigns it the role of "the instrument of knowledge" (396). As Catherine Hobbs Peaden explains, "Statements have no meaning unless they correspond to ideas present in the speaker's mind. The privacy and individuality his language theory entails leads to communicational skepticism . . . lack of faith in clear communication" (396). Locke declares that "it is impossible that every particular thing should have a distinct peculiar name" (326), yet that results in an inability to signify precisely our ideas about every particular thing: "it is easy to perceive what imperfection there is in language, and how the very nature of words makes it almost unavoidable for many of them to be doubtful and uncertain in their significations" (385). The realization that language, in principle, cannot precisely mirror the world to the understanding, or one mind to another, is nevertheless met by a desire to make language as accurate as possible. The desire to make language accurate is summed up by Bizzell and Herzberg:

> . . . there is no guarantee that the generality signified by a word will convey the same idea to all speakers. This is a serious problem, and Locke and his successors blame rhetoric for making it worse. If only stylistic extravagance were curbed, they say, language might be closer to the things it names—if not to things out in the world, then at least to people's clear and distinct ideas about them. For a number of seventeenth- and eighteenth-century rhetoricians, these complaints were a call for reform. Rhetoric was out of step with the times, it seemed, because invention re-

lied on outdated deductive methods and stylistic rhetoric impeded the already-difficult search for truth. . . . These reforms proved to be widely influential and later allowed for the development of a more epistemologically sophisticated rhetoric. (10–11)

The ideal of accuracy was largely expressed in terms of *clarity.* Campbell insists that the orator "must take care in the first place that his style be perspicuous, that so he may be sure of being understood" (215), and that "of all the qualities [of eloquence] above mentioned the first and most essential is *perspicuity*" (216). As Bizzell and Herzberg explain, "Thus, eighteenth-century rhetoricians endorse clarity as an ideal of style, support "natural" arrangement, and favor a rhetorical theory that follows 'human nature' in appealing to reason and emotions" (11). Furthermore, "Before the end of the seventeenth century, however, traditional rhetoric became the target of attacks by adherents of the new science who claimed that rhetoric obscured the truth by encouraging the use of ornamented rather than plain, direct language. Many philosophers called for broad language reforms in an attempt to purify communication, at least for science and philosophy. The call for a plain style, taken up by church leaders and influential writers, made *perspicuity,* or clarity, a watchword in discussions of ideal style during the ensuing centuries" (638). Clarity would help language come as close as it could to Locke's benchmark of exciting in the hearer the same idea that began in the listener.

The discursive practices of the newly developed sciences are often held up as models of perspicuity, of as close an approach to accurate conveyance of information as one might get. The emerging sciences sought epistemic efficiency and replicability in methods that relied on clear, reproducible procedures. Peaden notes that "[Locke's] *Essay* attempts to create a new scientific model of discourse as a model for what amounts to all nontrivial communication" (397). Likewise, the emerging techniques of industrial mass production required clear, simple, standardized procedures. From scientific discourse and industrial rationalization, Enlightenment rhetoric acquired a spirit of automation, of identifying a discursive mechanism that would produce accurate communication much as a machine would produce products or a scientific method would produce knowledge. Clarity of communication is homologous with the precise repeatable stamping-out of a product on a machine.

The machine spirit and processes of the Enlightenment are homologous with how the flintlock musket was used. This homology also has a practical dimension, since the flintlock musket was among the first mass-produced industrial goods. As Chant tells us, writing specifically in reference to the flintlock, "The first primitive mass-production techniques provided service weapons with a modicum of interchangeable parts, greatly easing the logistics aspect of weapon maintenance, and also markedly improving tactical reliability" (20). Early rifles required more hand tooling, and thus were rejected by armies more attuned to mass production and standardization, which was possible with muskets. Chant notes that "the rifle was more expensive than the musket, and so lacked attractions for the military rapidly becoming accustomed to the advantages of mass-produced standardization" (25).

The flintlock is hardly on the personal scale of the stiletto; it is on the outsized scale of the factory machine. It was quite long; illustrations usually depict it as taller than the typical soldier (22). Use of the flintlock explicitly did not depend on individual initiative. Instead, a clear procedure for military use was developed. The musket required a definite procedure to load and fire, which had to be followed precisely, or it became useless. Put the ball down first before the powder and the musket became inoperable. But the proper procedure was relatively easy to learn, and it remained the same each time one fired the musket. Clarity in language and orderliness of scientific procedure were paralleled by clarity and order in shooting. Rationalization of communication and of the larger epistemic enterprise was mirrored in the complete rationalization of firing.

Flintlocks were also fired in what was known as the "three rank system," in which soldiers lined up in three ranks (22). One rank would stand and fire, then sink to its knees to reload while the next rank stood to fire, and so forth in regular, rhythmic motion. The amassing of large rows of soldiers upon eighteenth-century battlefields was thus not the suicidal disregard for the common soldier that it looks like today, it was essentially the assembling of a human machine designed to produce large quantities of lead ball volleying off toward the enemy. The tremendous noise of battle made it impossible to hear verbal orders; much of the training of soldiers was largely to instill in them the instinct to follow automatically this three rank firing system. Chant emphasizes "the importance attached to perfect dressing and musketry drill for the infantry of the period. Only thus could a totally united face be shown to the otherwise overwhelming *arme blanche,* the cavalry" (20). The flint-lock musket was thus used in a homology of the machine, with well-trained soldiers rising and falling rhythmically as they went through precisely prescribed procedures to load and fire their weapons.

The development of faculty psychology and its use in rhetoric also parallels the rational processes of Enlightenment science and industry. Bizzell and Herzberg note, "[Enlightenment] Scientists shifted to the experimental method, and sought to name the innumerable parts that make up our universe and to discover the common features that linked these parts together" (637). Rhetoric followed that model. The naming of parts and how they are linked follows from a mechanical way of thinking, and it also underlay the faculty psychology that fueled the rhetoric of the period.

Enlightenment reliance upon faculty psychology reveals the same poignancy we observed previously in terms of accuracy of language. More than before, rhetorical theorists were thinking about how the human mind worked so as to appeal to it. Compared to earlier rhetorics that focused on the construction of messages, one could call the Enlightenment focused on the audience, with Ehninger: "In short, whereas the ancients had built a subject- or substance-centered rhetoric, the eighteenth-century theorists built an audience-centered one" (331). Campbell links the four "ends of speaking" to specific faculties in the mind to which each end is primarily directed: "to enlighten the understanding, to please the imagination, to move the passions, or to influence the will" (1).

Yet there is little concern in Enlightenment rhetorics for understanding how *particular* minds worked and how to appeal to them; there was perhaps even a presumption that all minds worked more or less alike. Such a stance might be expected in an age where the dominant epistemology was reason and a scientific method that was always the same, and where the dawning industrial spirit foresaw the easy mass production of identical parts. For instance, Campbell argues that the four faculties that correspond to the four ends of rhetoric must be appealed to in order:

> In general it may be asserted, that each preceding species, in the order above exhibited, is preparatory to the subsequent; that each subsequent species is founded on the preceding; and that thus they ascend in a regular progression. Knowledge, the object of the intellect, furnisheth materials for the fancy; the fancy culls, compounds, and, by her mimic art, disposes these materials so as to affect the passions; the passions are the natural spurs to volition or action, and so need only to be right directed. (2)

Note the generality and machinelike precision of this plan, how it assumes that all minds will work alike and according to this progression.

Campbell later explains how the speaker might consider the audience "as men in general, and as such men in particular" (71). The "men in general" consideration consists entirely in explaining the faculties that all people are assumed to share, and his discussion goes on at some length (71–94). His discussion of how to address "men in particular" takes barely more than a page (95–96), and is reducible entirely to the foregoing discussion of faculties, for he simply advises the speaker to consider that different people may have different passions, without questioning the presumed common centrality of that faculty and the other faculties in the first place. Enlightenment rhetoric yearned for greater fidelity in describing the audience, yet its audience is en masse, conceived of in terms of the general mass of humanity. Bizzell and Herzberg explain the assumption of universality in Enlightenment rhetoric and psychology:

> Psychology had been a concern for rhetoric since the time of Aristotle. Indeed, Aristotle has more care for psychology than most of his rhetorical descendants do. Most rhetorical systems focus on reasoning, discourse structures, and style but have little to say about appealing to a variety of audiences, beyond the rather obvious advice to adjust style and learning to their capacities. Ironically, perhaps, the new approach to psychology in the eighteenth century does not focus attention on audiences at all. In-

stead, it treats all minds as essentially the same. This approach conforms
to Locke's influential idea of universal psychology, it is democratic, . . .
and it is expedient for an expanded theory of communication. (12)

Indeed, it may be fair to say that a rhetoric based on faculty psychology
is not interested in moving particular audiences at all, but only in considering people as general types. As Bizzell and Herzberg note, "One
effect of the psychological turn was to be the emphasis on 'universal'
modes of discourse, modes that address not audiences but mental faculties. Thus rhetoric moves toward a more 'scientific' theory and takes a
proprietary interest in psychology" (12). Enlightenment rhetoric thus
aims to affect the audience, and constructs a message so as to do so, and
even has a theory about the audience, but it is not equipped to understand the changing characteristics of particular audiences. This is what
Ehninger means in saying that "[Enlightenment rhetoric] was largely
unrelated to and uninterested in speaking and writing as they existed in
the world about it. It was a hypothetical or "if, then" rhetoric—a self-
contained theoretical study" (332–33).

The military conception of the enemy, the opposing force, and the
best way to destroy it, is homologous with Enlightenment concepts of
communication, faculty psychology, and rhetoric. Flintlock muskets were
rarely aimed in battle; they were so inaccurate that there would be little
point in doing so at battlefield distances (say, over one hundred yards).
Their inaccuracy was due to their smoothbore barrels; unlike modern
bullets, which are made to spin as they emerge from the grooves of a
rifled barrel, the lead balls shot by muskets rolled and tumbled in flight.
Yet, when and if they connected with an enemy, their large size guaranteed a terrible wound. The flintlock works by way of generalities similar
to those undergirding faculty psychology and its rhetorics of mass appeal. As Chant notes, "The military also appreciated that the musket,
with shorter barrel and looser-fitting ball, was easier and thus quicker to
reload, allowing ranks of infantry to deliver devastating volleys of fire at
short ranges and over fairly protracted periods" (25).

The flintlock shared with Enlightenment rhetoric a grudging acceptance of the inherent inaccuracy of connection—with ball or word. Yet
the army went out as did the orator with the intent to do just that, to the
extent possible. The orator went with a generalized theory of the audi-

ence grounded in faculty psychology. The army went with the strategy of massed fire. Soldiers fired with the theory of raining down a hail of lead balls on flesh that must by its nature respond. As Chant notes, "Since the smooth bore was of poor accuracy, it was fired in volleys, rank by rank, to lay down a withering short-range carpet of bullets" (120). No particular Pierre on one side sought out the heart of a particular Hans on the other and aimed for it. Thus, the individual soldier's attention was devoted entirely to the process of loading and firing, although with the understanding that this was what was required to have an effect "over there." Ehninger's description of Enlightenment rhetoric as unconcerned with speaking and writing "in the world" is paralleled by the soldier's lack of concern for which target in the world his projectile hit. Chant tells us that the strategy of mass volleys lasted up through the American war of independence: "From this period onwards, therefore, the conventional military virtue of concentrated but short-range musket volleys was at first complemented and then ultimately replaced by rifle fire" (25), although there continued to be widespread use of the flintlock on the American frontier (26–27).

The seventeenth- and eighteenth-century soldier firing his flintlock musket is formally similar to the Enlightenment rhetor. Both embodying the spirit of the new scientific age, both presaging the coming Machine Age, they operate from a vision of total connection, of complete accuracy, even as they forsake hope of achieving it. They engage others en masse, as types, rather than as individuals. On several dimensions, then, a homology obtains between the era's rhetoric and its dominant military weapon. We turn now to the present age, to examine the final connection between the rhetorics of popular culture and the semi-automatic pistol.

Rhetorics of Popular Culture and the Semi-Automatic Pistol

Historians remind us of the difficulty of understanding the era in which we live. Understanding the rhetorical practices of the present age may well be just as precarious a venture. Nevertheless, many good theorists today have tried to do so. As with other eras, we must be careful not to generalize from a single theoretical model to all rhetorical practice, or to assume that the world of rhetorical practice will precisely match the theoretical categories we construct.

One rhetorical development of our age has been increased theoretical interest in what might be called the rhetoric of popular culture (Brummett, *Rhetorical* 1991). By popular culture, we mean those actions, objects, and events that are widely experienced by publics because they are generated in, stored in, and mediated to us by technologically grounded mass media. Popular culture is what most people experience, what most people know about, in the contexts of television, film, popular music, style and fashion, cyberspace, and so forth. While some form of popular culture has no doubt always been present, today's popular culture is often understood to be relatively more influential in determining public meanings and attitudes—relative to declining institutions such as family, religion, or even state. The rhetoric of popular culture is understood to be both a new form of discourse and a new problematic of discourse creation and reception that goes largely beyond traditional understandings of the public forum. Today's theorists of the rhetoric of popular culture therefore attempt to understand how meanings and attitudes are created in, shared by, or challenged through texts of popular culture such as movies or television shows, clothing choices, rap music, professional wrestling, and so forth, with the understanding that the structure and distribution of power in our era is influenced by such texts as well (see Fiske, *Understanding*).

Not coincidentally, a new kind of weapon was developed at precisely the same time, around the dawn of the twentieth century, that today's mass-mediated rhetorics of popular culture were developing. That weapon is the semi-automatic handgun, or *pistol*. A. B. Zhuk locates the time frame of its appearance: "By the end of the nineteenth century, the first true auto-loaders had appeared. . . . When the First World War began, great strides to perfect the auto-loading pistol had been made" (20). He notes the first emergence of the seminal Luger pistol around 1898 (21). Chant names the Borchardt as the first practical semi-automatic, appearing in 1893 (73). Edward C. Ezell cites as some classic examples of early pistols the Luger pistol, developed in the late nineteenth century (177), the Browning FN pistol introduced 1894–1945 (202–65), and the U.S. 1911 model (301–19).

"Semi-automatic," sometimes called "self-loading," refers to a kind of action that may be found today on any kind of firearm (rifles, shot-guns, machine guns). Cartridges consisting of a brass tube filled with gunpowder and perforated at the base by an explosive "primer," topped by a bullet seated into the neck of the cartridge, are generally loaded into a magazine or portable metal sheath. The sheath is inserted into the firearm and some mechanism (typically the "slide" or metal housing on the top of the handgun) is moved back and then forward to move a cartridge into connection with the barrel and readiness to fire. A hammer or striking pin is released by the trigger, it strikes the primer which ignites the charge of gunpowder, sending the bullet on its way down the barrel.

The key technical feature of the semi-automatic action is that forces created by the ignition of the powder in the cartridge—whether that be the backward motion of the spent cartridge or the gases created by the burning powder—are used to "cycle" the action. In the case of a hand-gun, the slide is automatically propelled to the rear and then moves forward again, picking up a new charge and moving it into position to be fired. This process happens in a split second. In short, semi-automatic actions are unique in their ability to allow the shooter to fire quickly and easily. Technical expertise is necessary to prepare the semi-automatic to shoot, and to deal with emergent problems such as jams, but a prepared semi-automatic is so easy and quick to shoot that a child (unfortunately) can do it. Zhuk remarks upon "the ease with which a conventional handgun can be carried. . . . All that the shooter has to do, therefore, is to take aim and press the trigger. Since unlocking, ejecting and reloading are accomplished automatically, shooting is very easy; the cycle is so rapid that the trigger can be pressed to fire another shot almost as soon as one has been fired" (22). (Parenthetically, trained professional shooters have been able to fire the old single-action "cowboy" pistol even more rapidly than a semi-automatic, but it is a technically difficult feat with no real world relevance.)

Different theorists have provided different conceptual schemes by which to understand today's rhetoric of popular culture. Here I rely on a theoretical description of that rhetoric that I developed in some earlier work (1994). In *Rhetoric in Popular Culture,* I argued that older, more traditional forms of rhetoric were usually *expositional, verbal, discrete, and hierarchical.* In contrast, the rhetoric of popular culture is *relatively* more *narrative based, nonverbal, diffuse,* and *democratic.* Based on that scheme, I will show how the semi-automatic pistol is homologous with today's rhetoric of popular culture.

Traditional rhetorics have been largely expositional, relying on the argumentative development of propositions. There have, of course, been notable exceptions of rhetorical theories and practices that emphasized nonexpositional order such as aesthetic rhetorics, but the balance of rhetoric has been reason-giving discourse. In contrast, rhetorics of popular culture that have developed since the start of the twentieth century are more grounded in *narrative* (Fisher, *Human Communication as Narration*). Often, these rhetorics are actual narratives such as films or television episodes. At other times they take the form of narrative, relying on interesting characters, creative tensions, and stock patterns of plot and plot development. A major reason for this shift in discursive form is that popular culture today must reach vast, fragmented, and complex audiences. Exposition depends on shared knowledge and shared assumption of correct forms of reasoning. When groups do not share those because of cultural, geographic, or other differences, they may nevertheless be drawn to narrative, which is more universal and which facilitates disparate readings more easily than does exposition.

In working out social meanings and attitudes through narrative, texts of popular culture *metonymize* or reduce large, complicated social issues into particular, focused, manageable stories and characters. The events of September 11, 2001, triggered a great wash of narratives throughout popular culture in which a wide range of complex issues engaging nationalism, religious bigotry, imperialism, and patriotism were metonymized and struggled over in stories and images. For every jingoistic story of an American "hero" there was a cautionary tale of a suffering Afghan or Palestinian victim of American or Israeli violence. In metonymizing narratives, the public works out great social and political issues that used to be handled more often in exposition.

The semi-automatic handgun is an instrument of narrative and metonymy fully as much as it is a weapon. It is, of course, a staple of the entertainment industry and a stock narrative element. Films, television shows, and music videos abound with pistols. They are the most recent iteration of the six-shooter of American Western myth, yet their smooth machine efficiency speaks to our hi-tech age. Pistols are characters in their own right, supporting players in films and television. Some of these mechanical actors acquire distinctive identities of their own, as in James Bond's signature Walther PPK.

I do not at all wish to claim that one would never have a legitimate reason of self-defense in owning a pistol. But in addition to whatever practical efficacy it may have, the semi-automatic handgun is also a celebrity. To have, to carry, or to use one is a performance, the enactment of a role. Often the user of the pistol is advised as to what that performance is by the latest action films or television crime dramas. The technical nature of the pistol's action even has narrative elements: once a cartridge is chambered, or made ready to fire, in a pistol there are springs compressed and held ready in tension. Some pistols are even somewhat difficult to be made unready to fire, unless one has expertise. The loaded, chambered pistol is thus a device of coiled potential, waiting to release energy, which is true of all good narrative devices.

The semi-automatic pistol also metonymizes important social issues. The pistol facilitates some predictable meanings. It is urban, whereas revolvers are rural. Its greater technical sophistication, compared to revolvers or other actions, plus its sleek design, gives it meanings of high technology. It is an instrument of personal empowerment rather than broad social cooperation. In popular-culture texts it is repeatedly associated with male action and domination. Controversies over handgun control arise, I believe, at least as much from this freight of meanings and wider implications than they do from clear facts and figures related to policy decisions. The pistol means so many different things that what is proposed or rejected for "control" is always those larger issues, never the individual machine itself. A pistol is thus a condensed site of metonymized meanings, a narrative in machine form.

Whether primarily expositional or aesthetic, traditionally rhetorical texts have been understood to be largely *verbal*. Of course, we find much advice about delivery, gesture, and intonation in major classical writers, but the balance of the rhetorical tradition conceives of delivery and vocal manipulation as icing on a verbal cake. Of course, an expositional rhetoric is also likely to be verbal, since language is the means of expositional development.

Rhetorics of popular culture have certainly not given up language, but the balance has changed; they are relatively more *nonverbal*. Even as texts become more based in narrative, narrative becomes more based in images. Special effects rule in the creation of images. Ever since Richard Nixon's five o'clock shadow did him in during the 1960 presidential debates, politicians have understood that appearance and image are as or more important than what they say. Verbal texts themselves shrink to the sound bite, the bumper sticker, and the brand name. One might sum up these changes by saying that rhetorics of popular culture are moving from the order of the word and logos into orders of aesthetics and kinesthetics. Hence the ways in which social issues are struggled over move at least in part onto that new nonverbal ground.

The semi-automatic pistol is a stylized, aesthetic product. It is produced and purchased with attention to design. As an image in entertainment narratives, the pistol takes on aesthetic dimensions that may actually be in conflict with its practical use; recent "gangsta" videos and films, for instance, show urban pistoleros holding their semi-automatics at a ninety degree angle, with the handle horizontal, or held oddly high, nearly above the head with the barrel pointing downward—both very stylized stances but both likely to result in jams after the first shot.

Such a stylized holding of the pistol emphasizes the extent to which it is an extension of the (urban) self in performance. Once one acquires the technical skill to make it work, using a semi-automatic handgun is quite easy. Zhuk notes the technical ease of firing in observing, "Truly modern handguns are generally easier to handle, more advanced technologically, and easier to make than their predecessors" (21). One points one's hand like a magician and powerful effects appear. Chant agrees in noting the Luger's "'pointability,' leading to good natural aim as the gun becomes a simple extension of the firer's arm and hand" (74). Use of the pistol is a kinesthetic experience, a wishing of power or destruction on a target followed almost simultaneously by that destruction and by a jolt of power felt in the hand. The pistol merges the body, power, and aesthetics.

Semi-automatic pistols display a machine aesthetic (Brummett, *Rhetoric of Machine Aesthetics*). While revolvers display the open workings and blue steel of older, Industrial Age machines, the pistol moves in the direction of high technology with its sleek frames and slides that enclose its workings. The surfaces are often a shiny or muted, brushed look of stainless steel or nickel, echoing the skins of aircraft, missiles, and "bullet" trains. The inner workings remained concealed and mysterious, exposed only for the millisecond taken for cycling cartridges during firing. As I have argued earlier (1999), such aesthetics combine meanings of strength and masculine force with meanings of hi-tech control over vast powers, mystery, and arcane knowledge.

We live in an age in which identity is proclaimed and turf is staked through aesthetic rhetoric, through what one wears or drives, through the music one plays or the entertainment venues one enters. That aesthetic management of rhetorical power is paralleled by the aestheticization of an instrument of actual physical power. Pistols need not be beautiful; early versions were boxy and ungainly. So the ubiquitous, intentional aestheticization of an instrument of physical violence today is meaningful, and can be linked homologically with the aesthetic means by which our culture increasingly manages its social meanings and its politics through aesthetic means.

Traditional rhetorical texts tend to be *discrete*. If an inaugural address is understood as a traditional text, it begins at a certain point and ends at another point. It is clear who the author or speaker is, even if there is dialogue with or heckling from an audience. Traditional texts are bounded in time and space and lie clear for all to see.

Texts of popular culture are relatively more *diffuse*. There are simply so many more of them than there used to be; one is hard-pressed to find a quiet corner in which messages are not present. The latest news story about a congressman's or entertainer's peccadilloes is a text in which social and political meanings are managed and spread out across quite a few signs in time and space. A month's worth of frantic news coverage, trailing off into a whimper of bored neglect, might constitute such a text. Or a text might be a series of advertisements on television, each one chaining into the next and received in terms of the series; but also, the series itself, broken and fragmented as its parts appear across different channels and types of entertainment. In a sound-bite culture, a whole text might consist of a cluster of such sound bites spread out here and there across news coverage of various press conferences. Furthermore, the ability of consumers of messages to shift and rearrange them, to channel surf, to tape, to time shift, to edit and reassemble, makes the notion of a text in popular culture a fluid matter. Technology and cultural practices have dispersed messages.

Most states now allow the concealed carry of handguns by suitably licensed citizens. In all states, handguns are widely distributed whether legally or not. Of more importance is that the perception that handguns are everywhere, especially in urban areas, is widespread. The image is largely embodied in the semi-automatic handgun, an urban weapon, and thus able to play a part in urban fears and myths of pandemic violence.

As an instrument of physical power, pistols are thus dispersed throughout the culture much as are messages. They are either ubiquitous or perceived to be so, often in fear. The fact that they must be concealed contributes to this diffusion. Either the laws governing concealed carry require that they be secret, or they are hidden away because they are carried illegally; in either case, the fact that a pistol may not be carried publicly contributes to the image that they lie beneath every jacket.

The ubiquity of the semi-automatic handgun in images of popular culture is also a kind of diffusion. The odds of finding a picture of a pistol in today's newspaper advertisements for current movies is great. If not there, one will find images of them on television programs or news reports. Pistols have become attached to so many different texts that they now chain out as an image throughout the interconnected texts of popular culture.

Another kind of diffusion of handguns is that they typically have no central, controlling connection to an institution. They are personal and decentered, much as was the stiletto. Soldiers carried their flintlocks as part of the army, but a female jogger may have a semi-automatic in her fanny pack for her own personal protection and comfort. Pistols are not "issued" to anyone outside of the police on a regular basis, and so their ownership is decentered.

A final characteristic of texts of popular culture may be understood in comparison with a dominant characteristic of traditional texts, which are *hierarchical*. By that I mean that traditional rhetorical texts are produced and consumed within a fairly clearly defined structure of speaker and audience. Even if everyone "gets their turn" to speak, while in the act of speaking a hierarchy is imposed upon the participants as one speaks and the others listen (even if they listen boisterously). In fact, though, historically some have been more empowered to be on the platform than have others, and so the hierarchical nature of traditional texts has sometimes been based in broad social inequities.

In contrast, texts of popular culture are more *democratic*. The Internet may serve as one example of the extent to which anyone with access may disseminate messages that might reach millions—without waiting in line to speak. Although access is certainly an issue, even the poorest of people can gain access to this means of rhetorical expression through schools and public libraries. Technology allows people as consumers of messages to manipulate what they receive; use of the wide range of channels and Web sites, and means of recording and rearranging messages, mean that sources of messages today may have very little control over the form in which their messages are received, much less over their rhetorical impact. Audiences today are more active in the reception, manipulation, and repackaging of messages.

One of the most visible and most controversial dimensions of semiautomatic pistols is their location in private hands throughout the population. Controversy has arisen for at least a century over whether the Second Amendment guarantees ownership of firearms as a private right, with some recent court decisions seeming to affirm that it does to the dismay of gun control advocates. If the Second Amendment does offer such a protection, it does so for purposes of securing the public's right, individually exercised, to the defense of person and home. The Second Amendment speaks to the use of violence in securing domestic safety; it is not about the right to hunt.

Semi-automatic pistols are uniquely suited to such a personal protection role. One can purchase cheaper models legitimately at any reputable gun store for two hundred dollars or less. Revolvers might have a number of purposes for hunting, which, as mentioned, the Second Amendment is not about. But due to their technical limitations, semiautomatic pistols *tend* to fire cartridges that are underpowered for hunting game yet well suited to homicide. For instance, Zhuk notes the merely "short range accuracy" of the pistol (22). And he notes that although for rifles, "The effect on an animate target at long range is comparatively unimportant; as the primary goal is simply to hit, it is not essential to disable an enemy immediately." In contrast, "Expectations of a handgun are quite different. Under normal conditions, it is vital to disable a target instantly to ensure that—for example—an armed opponent cannot continue to pose a threat" (22).

This location of pistols in the hands of the general public through private ownership is categorically opposed to corporate or government ownership or control over firearms, then. As such, the semi-automatic pistol is positioned against authority in one of its chief meanings (even if the police forces of many authorities also carry semi-automatic pistols). The semi-automatic handgun is uniquely my weapon for the securing of my protection and enjoyment of my property. It is my alternative, especially in the immediate moment, to calling upon the resources of government to protect me. This attitude positions the pistol against the hierarchical structures of government and makes its possession and use a democratic exercise, dispersed among the population.

If we take my earlier scheme (in *Rhetoric in Popular Culture*) as an operationalization of the rhetoric of popular culture, we see a number of homologies between those texts and semi-automatic handguns. Texts of popular culture embody a rhetoric that is relatively more nonverbal, narrative-based, diffuse, and democratic than are more traditional texts. Correspondingly, pistols are an aesthetic and kinesthetic nonverbal experience—they embody a narrative tension in their mechanism and they are found throughout narratives in popular culture. Their concealment and concealability make them potentially diffused throughout the population, and as such, they are instruments of democratic, individual empowerment situated specifically against governmental authority.

Implications and Conclusions

Homologies, formal linkages across disparate categories of experience, are lines of connection and influence. If I find a formal parallel between my experiences with a neighbor and a science fiction television series that leans heavily on the weekly repulsion of monsters, then a linkage is established between experience and text that allows them to speak to and to influence each other. I see the TV show a certain way because of my neighborhood experience, and I see my neighbor in terms of the TV show.

When the same kind of homology is asserted across several disparate categories of experience, the homology itself becomes more theoretically interesting. A formal parallel that keeps recurring may well tell us something fundamental about experience, texts, or both. In this study, the assertion of a formal link between rhetoric and a weapon in *one* era might be merely interesting, cute, or maybe even too clever by half. Discovery of the same formal link between rhetorics and weapons of three eras begins to suggest a deeper structure beneath texts and experiences that may be contributing to the ordering of both. Such a recurrence also illustrates how one transhistorical homological structure might underlie more historically inflected, historically specific homologies. This dual nature of homology occurs because the formal parallel that recurs here across history is a pattern in which rhetorics and weapons are homologous; how they are homologous is a subordinate homology emerging in specific histories. That rhetorics and weapons will be homologous is the transhistorical pattern; how they will be homologous is a historically grounded pattern that is newly ordered within new circumstances.

I believe that an extension of this study would show continuing parallels between rhetorics and weapons, and that alone is suggestive and interesting. Future research might identify linkages between the great classical rhetorics of Greece and Rome and dominant weapons of those times, for instance. This possibility would further confirm the claim that a fundamental super homology is at work here between rhetoric in general and weapons in general, that these two orders might well be vibrating on the same frequency no matter which era one investigated.

We are, of course, rhetoricians and not armorers. If we look at rhetoric with weapons as a foil (so to speak), what insights are generated about what rhetoric is at the core? Here we turn to the implications of a super homology between rhetorics and weapons across history. Rhetoric has of course been defined in many ways and on many dimensions throughout its long history. Often, theorists and practitioners have defined it in terms of the physical manifestation that it takes: rhetoric is public speaking, it is speaking in courts or the forum, it is the manipulation of style, and so forth. To see rhetoric as informed by weapons shifts attention to what I believe is a more fundamental way to understand rhetoric, and that is in terms of its social and political functions rather than its manifestation. The homology with weapons causes us to look to what both rhetoric and weapons do as the underlying strata that may define rhetoric more truly and more fundamentally.

I believe that this study emphasizes an insight into rhetoric that is not new, but is hereby nominated as central to rhetoric's functions: rhetoric is a way of connecting to humans so as to transform them. Call it the *transformative connection* if you want something catchier, following Burke's observation that poetics, rhetoric, and discourse about killing may all be "terms for transformation in general" (*Rhetoric of Motives*, 11), although no doubt something catchier still can be formulated by someone. Weapons are also fundamentally not the forms of steel, iron, leather, or wood in which we find them physically manifested throughout history. They are likewise a way of connecting to humans so as to transform them. Other dimensions of experience may be brought into this fundamental order; the reference earlier to Agrippa suggests that magic in all its forms and mutations is a transformative connection. It may well be that *religion* is yet another discourse and practice of transformative connection. Note that rhetoric, magic, and religion are clearly discursive in nature; might we see weapons as part of this group if we think of them as a kind of nonverbal discourse? If so, does the consistently discursive nature of transformative connections suggest that the whole point of discourse in the first place is to transform?

However transcendental may be the homological structure of transformative connection, I believe that it is fundamentally discursive. Its emergence in so many discursive structures such as magic and religion bespeaks a discursive DNA at the core of the super homology. But note that here we are going deeper, more fundamentally formal, in human experience, and we still find discourse and discourses of change. We find rhetoric and its textual kin. I believe this suggests that a transcendental human imperative to change the world is not only fundamentally discursive but also is the reason why we "have" discourse in human experience in the first place, because it is the mechanism of change. That suggests likewise that physical changes resulting from the finger that pulls the trigger or the hand that turns the spade are grounded first and most fundamentally in discourses that enable the very conception and form of transformation.

My suggestions here imply that transformative connection may be a transcendental discursive category of human experience, a crucible of experience from which different related dimensions of life emerge. Identifying such crucibles may be a way of understanding fundamental terms of experience. It may also be dabbling in an unfashionable structuralism, calling up the departed shade of Claude Lévi-Strauss from the purgatory of abandoned academic theories. I think that this suggestion need not be read as ahistorical and apolitical, though, any more than suggesting that language use is a transcendental category of human experience. Specific homologies obtaining among specific rhetorics, weapons, magics, and whatever else is a cousin to this category surely emerge in different eras to serve different political purposes, and having an eye to a fundamental supercategory of experience need not blind us to the different ways in which that category may be manifested and struggled over in history.

As I noted earlier, my concern is with rhetoric more than with its homological cousins. I believe the location of rhetoric in such formal families can help us to understand it better, however. Let us crawl back out of this crucible of transformative connection, keeping an eye on weapons as we go as a kind of informative metaphor for rhetoric. Suppose every author of a study announcing a rhetorical genre or strategy was required to identify a significant parallel between that rhetorical category and a certain weapon. The suggestion is absurd, of course, but it might well teach us something about rhetoric. If one writes about inaugural addresses, or apocalyptic pamphlets, or the lawyer's summation, what is the parallel weapon that can with some reason and insight be shown to be homologous? If an inaugural address, apocalyptic pamphlet, or summation is fundamentally a transformative connection, what sharp-edged, ballistic, or blunt-faced weapon parallel might help us to see the kind of transformative connection it is?

Likewise, as we climb back out of the crucible of transformative connection, might we not see violence and the instruments thereof as like rhetoric? Might these connections not encourage us to see violence as more nuanced and dimensioned than rhetoricians often do? So often rhetoric is opposed to violence as a monolithic category, the use of symbols opposed to the use of brute force. Violence may thus be understood more fruitfully as a cousin to rhetoric, a transformative connection that emphasizes this or that, that pushes here or there, but moves toward the same kind of relationship with others as does the speech, the incantation, or the prayer.

In our next two chapters we consider ways in which discourse responds to experiential exigencies. Recurrent sorts of exigencies may call forth recurrent sorts of discourse, as suggested by the genre theory alluded to in chapter one. In the next chapter, the rhetorical exigence of functioning as a "wise woman," or a "griot," for a diverse and mass-mediated society—and rhetorical strategies that meet that exigence—is studied. By studying ways in which two rhetors centuries apart met similar challenges, we find a homology underlying the structure of their rhetorical stances. Key to our discussion will be homologies structuring the personae adopted by rhetors in homological rhetorical situations, specifically the parallel personae of Sojourner Truth and Oprah Winfrey.

6

Oprah Winfrey, Sojourner Truth, and the Recurring Wise Women of Diverse, Mass-Mediated Societies

BARRY BRUMMETT AND DETINE L. BOWERS

One of the more enduring beliefs perpetuated in at least Western societies is that of individualism: the idea that we are each unique and entirely self-formed, self-motivated agents, autonomous centers of intension and creativity. No amount of postmodern decentering of the subject in academic journals has managed to call into question that cherished assumption that we all stand alone. Even people from more communal cultural backgrounds are likely to be strongly influenced by the individualistic beliefs underlying Western culture and economic behavior.

But those less individualistic cultures have it right after all. No one of us is an island. We are born into societies, or villages if you will, that are already in place. These societies have certain ways to be, certain kinds of personae or roles to enact, and the child growing up in a given culture is called to assume those different personae. The roles one takes on may be multiple and complex, especially in multiple and complex societies,

In this chapter we follow a convention concerning names. Oprah Winfrey has made her first name her trademark; for example, spelled backwards as Harpo it is the title of her production company. We thus refer to her mainly as "Oprah," not out of disrespect or diminution but in following her lead, in a sense. With that as a basic pattern, we likewise refer to Sojourner Truth mainly as "Sojourner." We do note that Sojourner Truth is a name she took for herself later in life. At birth she was named Isabella Baumfree by her slave master, although she later took the last name of Van Wagener. Of course, in referring to either Oprah or Sojourner, we are referring to their representations in these texts, not to any sense of the "real" person.

but they are not roles that the individual invents entirely anew. Ironically, even (perhaps especially) our notions of rugged individualism may be taken from discourses that are communally created and widely dispersed in a culture. We learn how to be isolated actors by watching the same cowboy or outer space movies that everyone else watches.

In particular, we wish to argue that the kinds of people we become, the kinds of *personae* that there are to become in a given society, are formed and encoded discursively. A society's narratives are the engines that cause individuals to grow themselves around the templates provided by discourse. Thus, an important kind of form is that which generates the personae that all of us enact in our daily lives. Such forms function homologically when different personae in different texts and experiences are structured similarly.

Neal Gabler argues that forms made available to us in the mass media, especially in forms of entertainment found in television, movies, popular music, and so forth, are used to structure who we become and how we live our lives. Life is increasingly becoming a movie, a form of art, he argues, as we enact fundamental forms found in entertainment. Not the least among those forms are those that advise us as to who we and others may become. We know how to be academics, and we know how to interact with others who are enacting academics, because we have seen movies about them. Note that because these characters, or personae, are formal they do not come in an infinite variety but rather group around a discursive structure that is the homology binding them together.

We also see the evidence of recurring, stock personae in popular expressions. He or she is or is not "my type" we might say, acknowledging that we think of others as types even if some of us insist that we ourselves are not. Similarly, a recently heard comedy routine on television wondered why people never recall being "reincarnated" as anyone ordinary; there must be millions of people who were once Cleopatra or Napoleon! The joke hides the truth that discourse of Cleopatra or Napoleon gives us those kinds of characters to become, along with a wide but not infinite range of other possible personae. It is a discursive if not a spiritual truth that many people are indeed the reincarnations of Cleopatra or Napoleon as they reindividuate patterns given to them in their society's discourses.

Any society will have certain kinds of characters that are explicitly embodied in its discourses more often or more powerfully than others. These are widely known characters, and especially in complex, mass-mediated societies they will be known only through discourse about them. Many of these characters recur throughout history, reindividuated in both famous and ordinary people. Saints are particular reindividua-tions of discursive patterns of virtue. Outlaws are particular reindi-viduations of transgression and refusal of order. Cowboys are particular reindividuations of the myth of rugged individualism. Homologies in discourse create these particular manifestations of types; one may say that a standard or stock persona is a kind of homology. It is not a ques-tion of who these people *really* are, whether Joan of Arc, Mother Teresa, or Princess Diana *really are saints*. The presence of the homologies of saintliness in a culture's discourse will from time to time throw up the local manifestation of that underlying form, creating a saint in public discourse who is wearing the flesh of this place and time.

Here we examine one such homology, the enduring and probably universal form of the Wise Woman. In particular we consider the special discursive challenges posed by the emergence of a Wise Woman in a highly complex, diverse, mass-mediated society. Our focus is on Oprah Winfrey and, to a somewhat lesser extent, Sojourner Truth. In this chap-ter we argue that Oprah embodies and enacts a powerful, fundamental form that is deeply embedded in many cultures. This form has clear rhe-torical effects, and understanding how it works is important in explain-ing Oprah's success. Of more importance are the social and political implications of this form, for who Oprah becomes as she enacts her "character" has connections to structures of empowerment connected to gender and race. We turn now to an explanation of who Oprah Win-frey and Sojourner Truth "really" are and the pattern and personae that they enact. Each of them enacts the same kind of character in response to the same kind of exigence; therefore, a homology underlies them and other, similar pairs of persona and exigence. In that sense this chapter, like chapter five, studies tiers or levels of homology.

Great Goddesses and Wise Women

There is a tradition in human history that goes back to the dawn of cul-ture, a tradition of the *wise women* of the tribe. These women provide stability and leadership for their social groups. They are repositories of knowledge, sites of collective memory, which garners them the title of "healer." The Wise Woman is connected to deep wells of healing power embodied in wisdom and intuitive knowledge, and thus likewise connects the society to that power. Her power is spiritual and cosmic more than it is physical. She contains wisdom rather than law, nurturing rather than physical force. The Wise Woman is present in every society but may be more visible in those societies relatively less influenced by Western skepticism and patriarchy (we later argue that Oprah merges these worlds of wisdom, intuition, and patriarchal intelligence as a business woman). In indigenous cultures of what is sometimes called the third world, and among people most directly descended from such cultures, we find the role of the Wise Woman most clearly enacted. She is thus founded on a very broadly based homology, a character type or persona, that has been central to many if not all human cultures.

The Wise Woman is a vicar for a still more ancient form, the Goddess. Monica Sjöö and Barbara Mor note this in tracing "The Great Mother in Her many aspects—maiden, raging warrior, benevolent mother, death-dealing and all-wise crone, unknowable and ultimate word" (xviii). Martha Ann and her colleagues trace the worship of "a primordial goddess" back at least thirty thousand years (1). The "powerful 'magic'" of these goddesses "could surely bless the tribe, the animals, and the environment to ensure survival" (1). They argue that "remnants of her presence have always been kept alive through the ages" despite the fact that the histories of many people, "notably Africans and Asians," have been written by more patriarchal societies (2).

Ann and her colleagues note the role of the Goddess in Africa "as supreme creator" (4). Among these African Goddesses was Oshun, "who represents the joy of being female" (6). In ancient Egypt, they argue, "women had a powerful place" which was homologous with the primacy of "primeval goddesses" (10). They note "positive signs that modern Egyptians may reclaim some of their rich goddess heritage" (10). As an example they offer Nut, Egyptian sky goddess, whose harmonious relationship with her husband represents "individuals using their unique talents while living their lives in a loving relationship" (12).

The Greek goddesses studied by Ann and her colleagues also include Hecate, Queen of the Night. Hecate would appear to be an early model for the Wise Woman, for she is "Goddess of Age and Wisdom," and is a "healer" and "a caretaker of children, flocks and vineyards" (18). In other words, the Greek goddess functions as a source of wisdom in support of the tribe.

Sjöö and Mor argue that since "the first environment for all new life was female" the Goddess is primary and primeval in human culture (11). Culture, they claim, is fundamentally female, based on the ability of strong women to nurture, advise, raise up, and reproduce (11–12). Sjöö and Mor particularly ground the worship of the Goddess in ancient Africa, in "the original black mother" of earliest human history (21). These early African societies were either matriarchal or strongly guided by central female figures (22). Repeatedly, they connect the ongoing tradition of Wise Women to foundational worship of the Goddess: "The Great Mother was the projection of the self-experience of groups of highly aware and productive women who were the founders of much human culture" (30). This means that "only black women, Oriental women, and Native American women can completely rediscover and reanimate the original Goddesses of Africa, Asia, and the Americas for us" (31). They point to the appearances of "Black Madonnas" in various European cultures as evidence that Wise Women, echoes of the Great Goddess, may in some sense be fundamentally African, fundamentally third world (31–32).

Sjöö and Mor's observations bring us to the present day, in which so much culture is not simply European, African, American, Asian, or some other unitary cultural/geographic descriptor. Culture today is international. Film, television, music, and so forth may in some cases originate from clearly identifiable geographic origins, but the entertainment industry that has become culture for so many is truly international in scope. The tribe is the Internet. What becomes of the Wise Woman under these circumstances? How is the homology grounding that persona manifest today?

We can, of course, point to a number of female figures who are widely known in our global, entertainment-oriented culture. But how do women attain the status of Wise Woman in such a diverse, far-reaching culture? How can someone be the matriarch for the tribe when the tribe numbers in the billions and is thus necessarily diverse, fragmented, even fractured? If the Wise Woman is a type, a role that homologously orders many reindividuations of the Goddess, how is that persona manifested today so as to appeal to and unify the vast tribe of her children? The recurring exigence of a diverse, mediated culture combines with a persona created in response to that exigence to create a more specific homology for postmodern times.

We argue that the Wise Woman today, and since the dawn of mass communication, must embody and express contradictory values, inclinations, political views, philosophies, and behavior patterns, yet unify them on the important dimension of *spirituality* (spirituality is the use of intuitive powers to transcend earthly adversity through access to the inner self and a higher power/source of knowledge than is visible on the earthly plane). A Wise Woman who is both Black and White, who says both yes and no, who goes both left and right, can body forth the Goddess to a wide and eclectic congregation. Indeed, if she is to be a Wise Woman to a mass-mediated audience rather than to a small, local tribe, she *must* embody and express contradictions. But she must find unity and hold together as a role on an important ground, and that ground is of the spirit, a language of healing and overcoming pain and suffering through a higher consciousness than is generally understood or accepted in the norm. The Wise Woman must in this sense be a kind of personal enactment of what Kenneth Burke calls a *constitution*. Burke argues that constitutions are symbolic structures that allow complex and contradictory behavior (since that is inevitable as times and situations change) yet provide a shared, unifying basis of motivation (*Grammar of Motives*, 323–401). In complex and fragmented electronically mediated environments, the Wise Woman likewise embodies contradictory values yet unifies them within the grounding motivation of healing oneself of life's pain and suffering, and victory over the adversities of struggle, a "spiritual motive."

To illustrate our argument we turn now to one main and one auxiliary example. We come to the auxiliary example first: Sojourner Truth, the great nineteenth-century African American fighter for emancipation and human rights. Living during a century in which mass communication was beginning its explosive, sharp trajectory of influence, she was widely known and came to be revered across the United States and abroad. She did so, we will show, by embodying contradictory impulses that were nevertheless unified on the ground of spirituality, wisdom in transcending pain and suffering through access to a higher power, and her inner self. Sojourner Truth was an example of a wise woman able to reinvent herself through the power of the holy spirit. An excellent, complete treatment of Sojourner's life and symbolic importance is found in Nell Irvin Painter's, *Sojourner Truth: A Life, A Symbol.* In that volume, she likewise notes the contradictions inherent in Sojourner and in her time, and examines the effects that her complex and polyvalent character had (3–11). Sojourner was a Wise Woman in an age when mass communication through the popular press and telegraph was beginning to resemble what communication would be in the twenty-first century. In that way, she foreshadowed the later manifestation of this homology, Oprah Winfrey.

The texts we examine require some discussion as well. We shall examine the *Narrative of Sojourner Truth,* by one Olive Gilbert, described in the introduction as "a sympathetic white woman [who] helped the illiterate Sojourner to record her remarkable life in writing" (v). We shall also examine *The Uncommon Wisdom of Oprah Winfrey: A Portrait in Her Own Words,* edited by Bill Adler—this book being a compilation of allegedly direct quotations from her speeches and writings. Neither text was written by the woman in question; in both cases they are representations of these women (certainly in Sojourner Truth's case, and probably in Oprah Winfrey's case, by White people). These books cannot be said to be *by* either woman, nor accurate as to either one's true thoughts and expressions, but they are important for our purposes because they are widely read *representations* of each Wise Woman, distributed en masse throughout the popular culture of the day (the Winfrey book, for instance, is number one on the list of Amazon.com books about her, at this writing). Each book thus helps us to understand, not who each woman is or was, but what each one means to the public.

Sojourner Truth

Sojourner Truth lived from 1797 to 1883, born in slavery in New York. The *Narrative,* which we examine here, went through several printings, first appearing in 1850 and re-emerging with supplements in 1878, 1881, and 1884. It is still in print and available today.

Spirituality is featured widely throughout the book, and is the common thread holding together what can be read as contradictory motives and attributions. Sojourner's religious instruction began at the feet of her mother, who told her, "My children, there is a God, who hears and sees you" (4). This early training stayed with her, as "she did not forget the instructions of her mother, to go to God in all her trials" (10). Happy developments in her life, such as deliverance from a cruel master, are seen as "answer to her prayer" (11).

Sojourner's escape from slavery comes after a discussion with God, for she "told God she was afraid to go in the night, and in the day every body would see her," but when the thought comes to her to leave at dawn she replies, "Thank you, God, for *that* thought!" (19). During her escape "she sat down, fed her infant, and again turning her thoughts to God, her only help, she prayed him to direct her to some safe asylum" (20). During her later trials and sufferings she "earnestly begged of God that He would show to those about her that He was her helper" (23). Attempting to rescue her son from slavery, "she felt confident she was to receive a full and literal answer to her prayer. . . . She had a short time previous learned that Jesus was a Savior, and an intercessor; and she thought that if Jesus could be induced to plead for her in the present trial, God would listen to *him*" (25).

One of the longest chapters in the book is "Isabella's Religious Experience," which describes her awakening to a fuller and more sophisticated spirituality (in the book's terms). The chapter is full of pious declarations: "Her faith in prayer is equal to her faith in the love of Jesus. Her language is, 'Let others say what they will of the efficacy of prayer, *I* believe in it, and *I* shall pray. Thank God!" (38). Likewise, "this perfect trust, based on the rock of Deity, was a soul-protecting fortress" (39). The trajectory of her spiritual growth is charted throughout the book: "As soon as Isabella saw God as an all-powerful, all-pervading spirit, she became desirous of hearing all that had been written of him" (63). Meeting an apocalyptic congregation, "she was invited to join them in their religious exercises, and accepted the invitation—praying, and talking in her own peculiar style, and attracting many about her by her singing" (65). The book closes with the pious avowal that "her trust is in God, and from him she looks for good, and not evil" (73). Sojourner's encounter with God brought her to the transformative moment in 1843 when she reinvented herself as she heard the voice of God proclaim that her name was to no longer be "Isabella," but "Sojourner Truth." In this crucial transformative moment of conversion, Sojourner Truth was able to reinvent herself and proclaim a higher level of spiritual consciousness. She was given the mission to travel up and down the land to teach God's truth. Her entire personhood became dedicated to following God's calling, a greater inner awareness of her earthly destiny.

With this grounding in a spirituality that her nineteenth-century audience would have found appealing, Sojourner is portrayed in Gilbert's *Narrative* as embodying several important contradictory impulses. She is represented as both acquiescing to and cooperating with the system of authority that was in place, as well as opposing that system. This contradiction would appeal to both sides of the nineteenth-century conflicts over what to do about legalized slavery. The contradictions are examples of how access to a godforce assists Sojourner in transcending deep levels of pain and suffering. The text also demonstrates her understanding of the power of authentically sharing these circumstances with a mass audience. She invents an authentic story of her journey to freedom.

On the one hand, we find many references to Sojourner's (and her family's) acquiescence and cooperation with the legal system in place in this country, one that clearly did not serve her interests. Her parents are described as virtuous in "their faithfulness, docility, and respectful behavior" (1), her mother as "proverbially faithful as a slave" (5). Her mother taught her children "to refrain from lying and stealing, and to strive to obey their masters" (4). Her father also is "a faithful slave" (9) and is described as "more helpless than ever before" as he advances in age, and indeed slaves generally are depicted as in need of guidance and control, for "Sojourner declares of the slaves in their ignorance, that 'their thoughts are no longer than her finger'" (8). The slave is described as having "creeping gait, the dull understanding, listless manners and careless, slovenly habits of the poor down-trodden outcast" (12).

Sojourner herself was so eager to support the system that oppressed her that "these extra exertions to please, and the praises consequent upon them, brought upon her head the envy of her fellow-slaves" at a time that "she then firmly believed that slavery was right and honorable" (14). Even at the time of the writing of the *Narrative*, "Isabella glories in the fact that she was faithful and true to her master" (15). Isabella/Sojourner's first husband is favorably described as "an obedient and faithful chattel" (16). The children she produced with him and with other men have this result: "she rejoiced in being permitted to be the instrument of increasing the property of her oppressors!" (17). In opposing the "fraudulent sale" of one of those children some years later, Sojourner wages her war entirely through legal means and in the court system rather than enabling him to simply run away (23–28). And her own escape from slavery is depicted in the most acquiescent terms: she had been promised her freedom but was then denied it, so that her escape was not really breaking the law (19–21).

These remarkable statements of cooperation with a system of brutal oppression are balanced by episodes (although fewer in number) of Sojourner's (and her family's) refusal of that system. The imbalance is interesting given that the *Narrative* was written at a time when Sojourner's activity in support of human rights was widely known. In one example, Sojourner's brother and sister are sold away from home as little children, but her brother "sprang from the sleigh, and running into the house, concealed himself under the bed" (3), a short-lived act of refusal. Although Sojourner's escape is explained as an entirely legally justified action, it is also presented as a defiance of slavery, if a mild-mannered one. And although her fight to regain her son is conducted through the courts, she is feisty in her adamancy that the courts should act:

> Esquire Chip next informed his client, that her case must now lie over till the next session of the court, some months in the future. "The law must take its course," said he. "What! Wait another court! Wait *months?*" said the persevering mother. "Why, long before that time, he can go clear off, and take my child with him—no one knows where. I *cannot* wait; I *must* have him now, whilst he is to be had." (25)

And so she does have him, but after more legal maneuvering. Finally, an enslaved friend of Sojourner's is described as taking her vengeance on a "brute of a man" who had killed her child but then fell ill and relied on this woman to help him:

> She was very strong, and was therefore selected to support her master, as he sat up in bed, by putting her arms around, while she stood behind him. It was then that she did her best to wreak her vengeance on him. She would clutch his feeble frame in her iron grasp, as in a vice; and, when

her mistress did not see, would give him a squeeze, a shake, and lifting him up, set him down again, as hard as possible. (48)

While hardly at the level of active insurrection, these refusals of slavery provide a counterbalance to the expressions of cooperation with oppression.

Another contradiction expressed in the *Narrative* is between examples of White, even slave-owner, kindness and instances of White cruelty and oppression. This opposition is more balanced than that between acquiescence and refusal. Let us consider some examples of White kindness and helpfulness.

Sojourner's early slave master, one Charles Ardinburgh, is depicted in generally positive terms: "She distinctly remembers hearing her father and mother say that their lot was a fortunate one, as Master Charles was the best of the family" (1). Charles does not live long, but his heirs grant freedom to Sojourner's mother on the condition that she care for her father in his old age, and "this important decision was received as joyful news indeed to our ancient couple" (5). When her mother dies, "the Ardinburghs, having some feeling left for their faithful and favorite slave, 'took turns about' in keeping him" (7). Other, later owners are described as possessing a "vein of kindness and consideration for the slaves" (12), or as having "kindness of heart" (17). In general, masters who allow slaves to work to purchase their freedom are operating from "latent humanity" (11).

Escaping from slavery, Sojourner meets a kindly couple, the Van Wageners, and she "was kindly received and hospitably entertained by their excellent mother" and is then employed by them, for "they never turned the needy away" (20). The Van Wageners are described in positive and egalitarian terms:

Dumont departed; but not till he had heard Mr. Van Wagener tell [Sojourner] not to call him master,—adding, "there is but *one* master; and he who is *your* master is *my* master." Isabella inquired what she *should* call him? He answer, "Call me Isaac Van Wagener, and my wife is Maria Van Wagener." Isabella could not understand this, and thought it a *mighty change*, as it most truly was from a master whose word was law, to simple Isaac S. Van Wagener, who was master to *no* one. With these noble

people, who, thought they could not be the masters of slaves, were un-
doubtedly a portion of God's nobility, she resided one year. (21)

Later she finds some Quakers among whom she is listened to "with patience, and soon gained their sympathies and active co-operation" (23).
Her son, rescued from slavery, is nevertheless not very law-abiding in his
life of freedom, yet his faults are tolerated by his employer: "wanting
money, he sold his livery, and other things belonging to his master; who,
having conceived a kind regard for him, considered his youth, and prevented the law from falling, with all its rigor, upon his head" (41–42).

These stories of White kindness are balanced by opposing stories of
White cruelty. Describing a dark and airless room in which slaves are
forced to live, the *Narrative* names it as "cruelty—for cruelty it certainly
is" (2). The slave's fate is one of "hardship and cruel bereavement" (5),
of "many miseries that his fellow-man had heaped upon him" (9). The
book describes the selling of slaves' relatives, "of whom they had been
robbed, and for whom their hearts still bled" (3).

Examples of cruelty to slaves abound. A slave named Robert comes to
visit Sojourner against his masters' wishes, and his masters follow him
and "both fell upon him like tigers, beating him with the heavy ends of
their canes" (15). The inability of slaves to maintain stable, legal mar-
riages is described as "an abominable state of things" (16). Another example was "of a little slave-child, which, because it annoyed the family
with its cries, was caught up by a white man, who dashed its brains out
against the wall" (47). And the book relates

> . . . the cruelty of one Hasbrouck.—He had a sick slave-woman who was
> lingering with a slow consumption, whom he made to spin, regardless of
> her weakness and suffering; and this woman had a child that was un-
> able to walk or talk, at the age of five years, neither could it cry like other
> children. . . . This exhibition of helplessness and imbecility, instead of
> exciting the master's pity, stung his cupidity, and so enraged him that he
> would kick the poor thing about like a foot-ball. (47)

Another female slave owner was described as "actually beating in the
skull of a slave-woman called Tabby; and not content with that, had her

tied up and whipped, after her skull was broken, and she died hanging
to the bedstead, to which she had been fastened" (48).

Sojourner's own experiences of cruelty at the hands of Whites are
numerous. A White fellow servant in one household "took every opportunity to cry up her faults" even to the extent of lying about them (12).
Her final master broke a promise to free her, which is described as cruel
and faithless (18–19). When she escapes, her master comes after her but
she refuses to go, and so he heartlessly says, "Well, I shall take the *child*"
(20). Her attempts to recover a son who had been illegally sold are met
with "demoniacal" ridicule by Whites:

> Her mistress heard her through, and then replied—"*Ugh!* A *fine* fuss to
> make about a little nigger! Why, haven't you as many of 'em left as you
> can see to and take care of? A pity 'tis, the niggers are not all in Guinea!
> Making such a halloo-balloo about the neighborhood; and all for a paltry
> nigger!!!" (22)

But Sojourner does recover her son and then discovers further evidence
of cruelty:

> She commenced as soon as practicable to examine the boy, and found, to
> her utter astonishment, that from the crown of his head to the sole of his
> foot, the callosities and indurations on his entire body were most fright-
> ful to behold. His back she described as being like her fingers, as she laid
> them side by side. "Heavens! What is all *this*!" said Isabel. He answered,
> "It is where Fowler shipped, kicked, and beat me." She exclaimed, "Oh,
> Lord Jesus, look! See my poor child! Oh Lord, 'render unto them double'
> for all this! Oh my God! Pete, how *did* you bear it?" "Oh, this is nothing,
> mammy—if you should see Phillis, I guess you'd *scare*! She had a little
> baby, and Fowler cut her till the milk as well as blood ran down her
> body." (28)

A third contradiction in the *Narrative* is between hardships suffered
and triumphs achieved. This contradiction allows the reader to summon
up either pity and horror or admiration, depending upon one's inclination. Sojourner's own experiences are harrowing: "she suffered '*terribly,*

terribly' with the cold. During the winter her feet were badly frozen, for want of proper covering" (10). Her own parents suffered hardships in later life, described in mournful terms (6). Her father becomes "so pitiable an object" who "bewailed his loneliness" (7) and progressively becomes "more helpless than before" with each passing episode of life (8). Death finally "relieved him of the many miseries that his fellow-man had heaped upon him" (9).

Sojourner's experiences of slavery were of course a hardship. For instance, "a slave auction is a terrible affair to its victims, and its incidents and consequences are graven on their hearts as with a pen of burning steel" (9). Her experiences are described as "torture," "trials," and "affliction" (10), and "a long series of trials" (12). Experiencing setbacks in her attempts to rescue her son from slavery, "the waters of affliction covered her soul" and "harrowed up her very soul to agony" (23). "'Oh Lord,' inquired Isabella, 'what is this slavery, that it can do such dreadful things? What evil can it not do?'" (46).

On the other hand, Sojourner's *Narrative*, much like we find with Oprah's life story, is a story of triumphs and successes large and small. In comparison with early hardship and ignorance, the narrator reports that "since that time, the subject of this narrative has made some advances" (17). Her active mind was evident early, as in the description of an ingenious device for suspending a basket with a baby in it from a tree branch so that it might easily be rocked and keep the infant safe (18). Sojourner is described as extraordinarily active in asserting her rights, as "when Isabel heard that her son had been sold South, she immediately started on foot and alone, to find the man who had thus dared, in the face of all law, human and divine, to sell her child out of the State; and if possible, to bring him to account for the deed" (21). This determination is portrayed in triumphant terms:

> "No," answered Bell, "I have no money, but God has enough, or what's better! And I'll have my child again." These words were pronounced in the most slow, solemn and determined measure and manner. And in speaking of it, she says, "Oh, my God! I know'd I'd have him agin. I was sure God would help me to get him. Why, I felt so *tall within*—I felt as if the *power of a nation* was with me!" (22)

Sojourner does triumph in the *Narrative,* and the triumph is set in appropriately spiritual terms, for she comes to believe of herself and her people that "although they may physically suffer for the sins of others, if they remain but true to themselves, their highest and more enduring interests can never suffer from such a cause" (30).

We have been considering Sojourner as an earlier iteration of the form of the Wise Woman in an age of mass communication, large and diverse publics, and multiple audiences. When one is a Wise Woman for a nation, one must embody contradictions within unity. Oprah Winfrey, like Sojourner Truth, shares her story of pain and suffering with the public, and demonstrates ways to overcome pain, suffering, and adversity, by being "every woman," a theme song Oprah embraces. Sojourner proclaims herself "every woman," having suffered the worse atrocities any woman could suffer at the hands of those in power over her. Both women invoke a godforce to help overcome these adversities and transcend the pain and suffering. Both create discourse for public audiences enamored with their stories, audiences who become an audience for Sojourner and Oprah. We now elaborate on the main focus in this study, Oprah Winfrey.

Oprah Winfrey

Bill Adler's "unauthorized" edited book, *The Uncommon Wisdom of Oprah Winfrey: A Portrait in Her Own Words,* represents Oprah as a Wise Woman for the mediated masses. As with Sojourner, we are not concerned so much with what is "true" about Oprah as with the construction of this character as a clear and powerful iteration of the homology of the Wise Woman in history. This representation makes clear and repeated claims that Oprah is successful in being a Wise Woman for the national, even international village.

Examples abound of statements that Oprah carries universal appeal because she understands the experiences of many, and many see themselves in her: "People don't treat me like I'm a star, or a celebrity. They treat me like I'm one of them" (114). Despite her fame, she identifies with all: "I'm the same person I always was. . . . You know, my theme for the show is 'I'm Everywoman,' because I think my life is more like other people's, in spite of all the fame that has come to me" (115–16). The theme is continued in this remark: "The reason I communicate with all these people is because I think I'm everywoman, and I've had every malady and I've been on every diet and I've had men who have done me wrong, honey" (238).

Referring to her wide range of personal experiences, she claims, "I'm thankful because I feel like I have an edge on a whole lot of other 'talk show people.' I have experienced so many different *kinds* of things" (2). She is represented as being able to empathize deeply with all manner of people, as in her saying that "it was very hard for me to all of a sudden become 'Ms. Broadcast Journalist' and not *feel* things" (37). Part of Oprah's declaration of universal understanding is her claim that people are fundamentally alike: "I feel that there's a common bond we all share" (67). This is an insight that would enable her to understand people universally: "People are no different in Podunk than in Chicago. [Here] they may dress differently and live in high-rises, but when it comes to human desires and human hopes, we are all the same" (50). She declares, "I think that I speak to the masses of women, because—women and men, but women more so because I am a woman and I identify with that" (123). The link she feels with women is thus especially strong. She later declares that "you want to be able to relate to a person woman-to-woman" (127). The book says that "she identifies with audience members and their problems with men: 'If you're a woman living, you've been done wrong by a man'" (191).

An entire section of Adler's book is devoted to "Letters," and in each case the message is that the public sees itself in Oprah: "You get a hundred letters from people who say you're wonderful. . . . I get all kinds of mail. . . . I get four thousand—an average of four thousand letters a week from people telling me what a difference the show has made in their lives. Every one is more personal than the next" (123–24). She even "started a monthly luncheon club for my hate viewers" so as to include them within her circle as well (124).

Some of what Oprah has experienced is hardship, such as childhood sexual abuse. Yet on those grounds, she connects to many people. Following one show, "the phones lit up with calls from women all over the country saying the same thing had happened to them as girls" (17). Her ability to share her own experiences links her universally: "People everywhere congratulated me" (18). Oprah's universal connection is revealed in her ability to speak not just for herself but for millions: "So I think if we can start to expose and to eradicate the problems stemming from the way we treat children, we can begin to heal ourself as a nation" (19)—the mid-word grammatical slippage to the singular in "ourself" is telling.

Oprah's stance as understanding and speaking for millions is expressed as an ability to bring about far-reaching change in people: "I'm really proud of this television show. . . . I think I can be a catalyst for people beginning to think more insightfully about themselves and their lives" (62).

Oprah's universal connections at one level transcend what some might take to be barriers to identification on issues such as race (although we will see that she also embodies contradictory values on that dimension below). In her college days, she says, "I felt that most of the kids hated and resented me. They were into black power and anger. I was not. I guess that was because I was struggling just to be a human being," surely a universal sentiment (34). "I refused to conform to the militant thinking of the time," she claims (34), and as a result, "race is not an issue with me. It has never been an issue with me" (35). Her universal identification is explicitly represented as consistent with dissolving racial lines: "I am those women. I am every one of them. And they are me. That's why we get along so well. White women stop and tell me, 'Everybody says I remind them of you.' And I say, 'But I'm much taller.' It crosses racial barriers" (69). Her television show, she believes, can "transcend race, sexual bias, and hatred" (264). Oprah's universal, transracial appeal even takes her to bastions of bigotry and prejudice in rural Georgia: "Our sole purpose in coming here is to try and understand the feelings and motivations of all-White Forsyth County. That's what we do every day on this show, explore people's feelings" (74). In that way she is able to represent herself more universally as crossing racial boundaries.

Oprah's ability to understand and to connect with so many people is consistent with her spiritual calling, which she identifies as central: "The spiritual dynamic of life is really the most important thing to me" (56). A series of chapters in Adler's book is devoted to the topics of Faith, God, Prayer, Spirituality, and Inspiration (231–37). Her day begins in this way: "What I do every morning is I go to my window. I watch the sun come up and I center myself and try to touch the God light that I believe is in all of us. Some people call it prayer, some people call it meditation" (227). That spiritual attunement to the God "in all of us" shows that her universal appeal is integral with her spirituality. When she was four years old she took this lesson from her grandmother's quoting of the Bible: "Despite my age I somehow grasped the concept. I knew I was going to help people, that I had a higher calling, so to speak" (5). Oprah's connectedness is linked with her spirituality from a young age: "I wanted to be a missionary for the longest time! I was a missionary for Costa Rica, let me tell you. I used to collect money on the playground every single day of the year" (9). It helps her to overcome barriers: "In first grade, six white kids were going to beat me up. So I told them about Jesus of Nazareth and what happened to the people who tried to stone him. The kids called me the Preacher and left me alone after that" (8). As with Sojourner Truth, spirituality is the consistent core that anchors her otherwise contradictory expressions; accessing a higher power, amidst pain and suffering is a prevalent theme.

Oprah's approach to the trials and stresses in her life is spiritual. Referring to her sometimes tense relationship with her mother, she beatifically avows, "I forgive her for any anger and hostility, and she forgives me. . . . I've made my peace" (13). Her success is expressed in spiritual terms: "Good Lord, I do feel blessed!" (58). And the imperative to do good to others is similarly grounded spiritually in "that divine reciprocity, reaping what you sow" (226).

Oprah's sense of purpose in her profession is also grounded in and expressed in terms of her spirituality: "My goal for myself is to reach the highest level of humanity that is possible to me" (81). Speaking to the judges in a beauty contest in her youth, she said, "I believe in truth and I want to perpetuate the truth. So I want to be a journalist" (32). With success, she frames her purpose in spiritual terms—note the word "blessed" in this avowal:

Television is the greatest medium in the world, and I think those of us who work in it are in a blessed position. We have a responsibility to enlighten, inform, and entertain, if we can. And as long as we do that, and do that with proof in mind, we won't fail. Success is about being honest, not only in your work but in your life. (63)

As if she were looking into the burning bush, Oprah declares that "when I look into the future, it's so bright it burns my eyes" (96). She claims that "it isn't until you come to a spiritual understanding of who you are—not necessarily a religious feeling, but deep down, the spirit within —that you begin to take control" (244). Even her worries about success are expressed in spiritual terms: "I have this fear they may promote me as the Second Coming" (61).

It is interesting that Oprah's story is so often connected to that other Wise Woman, Sojourner Truth: "I remember in high school, when I was competing in drama, I used to do matriarchal figures all the time, Sojourner Truth and Harriet Tubman, characters like that" (135). She specifically recalls reciting "Sojourner Truth's 'Ain't I a Woman?' speech" (140). And she refers to the character she portrayed in *The Color Purple,* Sofia, as "a combination of Sojourner Truth and Harriet Tubman and Fannie Lou Hamer and grandmothers and aunts of mine and other black women who have gone unnamed but who represent a significant part of our history" (143)—Wise Women all. It is telling that in each of these examples, Oprah recalls *enacting* Sojourner, just as we are arguing here that she enacted her homologically on the larger stage of life.

Now that we have a clear sense of Oprah's spiritual core, and her con-nection to Sojourner as an earlier manifestation of the Wise Woman, let us examine the contradictions she expresses to her diverse, international audience. The first contradiction has to do with expressions of racial at-titudes. Oprah is represented as expressing the view that African Ameri-cans are at some disadvantage in relationship to Whites, physically, so-cially, and economically. Even when she is only shown as expressing these ideas as notions that others might hold, her articulation of them gives some credence to them. As a child, she wanted to be White: "I used to sleep with a clothespin on my nose, and two cotton balls. . . . I wanted Shirley Temple curls; that's what I prayed for all the time" (3). It is clear that as a child, Oprah accepted White standards of beauty, for "I felt really ugly because the lighter your complexion, the prettier you were. My half sister was lighter and she got all the attention" (10). She says, "I was raised to believe that the lighter your skin, the better you were" (33).

A willingness to accept standards not supportive of her own physical characteristics continued into her adulthood. Oprah claims to suffer from "black-women's behind. It's a disease God inflicted upon the black women of America" (220). She describes an episode of submitting to "a French perm in my black hair" that burns her scalp and causes her hair to fall out (39–40). She does not describe her African American self in positive terms in looking back over her early career: "I thought, okay, I'm probably not going to get this job, since they're never going to hire a black, overweight female.... They're not going to put a black woman on at nine in the morning.... So when I was interviewed for my first job, I told my boss, 'You know I'm black, and that's not going to change'" (48). Of her present location in Chicago she says, "I tell you, Negroes weren't built for this kind of weather! We start praying for the motherland!" (51). Her staff is nearly all White, for which she has received criticism (89). Even speaking patterns are viewed from a White, racist perspective: "I never spoke in dialect—I'm not sure why, perhaps I was ashamed" (34).

Different patterns in child-rearing are explained, not to the advantage of African Americans: "as black children, we had a whipping every day of our lives. That's sort of like what you went through" (7). It is almost alarming to hear her refer to the numbers of African American children as if they were a problem; on the question of whether she intends to have children, she is quoted, incredibly, as saying, "but there are so many little black children out there" (214). And patterns in male-female relationships are likewise depicted as unfortunate among African Americans:

> If I could just get black women connected to this whole abuse issue.... I hear it all the time from black women who say, "Well, he slapped me around a few times, but he doesn't really beat me." We are so accustomed to being treated badly that we don't even know that love is supposed to feel really good. (68)

Her own relationships with African American men are similarly described in unflattering terms: "I have been in the backseat with some Negro with his hand on my breast—talking about, 'Baby, you don't have to,' in one breath and the next minute saying, 'If you love me, you really would'" (193).

Different economic conditions are racially grounded: "I had just started in this school called Nicolet, where everybody else was white. It's when I realized the difference. Up until that time I'd been poor but didn't know it" (11), thus equating her color with poverty. In that school, "the life that I saw those children lead was totally different from what I went home to, from what I saw when I took the bus home with the maids in the evening. I wanted my mother to be like their mothers. . . . But she was one of those maids" (22). These are not merely differences, they are differences that do not show African Americans in a good light, in Oprah's view: "For the first time I understood that there was another side. All of a sudden the ghetto didn't look so good anymore" (23). The paternalism of White racist structures through which she overcomes that economic disadvantage is described in not entirely oppositional terms by Oprah. Of an early job she says, "Sure, I was a token. But, honey, I was a very happy token" (36).

On the other side of this contradiction, Oprah is represented as expressing African American pride, strength, and resilience: "The drums of Africa still beat in my heart, and they will not rest until every black boy and every black girl has had a chance to prove their worth" (260). Her pride in her culture comes through clearly in this anthemic declaration she made at the National Council of Negro Women convention:

> I come here tonight celebrating . . . every African, every colored, black, Negro American everywhere that ever cooked a meal, ever raised a child, ever worked in the fields, ever went to school, ever sang in a choir, ever loved a man or loved a woman, every cornrowed, every Afroed, every wig-wearing, pigtailed, weave-wearing one of us. (274)

When a magazine describes her as "street-smart" she objects, saying, "I don't like the term *street-smart*. I think it's a term that gets put off on black people a lot. Rather than say intelligent, it's easier to say we're street-smart" (218), but she wants to claim the term "intelligent." She recalls periods of strong early family life: "My stepmother was real tough, a very strong disciplinarian, and I owe a lot to her" (9). Oprah recalls a moment of communal pride watching television as a young person:

> It was a night that changed my life forever. Sunday night, December 27,
> 1964. The Supremes were on *The Ed Sullivan Show*. It was the first time I
> had seen a black woman on television with such beauty and grace. I was
> a ten-year-old girl sitting on a cold linoleum floor in Milwaukee. I was
> inspired by the possibilities of what I could be. (106)

As a young person, she grew up in a time when "it was real hip to know
a black person, so I was very popular" (22). Her classmates wanted to be
around her "like I was a toy. They'd all sit around talking about Sammy
Davis, Jr., like I knew him" (23). Entering a beauty contest, "I was the
only Negro in the 'Miss Fire Prevention Contest.' I certainly never expected to win because, why would I? And I won" to her surprise and
delight (32). She takes pride in being "the only black—the first black—to
win the darn thing" (32). Winning the Miss Black Tennessee contest
later, she rejoices in her color: "There were all these light-skinned girls—
vanillas—and here I was a fudge child—real dark skinned. And Lord,
were they upset" that she won (33).

Oprah is often represented as finding her race or gender as either a
positive help or at least no hindrance in her life: "Truth is, I've never felt
prevented from doing anything because I was either black or a woman"
(34). A more positive expression of that idea is, "People see me and they
see that I am black. That's something I celebrate" (35). Oprah expresses
her sense of culture positively rather than in the form of a criticism of
others:

> We had a black father on talking about what he had gone through to pro-
> tect his daughter, and during the show I remember thinking this does
> more good than all the shows you could ever do about skinheads and
> KKK members and racism in which you say, "Listen to us. This is why we
> are angry." (67)

If on the one hand she is criticized for having a largely White staff, then
on the other hand her studio dramatizes the work of mainly Black writers: "Yes, most of the things I have bought so far have been black written
projects" (91). Oprah expresses her race as a positive motive for her professional success: "I just don't think you can allow yourself to be controlled. . . . I am more conscious of my legacy as a black person than

anybody. I have a responsibility, not only as a black woman but as a human being to do good work" (147). She generalizes that sense of responsibility to all people of color: "The truth is most black middle-class and lower-middle-class people . . . have a sense of ethics, want the best for your children, and try to do what's right" (151).

Racial tension is sometimes turned into a positive challenge that generates positive responses, as in this episode:

> It happened to me in Cap Ferrat at one time. I thought it was because I was black or something. I walked in, it was the Hotel de Cap or something, and there are these Germans in there, and . . . everybody put their forks down, and they turned and they looked at me. . . . So I thought that, "Gee, they're not used to looking at black people in here." So I thought, "Well, I am going to let them." You know what I did, to the whole room? I curtsied to them, and told them I was Princess Sheba from some island. (112)

The trials and sufferings that her character Sofia experiences in *The Color Purple* are likewise presented in positive terms: "I had a lot of time to think about the years Sofia spent in jail and how thousands of men and women, all the people who marched in Selma, were thrown in jail and what those years must have been like. Sofia finally speaking was a victory for all of us and for me" (143).

One would not think it would be possible to be contradictory on the subject of violence and sexuality in children. Yet Oprah manages to be represented as expressing a finely balanced strategic ambiguity between stances that abhor violence, molestation, and early sexual experimentation by children, and, if not approving of these practices, at least of putting them into social contexts that make them more comprehensible. Oprah does not condone any kind of child abuse, but she is shown expressing views that some practices may appear to be abusive to some but not to others.

Oprah condemns violence toward children. She has fearful memories of her grandfather: "I feared him. Always a dark presence. I remember him always throwing things at me or trying to shoo me away with his cane" (3). She recalls that "the reason I wanted to be white was that I never saw little white kids get whippings. I used to get them all the time from my grandmother" (3), clearly an injurious result of early discipline. The "whippings" were almost literally that: "My grandmother whipped me with switches. You go and pull a little limb off a tree and you bring it in. . . . She could whip me for days and never get tired. It would be called child abuse now," which is what she is in effect calling it (4). Clearly she resents these episodes: "What wouldn've happened if I had had the kind of grandmother who, instead of beating my butt, wouldn've sat me down to discuss, you know, my feelings over the matter? Perhaps I could've been more sensitive" (6). Oprah condemns the widespread social results of this childhood punishment:

> Our prisons are filled with older men who, as young men, had the living hell beat out of them. Every parent who beat them said, "I'm doing this because I love you." When my grandmother used to whip my behind, she'd say, "I'm doing this because I love you." And I'd want to say, "If you loved me, you'd get that switch off my butt." I still don't think that was love. (7)

The socially deleterious effects of child abuse are also identified in her claim that "our children in this country are not safe. They're not safe at the hands of strangers. Oftentimes they're not safe at the hands of relatives and friends and even their own parents" (248).

Oprah's own experience of childhood sexual abuse is also depicted as terrible and damaging: "I remember being at a relative's house and I had been left with a nineteen-year-old cousin and he raped me. And I knew it was bad and I knew it was wrong mainly because it hurt so badly. . . . So that's why I weep for the lost innocence. I weep for that because you are never the same again" (13–14). A result of this abuse is that "every time I had a stomachache, I thought I was pregnant and asked to go to the bathroom so if I had it nobody could see. That for me was the terror. . . . I know what it is like to lie in bed and know that other person is there, and you are pretending you are asleep, hoping he won't touch you" (14–15).

Conversely, while not condoning child abuse, Oprah is represented as identifying some positive results of what are otherwise seen as negative actions. She complains bitterly of the whippings she received from her grandmother, "But, you know, I am what I am because of my grandmother; my strength, my sense of reasoning, everything" (4). This in spite of, and perhaps even because of the punishment: "Sure, Grandma whipped me, she sure did. But she taught me about life, and I loved her so" (5). The punishment she received is sometimes presented as "discipline," as in her statement that "I was a child who was always in need of discipline" (28). Although she does not describe her father as beating her, some of his threats are draconian: "If you don't bring *As* into this house from school, you can't live here. . . . Be home by midnight, or, by God, sleep on the porch!" (29). Reinscribing her grandmother's behaviors, Oprah says of a Big Sisters group she has formed in Chicago, "I shoot a very straight shot: 'Get pregnant and I'll break your face!'" (52), which is surely metaphorical but just as surely a violent expression.

The ambivalence Oprah expresses in terms of sexual abuse is even more ticklish. While not condoning it by any means, she gives some reasons why it might occur and in the process of doing so mentions what seem to be some positive feelings. Of her first rapist, the book says, "She was grateful for the attention, thankful when he bribed her with presents" (14). Of a favorite uncle who abused her, she said, "I adored this uncle. Just adored him. And I could not, in my mind, make him be the bad guy" (15). As a result, "I blamed *myself*. I was always very needy, always in need of attention" (16). In *People* magazine she said that "she liked" the "sexual attention" she received: "If someone is stroking your little breasts, you get a sexy, physical feeling. It can be a good feeling, and it's confusing, because you then blame yourself for feeling good" (16). Her family assumes that a later pregnancy is her responsibility alone: "Because I had been involved in sexual promiscuity, they thought if anything happened, it had to be my fault" (27). Oprah no more condones sexual abuse than she does violence, but in both cases she is represented as uttering views that enable contradictory responses in the audience.

Another contradiction expressed in Oprah is the way in which she describes women. On the one hand she features them as strong and capable, even godlike: "See, God was looking out for you. Sometimes she does" (117). On the other hand she offers several examples of weak and ineffectual women, especially in her personal life.

Oprah proudly claims that "I came from a matriarchal family so I had to be the mama and had to tell the daddy what to do!" As a result, she enacts female roles early on: "If I was playing school, I wouldn't play unless I was the teacher. Or we didn't play house unless I was the mama" (8). From her childhood she remembers that her mother displayed pride in her appearance despite their impoverished circumstances: "My mother was the best-dressed maid ever known to woman. You know how you see women going to work at the nice white people's houses wearing slacks? My mother would put on high heel shoes and her suede skirt and go stepping" (12).

Of women who manage households all day, Oprah admiringly says, "I could not do what you do" (69). She declares, "The mothers who are home watching . . . those are my heroines. What it takes to do that. . . . To be able to create an environment that is stimulating, nurturing, teaching, a sense of moral values. What in the world is more important than that? The patience, the sacrifice . . . " (277). She admires women who struggle against poverty with great strength: "You find people in the projects who have as much desire for fulfillment and enrichment— to be somebody—as anywhere else in the world" (158). She likewise admires other successful female entrepreneurs such as "Madam C. J. Walker, one of the first black female millionaires—she invented the straightening comb" (137).

Oprah is proud of her own accomplishments as a woman, as when she completed a marathon: "I never felt anything like the sense of ac- complishment I had when I finished the marathon" (184). She discovers that "I must be somebody!" when people recognize her in public (111). She declares her independence as a female: "From now on I'm living this life for Oprah, not for some man. Women diet to keep men, everybody knows that. But I've decided men can go to blazes" (193). Yet Stedman Graham sticks around because, "I'm a neat girl" (203).

Oprah expresses some views that women, especially particular women in her experience, are weak and incapable. Her own mother is described in these terms: "I don't know why mother ever decided she wanted me. She wasn't equipped to take care of me" (8). Her mother is described as unable to provide enough love: "I started acting out my need for atten- tion, my need to be loved. . . . My mother didn't have the time" (12). In fact, her mother is indirectly blamed for Oprah's abuse and promiscuity: "Not getting the attention from my mother made me seek it in other places, the wrong places" (13, 28). The result of that abuse is described in contradictory, ambivalent terms insofar as women are concerned: "Everybody deals with their pain differently. Some become overachievers like me, and others become mothers who kill" (21), certainly a stark and contradictory opposition. Her mother's entire family is described as unsupportive in helping her deal with episodes of sexual abuse as an adult: "they criticized me for airing my dirty laundry in public" (20).

Her mother is sometimes described as full of false hopes: "I moved back to live with my mother when I was nine. The reason was that my mother would say, 'Come live with me. I'm gonna get married and we're all gonna be a real family'" (10), which proved to be illusory. Her mother's relationships with men leads Oprah to declare that "in ninety-nine out of a hundred cases . . . the female is the one who gives" (38) in comparison to the male. In Oprah's own relationships with men, she finds that too often, "I was a doormat" (41). Her mother's attempts at providing discipline and stability are ineffectual:

> I would break curfew. I'd stay out. I'd run the streets. Because I knew I could get away with it. . . . Because my mother would say, 'If you come in here late again, I'm gonna break your neck!' Well, I knew she wasn't gonna break my neck. So I would do whatever I could get away with. (24)

The contrast between her parents is stark, and not to the advantage of her mother: "My mother was so fed up with me at the time that she said, 'I can't wait two weeks. You've got to get out of the house now.' I was sent to live with my father in Nashville, and he changed my life" for the better (27). Even as an adult, her mother continues to be portrayed as ineffectual: "My mother is getting dunning notices from this landlord and never once tells me what's going on. What am I going to do with these people? I'm heartsick" (25).

A final contradictory we shall explore is between descriptions of Oprah's humble, impoverished origins and her triumphs and successes. She is thus able to relate to people who stand on both sides of the economic divide. She offers identification for those who are distressed and hope for those who seek to improve their situations.

Oprah explains her humble origins in life. Her family was materially poor: "We had an outhouse. You never forget it. No matter how many bathrooms you get, you never forget it" (1). She says, "I literally didn't wear shoes until Sunday. I was barefoot all the time because I lived on a farm. It was lonely. I had one corncob doll" (2). She lived with her grandmother, and "I don't know where our money came from. I really don't. My grandmother owned the farm and she did everything herself. She made my clothes; I never had a store-bought dress" (6). Almost comically, she recalls, "We were so poor we couldn't afford a dog or cat, so I made pets out of two cockroaches. There were lots of roaches available. You wanted pets, all you had to do was go in the kitchen at night and turn on the lights" (10).

In her later childhood, material poverty while living with her mother contributed, she claims, to her sexual molestation: "It happened over a couple of years with my mother's boyfriend. I was an open target living in that environment. . . . What caused me to be continually sexually abused was being in a family that I didn't think would support me if I told," and she makes it clear that the family's poverty contributed to these conditions (15). Her mother's inability to provide financially for her led to unfortunate social conditions, so that eventually her mother attempted "to have her put in a juvenile detention center in 1968" (27). Even in her adulthood, visiting her family, she finds, "I was so stressed at the end of the day. Everyone's so needy. They *need* so much" (26).

Oprah's expression of poverty, especially in her early life, is balanced by expressions of triumph and success. Some of this success was not of the material kind, but it came despite her material privation. Since her early youth, she says, "I've been the best talker and the best reader ever since I can remember" (2). Friends recognized these intellectual gifts and told her grandmother, " 'Hattie Mae, this child is gifted.' And somehow, with no education, my grandmother instilled in me a belief that I could aspire to do great things in my life" (3). Despite her complaints about her grandmother's disciplinary practices, Oprah acknowledges that "it was my grandmother who was responsible for developing my natural talents early" (6). Others also recognized her talents and intelligence. She wrote her kindergarten teacher a note saying, "Dear Miss New: I don't think I belong here," and her teacher agreed, promoting her a grade, which would happen more than once in school (8, 9). Oprah's own discovery of her intellect became a source of self-motivation: "I felt it happen in the fourth grade. Something came over me. I turned in a book report early and it got such a good response, I thought, 'I'm gonna do that again'" (21).

Of course, Oprah's intellectual success has continued into her adult life, as has a spirit of victory and success over adversity: "In 1987, TSU alumna Oprah was asked to give the commencement address. She agreed, but insisted that she finish her course credits first so that she could finally get her own degree" (35).

Oprah's success has also, obviously, been professional. She began as a rival to local Chicago broadcaster Phil Donohue, but "in February 1987 Oprah was topping Donahue's ratings. . . . she was awarded an Emmy that year." She indulged in some understandable triumph: "It's just that here we are stomping him in the ratings, you know, and suddenly—he's gone! It was maahvelous!" (54). Oprah recognizes the impact of her success: "Now I feel both the power and the enormous responsibility that comes with it" (60). She explains that "this medium of television is so powerful and has the ability to empower people and affect lives. . . . I changed the way I thought about television, and decided I was more than just a talk show host. . . . That it was indeed a way of being a voice to the world" (103). Success has also come with her development of Harpo Studios, which allowed her to "take ownership" of her own television show (90). Her professional success has also, of course, led to financial success. In regard to her own wealth, "I just read forty million the other day and I said, 'Oooh, got a raise'. . . . I'm blessed with more money than I could ever use" (240–41).

Because Oprah as modern, mass-mediated Wise Woman connects to so many people, her success is expressed in terms of empowering people: "That's the power in TV—not in making the Forbes list of richest Americans, but being able to say something that gets people to listen and take action" (97), and to "inform and inspire as well as entertain" (104). Her aim is "to empower, uplift, enlighten, encourage, and if we can entertain you" (103). She is strong and successful so as to empower her international electronic tribe. She says, "I try to use this show as a voice for raising consciousness, for doing good, for letting people see themselves in a way that makes their lives better" (78). Of her studio she claims, "The purpose of [Harpo Productions] is to invest in projects that we think are worthwhile" (92). In encouraging people to read through her book club, she also creates success for all: "This is going to be a book that really empowers people" (98), she said of a recent selection. Oprah's own success thus results in the success of others:

> I was in New York last week and I was crossing the street and a woman said, "I want to tell you how much I appreciate your evolution. I appreciate the fact that you are open enough to let us see it, because when I see that you can do it, I feel I can." I wanted to weep on the street cause I thought, "You get it!" (113)

Conclusions

In his biography of Charles Dickens, Peter Ackroyd notes that in Dickens's novels, "the same spirit is reincarnated, as it were, in a variety of human beings—Murdstone in *David Copperfield* becomes Merdle in *Little Dorrit* becomes Headstone in *Our Mutual Friend* becomes Durdles in *The Mystery of Edwin Drood,* all distinct but all related" (421). Ackroyd is clearly talking about a homology of personae. He also uses a language of the spirit, suggesting a spiritual dimension to homologies. For what is form but that which is unseen, with the flesh that form takes on as evidence of that pattern, of things unseen?

In this chapter we have argued that Sojourner Truth and Oprah Winfrey are in many ways "the same spirit" emerging in a long line of such "reincarnations" throughout history and across cultures and continents. Where else might we see the Wise Woman emerge? In South Africa, media personality Felicia Mabuza-Suttle emerges as a similar reincarnation of the Wise Woman, and discourse about herself and public discourse about her image in South Africa would be a fascinating future study. Mabuza-Suttle was trained in media in the United States, and returned to her native South Africa to become a television personality and entrepreneur. Human culture needs the Wise Woman, and the genetic instructions for her emergence are embodied in the stories, fables, and legends of people around the world. We all know those discourses at some level, for they will emerge in some kind of talk somewhere in most if not all societies.

The particular homology we examine here, manifested in the parallels between Sojourner and Oprah, is outside of history in its timelessness, *and* the homology also emerges in history and its struggles in the ways that both Oprah and Sojourner embodied contradictions that appealed to the multiple, diverse audiences of their times. We need not choose between a centerless postmodernity and a grand structuralism in understanding how Wise Women both recur and engage their own histories—we can have both. The pattern of wisdom, healing, strength, and transcendence endures, and the particular strategies of embodying contradictions arise as the pattern re-emerges in history. Sojourner and Oprah, two Wise Women, re-enact the grand pattern that makes them both, and they step forth from that pattern to confront, change, and heal their own eras. The student of rhetorical homologies thus needs to be attuned to both the timeless and the immediate situation, to transcendent discursive patterns and to history and politics.

Finally, this study suggests that homology itself might be a kind of spiritual experience, grounded in the ways and workings of discourse. If it is not spiritual in the making, then it is spiritual in the experiencing of it, as people confront a re-emerging character being born again from the flow of discourse in history. To be attuned to homology may ultimately need a kind of spiritual facility or attunement, a faith in forms unseen, an acknowledgment of the power that moves below the surface of discourse, language, and the human conversation. Explanations of how homologies can be rhetorically effective thus also requires a balance between acknowledging the ways that we are moved by timeless discourse and the ways that we are moved by the rhetoric of the moment.

In this chapter we have considered a homology of personae, in connection with a recurring exigence. In the next chapter we consider a homology grounded in the discursive property of a figure of speech, trope, or stylistic device, likewise in connection with a recurring exigence. We will study Kenneth Burke's claims that some discursive structures are teleologies, organized to move motivations toward a goal of perfection. Teleologies can be manifest in metaphors that imply a kind of perfection or summit. When exigencies arise in institutions or experiences that are also teleological, such as the American presidency, discourse is homologously ordered into teleological metaphors, as we shall see by examining several episodes of presidential crisis and discursive responses to those crises.

7

Burkean Perfection and the Presidency in Crisis

Of all the institutions and offices that make up the United States government, none is more exhaustively studied than is the presidency. In the discipline of Communication and in rhetorical studies specifically, the presidency as a communicative phenomenon has been the subject of much attention (Hart; Jamieson). Formal patterns that recur in presidential discourse and behavior have likewise been well explored; although few or none of them call these patterns homologies, that is what they are within the usage of this book. Decades of scholarship have explored the "Imperial Presidency" as one homologous pattern underlying the actions of several presidents (Schlesinger). The work of Robert Hariman suggests four different leadership styles that constitute formal patterns ordering the public faces of several presidents. As noted earlier in this book, one might take Hariman's styles as homologies. Other authors such as David Barber, James MacGregor Burns, and Stephen Skowronek have identified different patterns of psychology, character, and leadership that emerge in different presidencies. It would seem as if the presidency is a good subject for homological analysis, since taken as a whole it is an institution encompassing many disparate (and a few desperate) individuals *and* a smaller set of recurring situations and styles that the individuals enact. There is an important sense in which the nation and its presidents enact recurring scenarios based on homologies, enduring forms that emerge time and again into history.

One important recurrence connected to the presidency is crisis, specifically a crisis in the presidency itself: assassination (Lincoln, Kennedy), resignation (Nixon), impeachment (Clinton, A. Johnson), incapacity (Wilson, Reagan), questions over constitutional authority (F. D. Roosevelt), and so forth. When a crisis occurs that affects the whole country, the president is by law and custom the leader to whom the nation turns. At such times, the discourse to which the public is exposed both molds and reflects public motives concerning the crisis and also concerning how we expect presidents to respond to the crisis. When the exigency involves the presidency itself, discourse doubly molds and reflects the nation's motivations toward the presidency. Homologies that underlie discourse during presidential crises are thus powerfully motivating.

This chapter offers evidence that when the presidency is in crisis, some rhetorical responses encourage the public to embrace what Kenneth Burke calls perfectionist or *entelechial* motives toward presidential leadership. Entelechy is a kind of discursive structure that is homological because it consistently orders discourse of the presidency in crisis. As with chapter six, this chapter also studies tiers of homologies. Entelechial motives emerge in public discourse during presidential crises through at least four families of metaphors: *military, theological, business,* and *heart and brain.* Evidence of these four families of metaphors suggests a second, more historically specific homology: a pattern of discourse implying that presidential crises are regarded motivationally as much the same type of thing. The motivation to think about the presidency in entelechial terms is a transhistorical discursive structure underlying texts and actions, unifying them homologically. Furthermore, I shall argue that such homological motives may not be in the best interests of a democratic society and may hamper resolution of crises.

We have studied homologies unifying rhetorical events involving similar exigencies before, but here we turn to a new wrinkle in rhetorical homologies, and that is the idea of a rhetorical figure of speech, a trope, or stylistic device as a structural component of homology. Entelechies will be understood here as structures of discourse grounding motivations of perfection, and we will particularly examine metaphors that embody entelechies as the homological grounding that generates similar discourse across several presidential crises.

The chapter primarily examines reactions to the attempted assassination of Ronald Reagan on March 30, 1981. But since my argument addresses the presidency and not just Mr. Reagan, I shall also briefly examine some discourse reacting to the crises of President Clinton's impeachment, President Kennedy's assassination, and President Nixon's resignation. Let us first turn to some rhetorical theories of Burke to understand what is meant by perfectionist or entelechial motives.

Perfection and the Language Motive

Perhaps the most central concept in Kenneth Burke's rhetorical theory is the notion that "insofar as men 'cannot live by bread alone,' they are moved by doctrine, which is to say, they derive purposes from language" (*Rhetoric of Religion*, 274; see also *Grammar*, 33). Burke insists that the words people use do not name their motives, the words are motives (*Permanence*, 25). Motives are embodied in shorthand terms for situations (*Permanence*, 29–36), or ways of entitling situations (*Language*, 361). If one is interested in the motives that Americans have concerning the president, Burke would have the critic examine the words we use to describe the president.

People's motives are embedded in the terms by which they discuss their situations. But terms have implications; if one sets out to "master" a subject, for instance, use of that term implies that the subject will become a "slave." And since one uses a slave selfishly, with regard for one's own interests and not for those of the slave, the repeated declaration of a student that he or she will "master" a subject can imply that he or she will use it selfishly or destructively, with a thought to crass advantage rather than love of learning.

Language "ranges" in Burke's terms (*Rhetoric of Religion*, 290). It can add to or subtract from the concrete, physical situations in which people find themselves. Human motives follow the dances that words perform when they go beyond mere description of empirical reality (as they inevitably do). The ways in which language "ranges" are many. I should like to focus on one such characteristic, the principle of *perfection* or *teleology*, which "takes many forms. . . . Symbolism is unthinkable without it" (*Rhetoric of Religion*, 298; also *Language*, 16). What does Burke mean by the perfectionist motive, or as Aristotle put it, the *entelechial principle* (*Rhetoric of Motives*, 14; *Language*, 70–74; *Grammar*, 261)?

Burke argues that a vocabulary can be entelechial in at least two ways. Clearly, these two senses of entelechy are not exclusive and indeed are frequently found in concert in a given terminology. First, since every vocabulary embodies certain implications, an entelechial motive is the compulsion to pursue and perfect some of those motives. Among the many motives within Christian discourse for instance is an avoidance of sin. If one can avoid sin somewhat, another can avoid it even more, another more than that, and so on and upward to the saints. It is possible, as we see from many historical examples, to attempt the perfect avoidance of sin, and such attempts are driven by the perfectionist motives contained within a discourse of avoiding sin.

All terminologies have such implications, although some terminologies are more easily suited for entelechies. The perfectionist motive is the desire to develop and carry out those implications in words and deeds: "A given terminology contains various *implications,* and there is a corresponding 'perfectionist' tendency for men to attempt carrying out those implications" (*Language*, 19). Observations or conclusions may be *implicit* in a given terminology, quite in the sense that a grammar and syntax are implicit in a given language. One can be moved by a "'terministic compulsion' to track down such possibilities" (72).

Imagine a town that experiences racial conflict because of recent immigration by people of Arabian descent. Racist whites, egged on by prominent rhetors, begin discussing their situation in clearly segregationist terms such as "us," "them," "their side of town," "cultural purity," and "keeping them in their place." The rhetorical critic should be on the lookout for the entelechial principle; for example, if racists speak in terms of cultural purity, will they soon be talking about Arabs as an impurity, and then as a disease, and then begin discussing cures for the disease, moving "up" on a scale of the perfection of impurity? Here a sort of biological metaphor houses an entelechy of segregation. The interesting thing about entelechy is that a set of terms may have different implications; the terms may be perfected in different ways depending on which set of implications is pursued. Segregation and the terms it hides in may also be perfected legally, physically, geographically, and genocidally, and the direction of the perfectionist motive takes will be worked out publicly in discourse.

A second entelechy occurs when a discourse implies an ordered, sequential structure that has a perfection at one end. People will be powerfully motivated toward that perfection, and that motive will color the ways in which all other terms are seen. For instance, there is no perfect vegetable (carrots are neither more nor less perfect than turnips), and so a vocabulary of vegetables is unlikely to generate an entelechial fervor. But the vocabulary of academic ranks in most American universities puts the perfection of *Professor* over the less perfect ranks of *Associate* Professor or *Assistant* Professor (compare with non-perfectionist academic vocabularies of Lecturer, Reader, and so forth in which one rank is higher than another organizationally but not linguistically). Thus, an entelechial drive is created to reach that perfection, a motive that sours many who experience productive and honorable careers but retire at the less-than-perfect rank of Associate Professor.

When the language used in some arena of experience is entelechial, it musters strong motivations. Thus, the rhetorical critic as social critic should be on the lookout for (1) ordinary motivations and the terms they are embodied in, (2) indications in public discourse that the implications of those terms are being spun out, being pushed to an extreme form by the perfectionist motive, and (3) the particular form and direction such perfection takes. This vigilance is important because if people are motivated by ordinary terms, they are especially driven by the perfecting of those terminologies: "Symbolicity, for all its imperfection, contains in itself a principle of perfection by which the symbol-using animals are always being driven, or rather towards which they are always striving" (*Rhetoric of Religion*, 296). If such entelechial vocabularies are homologous, recurring in disparate situations, then we are dealing with discursive mechanisms that order powerful motives across time and space.

Clearly, the presidency is a subject matter that is well suited to a mode of analysis attuned to perfection. The presidency is a thoroughly entelechial institution, a perfect pyramid with the president sitting alone at the top. Within the executive branch, nearly all decisions and policies are ultimately adjudicable by the president. Power flows to and from the president as the sum of all leadership in the government, an influence that even trumps the legally (but often, not symbolically) independent legislative and judicial branches. So when that institution itself is in crisis, we should not be surprised to see discourse embodying perfectionist motives emerge.

In this chapter I examine journalistic commentary in the popular media intended to influence as well as to express public opinion in times of presidential crisis, specifically crises concerning the presidency itself. For the crises concerning Presidents Reagan, Nixon, and Kennedy, I examine discourse in newspapers and news magazines. For President Clinton, I examine some Web sites, where so much public discourse occurs today. I also want to note that I do not examine discourse related to the 2000 presidential election and the uncertainty over its outcome because I was unable to find much occurrence of our four key metaphors. I think this absence was because the crisis did not involve a sitting president: neither Mr. Gore nor Mr. Bush had an established position at the top of a teleology and thus perfectionist motives were not in play.

As noted, this chapter is anchored in reactions to the attempted assassination of President Reagan, with supporting examples from the other three crises. Following the Reagan shooting, the public was primarily exposed not to the extended oratory of a few leaders but to a flood of brief reactions and reports of statements in the press. I shall focus on some statements that were based on four root metaphors. I am not at all claiming that these statements were the only ones made, only that they occurred often. I shall show statements based on the same metaphors occurring in the Clinton, Kennedy, and Nixon examples. Also, in claiming that discourse sprang from four root metaphors, I am saying that it is spoken or written as if grounded in an explicit metaphor. To reiterate, the four root metaphors are *military, theological, business,* and *heart and brain.*

An important implication for a theory of rhetorical homology in this study is that a stylistic device such as metaphor can be a homological structure if we find similar metaphors being generated in response to similar exigencies (namely, presidential crises). The four families of metaphors studied here are easily commensurate with entelechies in that they each imply a perfection, a sine qua non, a desired and desirable pinnacle of motivation. Each metaphorical family carries the entelechial fervor into each rhetorical situation.

Military

The emergence of military metaphors in the discourse of presidential crises is a natural turn. The president is, of course, also commander in chief, a constitutional provision that merges the military within the entelechy of the presidency and its structures. On its own terms, the military is highly entelechial, with the Chair of the Joint Chiefs of Staff at the top of the uniformed ranks and then clear structures of the less than perfect all the way down to the enlisted personnel. Thus it is not surprising that military metaphors surfaced during the crises studied here. They are an entelechial way to muster motives about an entelechial subject, the presidency in crisis.

Although the president is literally commander in chief, discourse often pictures him in specific military roles that are more figurative than literal. A language of "command" or images of military or naval authority tend to put the president at the top of an entelechial structure. When President Reagan was shot, Alexander Haig's often-quoted denial of any need to "transfer the helm," for instance, paints Reagan as a sea captain (see Safire; Schram and Gerter). The military term "command" repeatedly refers to the exercise of both military and civilian power, making it a metaphor in that broader context: Senator Howard Baker declared that "never for a moment was there any interruption of the normal lawful chain of command" (Raines, "Meeting"). The *Atlanta Constitution* claimed that Reagan had set up a chain of "command authority" ("Who's in Charge?"). The *Washington Post,* referring to Reagan's good humor in the emergency room, declared that "the president's jokes . . . bolster the impression of a leader in command" (Lescaze and "Reagan Looks Robust" reported that Mr. Reagan had "resumed command of the Republic"). The *New York Times,* conversely, editorialized that "for a few hours while Mr. Reagan lay anesthetized, there was a problem of command" ("Who's Minding"). A related expression was the claim that Reagan was still "in charge" (" 'Didn't' "; also "Reagan Shows").

This same metaphor also surfaced during the Clinton, Kennedy, and Nixon crises. The Clinton impeachment was seen in military terms, with "sexuality and human rights double standards as vehicles for political assault" on the president-as-fortress, thus requiring "Clinton's defense" (Lockard). Similarly, Republican attacks on Clinton were described militarily as "a grotesque eruption of the American old guard" and a "very dangerous attack" created by their "need for an enemy" (World Socialist Web Site, "Week"). Clinton was not without defenses, and Robert G. Kaiser repeatedly described his strategies as "aiming" or "targeting" certain issues and audiences. Similarly, David Broder is asked online, "Have you ever witnessed a president as much under siege as this one?" by a writer who wonders how Clinton "could have survived such an onslaught" ("Direct"), making Clinton a castle, or the fortified military seat of a strong ruler.

Kennedy's death brought the more literal reassurance that "the United States yesterday was never without a 'Commander-in-Chief'" ("Instantly"). A more frequent and metaphorical usage emerged after Nixon's resignation. Just before leaving office, "on his yacht cruising the Potomac . . . he was the tough field marshal, devising some grand strategy" (Sidey). Commentators remembered Nixon as being "second in command" under Eisenhower, and described his Watergate behavior as "waging war, not politics" ("Down"). Gerald Ford was expected to avoid "open warfare" with the Congress ("Newsgram," August 19). He was, however, to participate in election "campaigns," to risk "victory and defeat," and to press "sharp attacks" ("Newsgram," August 16). Ford is described in the metaphor of the sea captain as "setting a course," a captaincy in which he would fire "opening shots in his declared war on inflation" ("Ford Sets").

Theological

What structure of motivation can be more entelechial than a theology? What vocabulary can point toward a perfection more clearly than one that includes "God"? When the presidency is in crisis, we find metaphors emerging that, if they do not explicitly call the president a god, at least cloak him with deistic connotations and trappings.

None of the discourse examined explicitly equated Mr. Reagan with God. However, a theological metaphor underlies some statements. The *New York Times* implicitly deified Mr. Reagan by declaring that "the only thing anyone is inclined to shout at Ronald Reagan today is hallelujah" ("Presidency"). Russell Baker departed from his often humorous style by structuring an article around the anguished use of the expression "My God" in reaction to the shooting (29). Evans and Novak incidentally referred to David Stockman as a Reagan "disciple" (21). Representative Morris Udall found a supernatural illumination around the stricken leader: "There is an aura there that wasn't there before" (Broder, "Rise"). David Broder also saw an "aura" around Mr. Reagan. Broder argued that "the survival of the hero in conditions of imminent danger is taken as a sign of divine favor—a token that he has been saved for a reason" ("End"). A number of editorials referred to prayer (he is in our prayers, our prayers go out to him, etc.) when discussing the shootings (Wagner; "Bullets"; "A Strong"). The *Indianapolis Star*, discussing Haig's behavior, placed the Cabinet only a little lower than the president: "Cabinet members are not demigods, even though at times they might not mind being taken for semi-divine," inviting one to extrapolate upwards toward the all-powerful president ("All"). The Reverend Oral Roberts was quite explicit about Mr. Reagan's heavenly connections: "This is a conspiracy not of man but of the devil to destroy the last free nation on this earth, because the devil knew that here is a man who can rally this country. And the recovery of Mr. Reagan will give us our best chance" ("Devil").

A more subtle form of theological metaphor portrays the president as a source, rather than a mere wielder, of power. Despite George Reedy's claim that "there is no power in the Presidency" because he holds the office by the sufferance of the people, discourse sometimes views him as the source of power in the government just as God is the source of power on a cosmic level (4). Thus there was much denial of the need to transfer the president's power, which treats power as originating in Mr. Reagan (Weisman; "I Am"; "Lawmakers"). Power is made physically to reside in the president by the claim that "the power of the presidency never actually left Mr. Reagan" ("I Am"). The *Atlanta Constitution* agreed that Reagan "retained Presidential powers" ("Who's In"). If the president is the godlike generator of vitality, his absence from centers of government leaves them bereft of life: "Confined to George Washington University Hospital, his administration's vital force is depleted" (Evans and Novak). Such a state of affairs caused much concern that a "power vacuum" might exist ("Cool"; "Haig"). A number of writers speculated that because the president is the locus of power, he actually draws assassins to him (Lewis; Tugwell and Cronin). Finally, just as a defining characteristic of God is the ability to create, so Mr. Reagan demonstrated power of Executive Creation, the signing of a bill into law: "To demonstrate his authority, he signed a bill" (Lescaze, A12).

President Clinton was referred to in theologically charged tones as well, perhaps ironically given the moral nature of some of the charges against him. David W. Sedgwick makes Clinton continuous in a direct line not only with kings who "carr[y] our self-image" but also with kings conceived of as "being 'gods,' or God's representatives on earth." Sedgwick identifies "the president [as] a collective image" of the country that "transcends and permeates our awareness and our outer and inner relationships," language with clearly spiritual, even deistic implications. Joe Lockard argues that Republicans accused Clinton of "polluting the civic temple of government" such that "the civic temple would be cleansed," but then he reverses the metaphor to make Republicans the real defilers and Clinton, by implication, the Holy of Holies: "Another sort of cleansing is needed though." Similarly, the World Socialist Web Site, in claiming that "Ken Starr is diabolically evil," implies that his polar opposite, President Clinton, must be the polar opposite of the devil, and hence divine ("On"). Less direct theological attributions include those such as Robert G. Kaiser's reference to Clinton's "energy, his appetites, his life story" as all being "unique," as God's attributes would be, and to Clinton as one of "the shapers of this era," a creative role that may be godlike.

Theological metaphors were found in other crisis discourse as well. President Kennedy was often referred to as a "martyr," a term with traditionally religious connotations ("John"). Prayer was also asked for Kennedy and Johnson, as it was for Reagan ("John"; "I Will"). Gerald Ford, upon taking office, also raised the theme of prayer ("Ford: 'Our' ").

Business

In capitalist economies, most businesses are highly structured with clear lines of authority. They are therefore amenable to entelechial motivations. Business metaphors contain terminologies of command and decision making that are homologous with the placement of the president atop the executive structure of government.

Much discourse equated Mr. Reagan's administration with the running of a business. Mr. Reagan did so himself by asking, "Who's minding the store?" a question repeated in headlines in the *New York Times* ("Who's Minding"). "Management" is clearly a business term; shortly before the shooting, disagreement had arisen over whether George Bush or Alexander Haig should take charge of "crisis management" ("Haig"), and of course that term surfaced again after the shooting ("I Am"). The president's incapacity meant that "others moved in to manage the situation as best they could" ("Cool"), a statement that makes the president a consummate manager by comparison. A related pronouncement was Senator Baker's claim that "the president is running the country" (Lescaze). The most explicit business metaphor, however, stemmed from aide Lyn Nofziger's claim that "in the meantime the business of government is going on normally and we expect it will continue to" ("Cool"). That metaphor was echoed by Edwin Meese: "Basically, the message is that this government is doing business as usual" (Cannon). The "business as usual" theme was sounded repeatedly by Mr. Reagan's aides, leaders in Congress, and commentators in the media ("'Didn't'"; "Bush").

Clinton is put in the front office of a business rather explicitly by the World Socialist Web Site in its claim that "the President should be able to conduct business for at least the end of his term without more torment" ("On"). Robert Kaiser described Clinton as uniquely able "to sell 'progressive' government in the late 1990s," thus making him the consummate businessman. David Broder is asked online whether he "gave the president full credit for balancing the budget," the act of a businessman, and Clinton's goals are described in profit-loss terms as pursuing "selfish gains."

The Kennedy assassination provoked several business metaphors. One headline in the *San Francisco Examiner* announced, "Business Halts" (1). Looking to the new president, commentators remembered that Lyndon Johnson "ran the Senate like a factory production line" (Albright), and remarked that he would soon attend to the "first order of business" ("Government"). The *National Review* hoped that the new President Ford would act like a "hardheaded Yankee trader" and that he would "deal with the items of unfinished business" left to him by Mr. Nixon ("A Ford"). Other observers of President Ford described him as "all business" ("What") and claimed that "he plunged quickly into the first business of his Presidency" ("Seven").

Heart and Brain

The human body is a whole, integral organism, and every organ is important to its functioning. But there are two organs that are often spoken of teleologically, as the *most* vital, as the sine qua non. These are the heart and the brain, which may thus be thought of as the most perfect organs in the human body. Metaphors based on the heart and brain surface when the presidency is in crisis.

George F. Will wrote several days after the shooting that "the presidency is so central, not only in the constitutional system but also in the nation's fabric of reverence and affection, that a physical attack on the President is an almost physical trauma to the people in their corporate existence—to the body politic" (24). Will's use of a physical metaphor for the president's relationship to the rest of the country was echoed in other discourse. Some discourse viewed Reagan as if he were the heart of government. Spokesperson Larry Speakes claimed, "The important thing to note is that the White House did not skip a beat, the government did not skip a beat" (Weisman; "'Didn't'"). Chrysler president Lee Iacocca said that the administration "won't skip a beat" (Noble).

A less explicit metaphor saw the president-as-brain. Referring to a statement by attending physician Dennis O'Leary, the *New York Times* reported: "Let the anesthesia wear off, he assured the country, and the President could decide anything" ("Who's Minding"). Anesthesia affects the brain primarily; furthermore, the brain is the organ of decision. References to the president's ability to make decisions despite his wound pictured him as the brain of his administration, the center of its decisiveness. Concern for the president's ability to decide was expressed quite often: "Mr. Reagan is capable of handling the few things that absolutely require his decision" (Reston), "decision-making control of the Government remains in Mr. Reagan's hands" (Raines, "Reagan Sees Aides"), "Reagan, from his hospital bed, will be able to make the decisions that are required of a President" (Cannon; Lescaze), and so forth.

Clinton as the nation's brain is the clear implication of David W. Sedgwick's argument that "we are, psychologically speaking, organically attached to our leaders." David Broder declines online to "offer any psychological insights about how the president keeps going under stress," pursuing the same theme ("Direct"). It follows then, as the World Socialist Web Site charged, that a political disorder in Washington must be "true psychosis" ("Week").

After the Kennedy assassination, Ladybird Johnson described the loss of a president as the loss of the heart: "We feel like the heart has been cut out of us" ("I Will"). Yet another "heart" had taken its place in the body politic in the form of Lyndon Johnson, and so the organic metaphor emerged in a headline, "The Government Still Lives" ("I Will"). The transfer of power to Ford was described in terms exactly paralleling the heart metaphors following the Reagan shooting: "Not a beat was missed" ("A New"). Gerald Ford referred to both brain and heart in declaring that "this is an hour of history that troubles our minds and hurts our hearts" ("Ford: 'Our Nightmare'"). Richard Nixon was described in medical terms as if he were a failed organ, perhaps even a tumor: "The American system slowly and carefully excised him from the body politic" ("Time").

Perfection and the President

We have seen the emergence of four families of perfectionist metaphors during times of presidential crisis. The recurrence suggests a homology of motivation underlying those times when crisis erupts in the presidency itself. But vocabularies are changeable and changing, and even the course of homologies can be altered or overturned. Is it desirable that these four metaphors should emerge? I should like to give some reasons why I think not.

Some writers have noted that motives toward the presidency are contained in the terms "unity" and "power." As ordinary motives the terms seem unobjectionable, for presidents ought to unify the nation and be strong. "*Unity* is the key word to describe the nature of the Presidency: unity of constituency, unity of representation, unity of membership, unity of authority" (Andrews, 40). The president is "the state's unifying symbol (Finer, 41), insofar as he represents all the people (Hutchins, 38; Cronin, 175), and he serves as "the one-man distillation of the American people" (Rossiter, 5), "the embodiment of the nation itself (Rossiter, 25).

The public expects that the executive branch should be a "seamless unity," "a one-man job in the Constitution and in the minds of the people" (Rossiter, 27). The public demands that the Babel of Administration be stilled and unified in the president, which is a major source of its entelechial power: "The contemporary phenomenon of Presidential autocracy was created by the considered preference of idealists for a kind of decision-making that somehow seemed more just because it was made on high by one man" (Hutchins, 51). Diversity of policy, initiative, and decision if not ultimately unified on one ground is intolerable: "The establishment of a single President is, of course, the foundation on which the entire subsequent development of the executive office rests" (Pritchett, 18–19).

Another motivation that people have is the expectation that the president be a symbol of strength or power (Fisher, "Reaffirmation," 164). The public attributes to him "powers that make for independent strength of tremendous effect" (Finer, 175) with "power of life or death" over government (Fenno). Gallagher notes that "we are taught in school that the President is the most powerful man on earth" (Gallagher, 217–18).

The four root metaphors examined earlier are developing implications of power and unity to an extreme, to perfection. The form or direction each perfection takes is convergent, such that the perfectly unified president is perfectly strong and vice versa, perfectly strong because perfectly unified. Furthermore, although the content of each metaphor is different, they each express the same perfected form of power and unity. The metaphors express a public desire for the president to be the *one and only* individual who exercises ultimate power in times of crisis.

A "representative anecdote" that expresses that attitude is the confusion over who was "in command" while President Reagan was undergoing surgery, especially with regard to the nation's defenses. The public seemed exquisitely anxious over any ambiguity in the executive branch, over any uncertainty about which one person held the power to make final decisions. Nobody seemed content that decisions be made and actions initiated by a group, by a gaggle of aides or Cabinet members. The press and public itched to know which single finger hovered over the nuclear button, as they did when President Kennedy died ("Instantly") and when President Nixon resigned (Osborn, 358).

When perfected, the values of unity and power are merged, for the public seeks in presidents a perfect unity that removes any check on his or her power to act. A perfect presidency is the one place where the buck stops, the one officer who makes things happen, the one center to which all administrative roads lead, and the one court of ultimate appeal. The perfection and subsequent marriage of unity and power motives tolerates no decision without the president's explicit sanction.

The four root metaphors reflect, in moments of uncertainty over power and unity, a need to be reassured that a Single Great Backstop still existed. The military structure of command depends on one final level of command at which ultimate power is wielded. Along the chain of command, decisions are typically made by single individuals whose power, unless superceded by a higher officer, has final authority for that company, division, or brigade. On a ship at sea, the captain is the single person whose decisions settle any disagreements. Clearly, theological metaphors reflect the perfection of unity and strength, for God is the one source of all action and power. In business, the chief manager or owner is the final maker of decisions within the bounds of the law. Even corporations headed communally by a board of directors are treated legally as single corporate persons, and they typically elect executive officers to embody the unity of their decisions and to exercise solitary power. Finally, the heart is the chief organ without which the body cannot function physically and the brain is the one organ without which the person cannot function cognitively. They are the ultimate members of mind and body, and might be said to define those respective spheres. In each of the four root metaphors, then, there is a yearning for a clear "bottom line" of power and control.

Implications

Because the metaphors examined here are by no means the whole of what people say about the presidency in crisis, it would be wrong to conclude that the public has only these motives. But these perfectionist metaphors are there, seeds that might grow into action, signs of a latent, ever-present motive force. If, in the future, the public is led to speak of presidents in crisis more and more in these terms, what dangers does that pose? What symbolic problems should we watch for in these metaphors?

Clearly, the images contained in the root metaphors militate against shared decision making, especially popular democracy. A nation that yearns to be piloted through stormy seas by a strong captain will not tolerate participation in decisions by the legislative or judicial branches. Putting questions of crisis resolutions to the crew, the general public, is out of the question. Debate or dissent is avoided. Increased use of these metaphors could signal a danger to the public's democratic birthright.

Reliance on the root metaphors, should they become a predominant mode of speaking about presidential crises, would also reflect a public preference for resolving those crises through an intensification of power and unification in the president. But if the crisis is born of too much concentration of power and unity, as was the case with Mr. Nixon, then public use of the metaphors may preclude resolution of the presidential crisis by reinforcing the undemocratic motives that spawned the exigency in the first place. Perfectionist motives can hamper resolution of crises stemming from improper use of power and unity.

As a final warning, let us try to extend the application of this study. I have focused on motives concerning presidential crises. But further research may well find perfectionist motives aroused in all sorts of national crises. Michael Osborn's work suggests that the perfection of power and unity is sought by the public during crises in general. Osborn's interesting analysis of the "archetypal sea" suggests that the ship-of-state metaphor, which employs the image of leader as captain, usually arises in times of public fear and disunity when people want decision-making power concentrated in one body:

> People in the grasp of fear look for the strength which can save them, especially for the collective strength of a united society. They become intolerant of that individualism which defies group purpose, and they yearn for strong social leadership. The ship-of-state can serve them well, for the image bends easily to advocate greater social discipline. Ship society can be made to represent a tightly structured hierarchy, all citizens performing their assigned tasks in harmony with the needs and interests of the vessel as a whole. Commanding this symbolic society is an enhancing projection of ultimate authority, the all-powerful sea Captain. (358)

A nation that yearns for a captain, a manager, a god, a supreme heart or brain to lead it through crisis is not searching for an alternative to the Imperial Presidency. But while this chapter has attempted to sound warnings, they are warnings contingent on increased use of the root metaphors in public discourse. As noted before, that these motives are present in discourse does not mean that they are the only motives he public might accept. The Ultimate Manager is not the only direction in which the otherwise admirable values of power and unity might merge. Part of the rhetorical critic's task is to ferret out dangerous extremism from its hiding places in seemingly innocuous usages and metaphors. Critics should also offer counter-statements, different ways of talking about situations that entail different motives. The perfection of power and unity might take a less dangerously authoritarian form; one example that comes to mind is the metaphor of the Orchestra Conductor.

The orchestra conductor is the locus of unity in the group, for his or her baton dictates a common rhythm, his or her score contains all the individual parts, he or she receives applause as the representative of the group, and without the conductor's guidance the ensemble falls into disarray. The conductor represents power: the baton dictates rhythm, the hand calls for changing dynamics, and the orchestra responds.

The metaphor is more democratic, participatory, and pluralistic (if only in degree) than the four metaphors discussed earlier. Each instrument and each grouping of instruments have their unique parts to play that are directed toward the common good. The conductor's role is not to coerce others (as does the keyboard of an organ, a musical metaphor close to the Sea Captain) but to use power in coaxing the best from each player, which will contribute to the unity of the group. The conductor is thus the Great Mediator and Persuader as opposed to the Great Backstop.

Let the metaphor serve as the counter-statement of this chapter. We have seen that some discourse about the presidency is centered on the motives of unity and power and develops terministic implications of those motives toward perfection through business, theological, military, and heart and brain metaphors. Such a direction of perfectionist development is contrary to the interests of a democratic society. This chapter has called attention to that motivation and has proposed a more constructive direction it might take.

We have also seen that the implications of homologies may need to be studied with special care, because the operation of homologies is so often out of awareness. One may certainly be aware that the president is referred to in terms of military command, or as the heart of an administration, but the "big picture" that one may see of the unity among all these four entelechial metaphors may be lost if one does not think homologically. The homology here does not lie in the occasional metaphor but in a network of discourse that, in its many nodes, supports entelechial thinking about the president. Homologies, like any rhetorical device, may have both desirable and undesirable consequences. Rhetorical critics need to be vigilant in their examination of homologies so as to better advise others as to the implications of public discourse.

Conclusion

As a people, we are obsessed with correspondences. Similarities be-
tween this and that, between apparently unconnected things, make us
clap our hands delightedly when we find them out. It is a sort of national
longing for form—or perhaps simply an expression of our deep belief that
forms lie hidden within reality; that meaning reveals itself only in flashes.
                    —Salman Rushdie, *Midnight's Children*

By way of conclusion, I want to review the critical application chapters of this book, chapters two through seven, to try to identify some major themes and movements of the ideas developed there. Then with a sense of the different kinds of rhetorical homologies and the ground they cover, I want to return to some broad issues raised in the first chapter. I will crawl out on a theoretical limb to make some claims for rhetorical homologies as central to postmodern life and how we understand it.

In an important sense, the trajectory of homologies studied in this book has moved from broad but single-level homologies to more fo-cused yet multi-tiered homologies. We have moved from fairly simple and straightforward discursive structures governing broad ranges of experiences, including textual experiences, to homologies of homolo-gies, super homologies, and homologies that both transcend and emerge within history. Let us review this progression of understandings of ho-mology.

Chapter two was based on the understanding that everyday injuries and slights are transformed discursively into ritual injury. The form of ritual injury was described as a homology underlying several discourses found over a wide span of time. Ritual injury enacts a pattern of mea-sured, deliberate, gestured receiving of injury that provides an audi-ence with a way of understanding their everyday affronts and thus re-sponding to them. Discourse in the form of ritual injury advises people how to see and respond to everyday injury. The homology of ritual injury energized the texts examined to encompass everyday experience by grounding motivations and strategies for response. Some texts seemed to advise people to see their everyday slights as earning stars for their crowns in heaven by depicting ritual injury as an act of sainthood. Other texts seemed to advise people to see their everyday injuries in a more comic frame, downplaying the importance of these hurts.

The chapter therefore emphasized the rhetorical effects of the ways in which content is carried to an audience by form. Although the form of ritual injury was at one level in each case the same, the different content or information through which the homology was manifested in texts varied in the responses it urged upon an audience. It makes a difference whether the form of ritual injury is clothed by a saint's martyrdom or by a comedian's pratfalls. We considered the possibility that as the homology has moved forward through history, it has clothed itself in increasingly ironic, slapstick, and otherwise generally debunking content. Such was the trajectory of the examples studied in that chapter, from pious representations of martyred saints to the grotesqueness of professional wrestling. That homology maintains the underlying form of ritual injury but offers historically specific and changing advice to audiences that may alter the form itself.

New reindividuations of the form in new content add new permutations to the homology; form itself grows, expands, and adapts to history. If the homology of ritual injury is always reindividuated in saints' narratives, a *kind* of saintliness becomes part of the homology. If in recent times the homology of ritual injury is increasingly reindividuated in slapstick and burlesque, a kind of comedy enters the homology, and thus a kind of comic attitude toward injury enters the DNA of the form.

The familiar form of myth was treated homologically in the third chapter. I argued that numerous discourses and experiences are ordered according to a White liberal version of American history that treats people of color in a paternal, condescending way. In a sense this was one of the narrowest chapters, focusing as it did on one main text and offering only brief descriptions of other manifestations of the homology.

Yet the third chapter illustrated the importance of form as a rhetorical device with its own power, in spite of the content it conveys. For the text studied, *The Horse Whisperer,* would seem to have no content whatsoever that matched the myth in question. The usual content of race was absent. Yet I argued that the form of race relations in the myth was very powerfully present, and detectable at the level of pattern rather than information.

Chapter three showed how texts can do social and political work because of their homological grounding despite of, even because of, a content that seems not to match the form. For a content that seems not to fit the homology is also a way of disguising the nature of the form at work. A pattern that is nearly always manifested in a content having to do with race may continue to effect social and political attitudes, and may perhaps especially do so, when it works in a text that does not have that usual content. This disguise was effected by the reversals in the film, in which White people are formally people of color, male and female traditional roles are reversed, and so forth.

The chapter not only illustrated the centrality of form as a persuasive device, but also suggested that other categories may be more formal than previously understood. Race itself may not be so much a matter of specific physical attributes as it is a model of expectations, relationships, perceptions, and behaviors modeled on a discursive structure. Race, in other words, may be a homology pushing up behaviors and texts. One might see that clearly through a text that is formally homologous with the myth but shares little of its content or information. Attention to the centrality of homologies may refocus attention toward underlying patterns of domination and control that lay bare the heart of the matter in racial politics today. And if race may be seen as primarily, fundamentally a kind of homology, so may other human categories in today's dialectic of social organization.

The fourth chapter took a new direction. Chapters two and three had been based on homologies of discursive structures largely in narrative form, chaining out syntagmatically in a linear fashion. Although retaining that sense of homological structure, the fourth chapter was based on a complex pattern of meanings facilitated by a complex sign, or family of signs, The Chair. The Chair was described as a structure of connected signs and experiences, ordered according to fairly predictable, recurring patterns of empowerment and disempowerment. There are predictable circumstances under which sitting (as sign or practice) is empowering and likewise there are conditions under which standing (as sign or practice) is empowering. This structure, this homology linking together the whole tribe of signs that comprise The Chair, is a kind of reservoir of meanings that texts and experiences can access and activate for rhetorical purpose. Those experiences and texts are therefore homologous with one another as part of The Chair's structure of signs.

We have considered "experience" as an overarching category that is ordered by homologies, whether material, everyday experience or the experience of texts. Chapter four added to this understanding the idea that experiences of media are also ordered in homologies. The chapter advanced an argument made in earlier research that the more experiences that are homologically ordered, the more powerful the effect of the homology. If an audience's textual, technological, and quotidian experiences vibrate to the same homological frequency, the rhetorical effects of the homology are increased. And thus, the rhetorical uses to which the symbolic resources of The Chair may be put are increased if the experience of The Chair in everyday life is homologous with how it is portrayed in a text such as the film Get on the Bus as well as in the medium the audience uses so as to experience the film. That film, the chapter showed, moves the audience in a trajectory from empowered sitting to empowered standing, in sync with how the characters in the film are moved, and both audience and characters are challenged in parallel fashion to stand and act as a result of the experience.

This book took a somewhat different turn with chapter five. This was the first of the chapters to consider tiers or layers of homology. I argued that recurring formal resemblances between the dominant rhetorical theories and practices of a period on the one hand, and dominant weapons on the other, formed a kind of super homology. *Some* kind of formal parallel between rhetorics and weapons was likely to obtain, I argued, and examined such a parallel in three eras. Renaissance rhetorics were paired with the stiletto, Enlightenment rhetorics with the flintlock musket, and today's rhetorics of popular culture with the semiautomatic pistol.

The nature of each homology varies, but the linkage is always homologous, that is to say at the level of form rather than content. Each specific homology between rhetoric and a weapon is specific to its historical period and conditions. The homology between Renaissance rhetoric and the stiletto is not the same as the homology between Enlightenment

rhetoric and the flintlock musket. Chapter five thus illustrated how homology can operate on a transhistorical level (rhetorics and weapons
will always be, or will tend to be, homologous) as well as more historically specific ways (rhetorics and weapons are homologous in this particular era, or for this particular culture, in more temporally and socially
specific ways).

Chapter five included theory, which we had not previously considered, within the experiences and texts ordered within homology. Posit-
ing two tiers of homology, the chapter also explored some implications
of the super homology of recurring formal linkages between rhetorics
and weapons. The chapter suggested that a pattern of transformative
connection may be the bedrock formal linkage creating this kind of recurrent pattern. If so, I argued that discourse itself may be fundamentally transformative—rhetorical, religious, or magical—at its very core,
and that transformation may be of the essence in how discourse orders
our world for us.

As in chapter five, the sixth chapter studied tiers of homology. A persona can be a kind of homology, a form structuring appearances of the
same type of character or role in different times and places. Another,
related homology is the way in which personae connect with recurring
exigencies or rhetorical situations. The pattern of specific connections
between persona and exigence may also be a homology. As our understanding of the homology becomes more specific, moving from the form
of a persona to the form of a persona responding to a recurring exigence
(to a form of exigence), the homology comes closer to historical specificity and moves downward on the scale of abstraction.

In chapter six we argued that the Wise Woman is an ancient, recurring persona, grounded in third-world cultures but found all over the
world. Most if not all societies value the Wise Woman as a source of wisdom, guidance, and spiritual leadership. However, the historical roots of
the Wise Woman are in the local tribe; how does one enact this persona
for a complex, fragmented, fractious society? That exigence of how to
provide spiritual leadership for mass-mediated, postmodern societies
recurs as does the persona of the Wise Woman, and the chapter considered how the persona follows new forms to adapt to the recurrence of
the exigence.

We argued that Sojourner Truth, at the dawn of mediated, postmodern culture, and Oprah Winfrey in our own era, enact the persona of Wise Woman. But to serve in that role for their respective large, complex societies, they need to represent contradictory values of empowerment and disempowerment. The contradiction is resolved on a ground of spiritual unity.

As in chapter five, we showed in chapter six how homology can be transhistorical at one level and grounded in historical particularities at another level. In the first chapter I argued that abstract form and specific content or information are on a continuum rather than sharply distinct. It follows that homologies, although always formal, may be more or less formal, more or less transhistorical, more or less patterns adapted to the specific historical moment.

Chapter seven also studied levels of homology. There I proposed that homology can be a teleological structure, that an entelechy can be a formal pattern underlying different kinds of discourse. Because most discourse contains a teleological motive to some extent, although some more than others, a homology of perfection is transhistorical in cutting across many different times and places.

The chapter argued that when the type of rhetorical exigence that is a presidential crisis recurs, four kinds of metaphors tend to emerge that express the teleological motive. This chapter therefore identified a homology of linked exigence and response, as did chapter six. The second layer of homology, that of four families (forms) of metaphors arising in response to a focused category of presidential crisis, is a more historically specific level of homology.

I argued that the four families of metaphors embodying an entelechy are used to create images of presidential action and unity. The peculiar conjunction of perfection, perfectionist metaphors, and calls for forceful action without meaningful dissent may, I suggested, be an unfortunate combination of rhetorical devices. The homologies at work in presidential crisis rhetoric may therefore have unfortunate political and social consequences. I suggested that attention to homologies may facilitate the kind of rhetorical judgments and warnings that critics are sometimes obliged to give. Having now reviewed the range of critical application chapters, let me turn again to some of the theoretical issues discussed in the first chapter, and make some claims concerning the importance of rhetorical homologies.

Magics, Orders, Discourses

In chapter one I noted some of the different groundings that have been proposed for homologies: Marxist, biological, theological, and in this study, rhetorical. A rhetorical homology is grounded in discursive properties. A *grounding* in that sense is the effective cause for different kinds of texts and experiences to follow the same pattern. So depending on grounding, one understands formal parallels in experience as based on economic experience, or the will of God, or discursive properties, and so forth. I facetiously claimed that a choice of grounding is a choice among *magics,* and which magic one habitually prefers for casting everyday incantations will determine that choice. Let me revisit that claim more seriously.

If one sees an order underlying the objects, actions, and events of the world, one sees homology, for one sees some sort of prime mover in some part of the world pushing up the stuff of experience in array. We are surrounded by homologies, large and small. To see the world as ordered at all is to see it homologically. The small homologies do not interest us, nor do they trouble us: there is a homology behind the way the books sit on my shelves, and probably on your shelves as well, but few will think this entails social or political dominance, hegemony and refusal, or any other arrangement of power. It is when one asserts homologies ordering wide ranges of experience, even life itself, that questions arise of what sort of homology this is, how it is determined, and with what political and social biases encoded into what seems to be a formal DNA of pattern. A theory of wide-ranging homologies tends to be structuralist, and structuralisms are often shunned for the ways in which they enshrine as universal some assumptions that may not, are not, or ought not to be universal. From an aversion to declaring that Pattern X rules the universe only to find that Pattern X is covertly misogynist, racist, or capitalistically exploitive, is born the poststructuralist impulse to avoid asserting homologies at any significant level.

As an illustration of the problems involved in declaring *or* in refusing to declare a structure, let me turn to some recent work by some Australian critical scholars, Gavin Kendall and Gary Wickham, and Toby Miller and Alec McHoul. Kendall and Wickham "propose Cultural Studies as the study of ordering" (2). That stance is appropriate because for them, "culture is ordering. . . . Any time and any place you find ordering, by our account, you have found culture" (24). Their approach would seem to be thoroughly homological, for they argue that "ordering is everywhere. Ordering is part of human life, whatever we think of it" (25). As does I. A. Richards, they place ordering at the core of human perception and experience: "objects are given to us, as 'the world,' only in and through ordering. As such, ordering can be considered characteristic of all human life" (28). They even argue in ways that seem compatible to what I have presented here as tiers or levels of homology, claiming that "every ordering practice is itself subject to ordering" (41). Similarly, as I noted in the first chapter, Miller and McHoul use our terminology explicitly in claiming that "structural homologies with industrialism are obvious" in sports' valuing of "training and discipline" (82).

These scholars also argue, however, for a tight focus on the local, specific, and historically immediate. As Miller and McHoul note, "Everyday cultural objects arise out of local conditions—conditions which are highly specific and far from spectacular" (x–xi). By "spectacular" they mean "speculative," and by that they mean asserting connections between specific behaviors and practices and "broader sociopolitical agendas of race and sexuality. . . . [I]t is speculative because it simply assumes that the everyday event represents that much broader field of contested sexuality" (ix–xi). Kendall and Wickham prefer that culture be "theorised in practical intellectual fields" rather than "as an abstract problem" (9). They complain of much in current Cultural Studies that moves to what is for them too abstract a level of form. When studies always connect local practices to grand structures of domination and resistance, they argue, "this style of engagement with power further weakens the discipline and sets it adrift in a world of baseless grand theorizing" (14). The kind of ordering they would prefer to find is emergent, arising from historical specificities instead of transhistorical form: "They are contingent patterns, not a priori patterns" (44). Miller and McHoul agree in championing "ethnomethodology," which they argue "understands language as a mode of action in its own right, rather than as the representation or transmission of other, more authentic messages" (25). By those "other" messages they mean broad implications of power and meanings beyond the immediate moment of usage—precisely the sort of implications I have been exploring here.

I believe we see in Kendall and Wickham's distaste for the a priori a distaste for structuralisms. At least three difficulties with this stance arise, in my view. First, it is unclear to me how we know that some practice is an ordering practice without an a priori understanding of what ordering is and what patterns look like. Kendall and Wickham's preference for discovering "contingent patterns" (44) is an oxymoron; as soon as something is a pattern it anticipates the part of the world that it orders. I could have declared of my daughters' rooms when they were teenagers that they were nothing like "ordered" only because I knew what order was, I knew what some of the patterns were by which rooms are ordered, and their rooms matched none of those patterns. Second, Kendall and Wickham's endorsement of theories that place ordering at the heart of perception, of object-giving, would seem to make order a priori to the objects and perceptions it gives to us. Third, why should we read Kendall and Wickham's later chapters in which they analyze how ordering has occurred in various historically specific times and places if the forms they find cannot be or ought not be extended beyond those locations? We need to be able to think about how ordering occurs in the moment without staying trapped in the moment and without ignoring the moment through application of forms that perforce go beyond the moment. I believe that is precisely what a rhetorical homology, among other homologies, helps us to do.

How to avoid the two extremes of the trivial and the overgeneralized and yet say something significant about experience? A significant statement about experience applies beyond the here and now—it cuts across history—it is for that reason formal. Can one be a scholar, a critic, an observer of life and not suggest a homology? I think not. The most dedicated poststructuralist will go to school to learn the rules and principles of poststructuralism, and thereafter fiercely enforce those structures in any book or article that dares to enter the temple. To claim that one can or should escape structure, form, homology is to engage in the very privileging of position that prompts the poststructuralist deferral in the first place—in that case, a privileging of unstructuredness. Let me say parenthetically that I think this same fault line underlies some battlefields in what are sometimes called the "culture wars," in which structuralist, modernist insistence on seeing the world in specific ways (that may encode cultural bias) clashes with postructuralist, postmodernist refusal to structure the world in enduring ways (that may court trivial conclusions). I believe it is more politically and socially responsible to recognize that one *will* see the world as ordered, understand what order one uses and what is its domain, assess the implications of such ordering, and then struggle over the implications of that ordering.

How shall we understand the ways we order? In the same way that we do the ordering, or perform the magic, in the first place. When we perform magic we order the world by using gesture, fetish, and word; in other "words," by using signs and symbols. By using discourse. And what have you been doing, Gentle Reader, but ordering the world with me (or resisting my attempts by offering up your own ordering) through signs and symbols for many pages of our discourse by now? If you struggle with my reasoning by opposing your own Marxist or theological homologies, how do you do it except through signs and symbols, ordered into the busy discourse that buzzes in your head?

I believe this takes us back to Kenneth Burke, who got "here" decades before any of us, in claiming a privileged position, beyond which humans cannot go, for a method and a philosophy of understanding the human experience that is keyed to language. Burke's claims for the logical and logological priority of his system are explained at length and throughout *A Grammar of Motives,* but are adumbrated most clearly in *Permanence and Change* and in *The Philosophy of Literary Form.* Burke well understood (as far as, and in the way that, humans understand) the role of the nonlinguistic in human experience, but likewise understood that even nonlinguistic experience is not understood by us except through symbolic systems. For Burke, ordering and symbol systems are one and the same process, and methods designed for understanding experience must be keyed to, and grounded in, such systems. This equation between order and symbols was likewise asserted by such scholars as Mikhail Bakhtin and I. A. Richards. This book has expressed that equation in terms of a *rhetorical homology.* The magic that rules the world of formal resemblance, I have argued, is discourse itself.

Having begun in the first chapter with presenting rhetorical homology as one among many stances one might take toward order in the world, I have now come around to offering it as a bedrock way to understand such order. Such a view is clearly structuralist, but I believe Burke likewise to have been structuralist. Yet I believe that one can be a structuralist, and claim a privileged position for a method or philosophy, and yet understand the social and political implications of one's stance. Some structures, I think, are more transcendent than others. One can see the world both as structured and as bending to history and to struggle within structure. If one is to be a structuralist, I believe a structuralism grounded in rhetorical homology is the most defensible and flexible because it knows when to bend to history.

Among the many choices of magics to ground one's homological structure, discourse contains an inherent balance between permanence and change. To privilege discourse over, say, DNA or chemical processes as productive of the web of homologies that pushes up experience is, at least, to privilege a tension between fluidity and structure, just as language itself is in constant tension between meanings, grammars, and syntaxes that are stable for the moment yet are always in flux and struggle. Permanence comes from recurring discursive properties (which language has because it is a structure anticipating history), and change from the moments in which language enters history (which it must enter because language is also a practice). To put rhetorical homologies at the center of how we understand the world is to make it not a center but instead a parameter, an exoskeleton for unstable historical moments, yet a surrounding framework always nibbled at by social struggle and by the dynamics of symbolic instability. Surely that uneasy tension has implications for how one sees power arrayed in the world. To ground one's understanding of order in *rhetorical* homologies is a way of understanding homology, order, in a rhetorical way, as something that is always already being argued and struggled over within discursive structures that always already give a stable arena for struggle. Struggle in history requires a discursive stability to work within, with, or against—a symbolic maypole to dance around. Rhetoric is the dual ability of discourse to *structure* transhistorically the parameters for historical *struggle*. Because rhetorical discourse requires that tension, I believe it provides the happiest possible structure even for squeamish poststructuralists.

Postmodernist scholars and activists may oppose any kind of structuralism because they insist on understanding how experience works in the particular moments of history that situate what we do and say in networks of empowerment. Privileging any kind of stance is thus seen as an attempt to escape history. Let me co-opt that very argument to make another bid for the centrality of rhetorical homologies as a method and perspective on experience by entering history.

Suppose we lived in a world that was increasingly becoming one of signs, symbols, representations, simulations, rather than a world of un-alloyed "reality" in anyone's sense of the word/world. That would be a world of engrossment in texts, and the more engrossing the text the better. It would be a world in which people would prefer to play video games about driving cars than to drive cars, to tape their children's pivotal life events rather than to put the camera down and to watch the event, to view reality television shows rather than to walk out and experience reality itself. It would be the world we do live in.

If we live in a world that is increasingly constructed of signs, then the privileging of rhetorical homologies as perspective and method enacts precisely the kind of historical specificity called for by the postmodern refusal of structure. A world of discourse is just exactly the world we live in today, and in such a world where is there a place for systems of order keyed to "real" chemistry or biology, to the gods, or even to some sense of mystical economic relations occurring outside of texts? A rhetorical understanding of homology becomes *appropriate,* if one does not like the idea of *privileged,* under such circumstances. The method of rhetorical homology, identifying discourse as the generative ground of formal parallels, is attuned to the discursive, textual world that global culture is increasingly becoming.

In such a world, the idea of rhetorical homology, or rhetorical ordering, becomes a redundancy. The idea that rhetoric orders the world for rhetor and audience is far from new. The idea of rhetorical homology makes ordering the sine qua non of rhetoric. Stepping into the middle of an ongoing ordering process, let us suppose that one is experiencing a "war" in some sense. The same exchange of blows and bullets might well be ordered in alignment with *M*A*S*H* or with *Saving Private Ryan.* A "terrorist" bombing may be discursively crafted to fit with patterns of heroic struggle between good and evil or to fit with patterns of overreaching strength receiving its comeuppance at the hands of the dispossessed. We make the world by ordering it and we order the world rhetorically—to be rhetorical is to order it, and in ordering it we do so with one or another social and political outcome. This "war" that we are experiencing now we experience as in alignment with discourse

X or with discourse Y; rhetorical struggle lies in crafting discursive resonances with one pattern or another. The perspective of rhetorical homologies thus sees rhetoric, and all rhetorical struggle, as manipulation of the resources of King Discourse, the ground of life's patterns, so as to claim the resources of one pattern or another.

Rhetorical homologies thus merge distinctions between traditional, expositional forms of rhetoric and the more fragmented, nonverbal, narrative forms of popular culture. The same order is culturally available to align a given exigency with a speech, a film, or a sidewalk performance of guerrilla theater. A presidential address and a late-night television comedy monologue may both be pushed up by the same discursive form. A rhetorical homology is thus an alembic for the healing of a fractured academy, a distracted critical eye, and a public divided by cultural wars that offer up Homer on one side and Homer Simpson on the other. We need not choose if we look for ways in which discourse has in the long march of history linked text and experience in ways we may not even have suspected.

Appendix

One significant use of homology is in mathematics. Peter Hilton and Shaun Wylie, for example, review the use of homology theory in algebra. The development of homology theory is cited by Michael Atiyah as one of the developments of twentieth-century theory in mathematics. In addition to formal homology theory, Brian Rotman suggests "a homology between virtual reality and mathematical thought in terms of their conceptual framework" (389), pointing to other uses of the idea of homology in mathematics.

Homology is also a widely used concept in natural sciences such as biology, medicine, and child development. Paul Griffiths notes its origins in Darwinian thought, in which homology was conceived of as a shared ancestry that accounted for shared characteristics among organisms. N. Jardine agrees in noting that "most recent textbooks define biological homology in terms of common ancestry," which is "contrasted with analogy, resemblance due to common function" (125). Jardine says that historically, biological homology has been judged in terms of "conformity to type" (125). In that vein, Jack Wilson reviews some work in "the study of homology within multicellular lineages," also an ancestral understanding of the term (S301). Other thinkers such as Bruce Young have suggested that biological homology should be understood in terms of similarity, not ancestry. One example of a collection of studies addressing the issue of biological homology is Lance Grande and Olivier Rieppel's volume.

Kenneth Schaffner discusses biomedical science's use of "deep homology" in investigating "model organisms" (276). Homologies have been used as a way of determining significant, real biological differences; Winfried Schleiner notes that in the history of biology, the "Galenic 'one-sex model'" was based on "a homology between male and female genitalia," using an analysis of formal resemblance to argue that male and female are but variations on one gender (180). Donna Thal notes the use of different models of homology in child development to account for the parallel patterns of development through which children typically move.

The use of homology in the social sciences and humanities is, of course, closer to the interests of this study than is homology in mathematics and the natural sciences. The base concept of formal resemblances or linkages is used in several related ways in this vast literature. Claude Lévi-Strauss articulates what may be the strongest, most determinant view of homology in social science. He studies myths across cultures as iterations of the same basic structure; thus, examination of those connections reveals homological "laws operating at a deeper level" than surface content as well as "a pattern of basic and universal laws" of the mind (*Symbolic*, 202–03; also *Raw*, 10–11). Another widely respected scholar of myth, Joseph Campbell, thought homologically in identifying the myth of the hero's journey as a form underlying quite a large number of stories occurring across time and space; identifying such a homology, he argued, revealed a fundamental form of thought shared across cultures. In turn, Edmund Leach believes that homologies reveal "human universals" ordering material experiences (40).

Other theorists identify homologies underlying disparate experiences without claiming such lawlike, determinant status for them. Often the focus of these studies is to show homologies ordering and linking texts and material experiences. In studying "the homology between the classic novel structure and the structure of exchange in the liberal economy" (122), Lucien Goldmann argues that "the novel form seems to be the transformation on the literary plane of everyday life in individualistic society born of production for the market," thus identifying homologies between economic experiences and texts (127). The depiction of difficult or eccentric people in literature is shown to be homologous with those who cannot or will not work within capitalist structures, for instance. Goldmann argues, "Thus, the structures of an important novel genre and of exchange prove rigorously homologous to the point that one can speak of a single structure manifest on two different levels" (128). Homologies among texts and experiences are likewise identified by Raymond Williams, who sees them as "resemblances, in seemingly very different specific practices, which may be shown by analysis to be both direct and directly related expressions of and responses to a general social process" (104).

For some researchers in humanities or social science, a homology is the discovery of a meaningful formal connection bridging experiences that have not been consciously ordered together. Phil Francis Carspecken studied a group of residents who took over and illegally ran a school in Liverpool, England, for a year. He attributes the "coordination of routines through face-to-face interactions" to a shared "paradigm," while similarities in "routines separated in time and space" he attributes to "homology" (1). If people seem to follow a similar pattern in actions performed across time and space, without having coordinated their actions, there is a homology underlying those actions. This usage suggests that homology is a linking device across orders of experience that otherwise seem dissimilar; it appears to be a higher order of abstraction than a "paradigm" that orders the immediate, local performance of shared tasks. There seems to be a sense in which the routines separated by time and space are nevertheless ordered or partially determined by the homology in which they participate. Likewise, Lynn Meskell finds a "narrative homology" between the houses and tombs and the writings of the Egyptian New Kingdom village, Deir el Medina (c. 1500–1100 B.C.); that homology allows the demonstration of "conjoinings and ruptures between various levels of evidence" (405). Homology for Meskell appears to be a way of confirming conclusions that might be drawn from one set of data if formally similar conclusions might be found in another set. Homology is thus a way to triangulate from different dimensions of a culture so as to generate some general conclusions about the culture. To understand two levels of Islamic culture, Margaret Malamud asserts "a homology between normative relations among Sufis and normative relations in the larger [Islamic] world" (89). A model of hierarchy structures both sets of relationships and creates a deep cultural homology; her argument seems to be a way to show how some dimensions of Sufi culture came to be that way through at least partial determination by their homological relationship with Islam in general. Likewise, Nicole Revel finds that "the values of a society" in the Philippines form "a homology binding together" several art forms that express those values (7). Willard Van Orman Quine argues that the translation of observation sentences "calls for a sharing of homology of stimulations by a translator and a native" (159). In these studies (Carspecken, Meskell, Malamud, Revel, Quine) the orders of experience brought together are not sharply different; they are different kinds of apples shown to share the same pattern, rather than apples found to be formally similar to oranges.

However, we can see a use of homology as a form ordering sharply disparate orders of experience in Thomas Kavanagh's study asserting "a strong homology" between social thinking about relationships between the sexes and the social practices of gambling in eighteenth-century France. His discovery of "homologies between sexuality and gambling" speaks to a deep cultural mechanism that erupts in more than one face of any given culture (505). In the same vein, Phillippa Levine asserts a "homology between sexual and political dominance" in British colonial India, which suggests a way of "integrating gender history with political and imperial history" (585). Christopher Keep and Don Randall identify "an implicit homology between the punctured body of the English detective [Sherlock Holmes] and the body politic of England itself in the wake of the Indian Mutiny of 1857," a homology suggesting connections "between addiction, empire, and narrative" (207). Homology in this case seems to be a structure connecting disparate orders of experience, although whether the authors believe the form generates those experiences is not explicit. Similarly, Toby Miller and Alec McHoul observe that "structural homologies with industrialism are obvious" in sports' emphasis on "training and discipline" (82).

Sometimes homology is described as a formal linkage among practices, asserting some similar procedure, goal, or determinant of the practices. A. E. Denham asserts "a basic consistency, a deep homology" between Iris Murdoch's philosophy and her literature (602). The homology seems to assert that both grew together out of the same underlying pattern. Meredith Shedd studies the practice of ekphrasis, whereby art objects may be described so that one may visualize them, and finds "a structural homology between making and describing sculpture" revealed by ekphrasis (315). The link between sculpting and describing would thus seem to make each part of the same more general patterned process. The practices of making and appreciating art are similarly found to be homologous in Thomas Pfau's study of how "interiority" was conceptualized, in which he assets "a homology of the artwork's formal composition with its beholding intelligence" (321).

Homology may also be used to suggest that two different constructs, or theorized entities, are essentially the same or share a common ancestral influence. Simon Critchley finds homology between the theorized ethical subjects of Jacques Lacan and of Emmanuel Levinas, and uses this link to enrich the theories of each with insights from the other. Daniel Pigg addresses the question of whether Geoffrey Chaucer was familiar with William Langland's *Piers Plowman;* unable to say that he was, Pigg nevertheless argues that both Chaucers and Langland's work "form a homology to the confessional" and that "both recognized the power of the confessional," thus linking the two through a shared formal resemblance with a third discursive pattern (428). Similarly, Ronald Martinez, in trying to trace the effects of the *Lamentations of Jeremiah* on Dante's *Vita Nuova*, finds a "homology of parts and parts of parts, or sufficient articulation" between the two to suggest an influence (1).

Homology may create a structure underlying and unifying far more than specific entities and practices. Colin Beer suggests that homologies underlying large social structures arc more stable (perhaps in some sense, more real) than are those underlying specific behaviors. Walter Brennan also takes the wide view when he argues that homology is the basic method in the writings of Mircea Eliade, and that Eliade's homological method is based on Platonic idealism. If correct, this view identifies a powerful use of homology, for the forms underlying the world are a more basic reality than are the content-specific individual manifestations of form. Homology is used as a rather widely cast net also in Keith Livers's assertion of a "cosmic homology of food and filth" that emerges in different literatures; he finds it in a novel by Russian writer Andrei Platonov (154). The language of cosmology suggests that homologies are fundamentally generative structures beneath different immediate material manifestations.

Some writers are more hesitant to draw conclusions about a culture based on the discovery of a homology, however. Although Reinhold Kramer asserts a homology in Canadian law and literature on the issue of whether the body may remain free from state authority, he cautions against asserting "a general cultural bifurcation" based on that homology (385). This use of homology is suggestive but not conclusive in the identifying of a cultural mechanism that emerges in different orders of experience. Another more cautious use of homology is found in Konrad Lorenz's comparison of homology with analogy; the former is a stronger claim about the reality of connections among disparate things, and should be used carefully, he argues. Likewise, Angus Gellatly argues that a widespread assumption that young children have "a theory of mind" should be treated as an analogy, not a homology; homology, he implies, suggests a more powerful connection and perhaps a shared generative mechanism.

I have used the idea of homology in my own work (*Rhetorical*, 87, 96–98). In one study I identified a homology among the content of pornographic videos, the medium of the VCR for home use, and patriarchal domination of men over women, arguing that the connecting device of the homology intensified the negative, patriarchal effects of pornography ("The Homology"). In a slightly earlier work ("Electric") I had made much the same argument, without calling it homological, in arguing that formal parallels among the content of haunted house films, the experience of viewing a film in a theater, and certain "real life" experiences enabled the films to address those experiences in more powerful ways. In an earlier line of work, I developed a thoroughly homological method although I did not call it by that term. Developing the possibilities of Kenneth Burke's concept of the "representative anecdote" as a method for rhetorical criticism, I argued that simple story lines, described in starkly formal terms, could be shown to underlie different orders of discourse. I argued that several evangelical Christian rhetors, although widely divergent politically, were all formally similar to certain biblical parables expressing a kind of fortress mentality; by identifying that formal pattern, one could understand more clearly the rhetorical perspective taken by evangelical rhetoric ("The Representative").

References

Ackerman, Peter, and Jack DuVall. *A Force More Powerful: A Century of Nonviolent Conflict*. New York: Palgrave, 2000.

Ackroyd, Peter. *Dickens*. London: Sinclair-Stevenson, 1990.

Adler, Bill, ed. *The Uncommon Wisdom of Oprah Winfrey: A Portrait in Her Own Words*. Secaucus, N.Y.: Carol Publishing, 1997.

Albin, K. (2001). "Rosa Parks: The Woman Who Changed a Nation." <http://www.grandtimes.com/rosa.html>.

Albright, R. C. "Johnson Grooming for High Office Started in His Infancy." *Washington Post*, November 23, 1963, national edition, A4.

"All Too Human." *Indianapolis Star*, March 31, 1981, national edition, 6.

Althusser, Louis. *Lenin and Philosophy and Other Essays*. Trans. B. Brewster. New York: Monthly Review Press, 1971.

Andrews, William G. "The Presidency, Congress, and Constitutional Theory." In *Perspectives on the Presidency*, edited by Aaron Wildavsky, 35–42. Boston: Little, Brown, 1975.

Ann, Martha, Dorothy Imel, Lee Redfield, and Barbara J. Suter. *The Great Goddess: An Introduction to Her Many Names*. Boulder, Colo.: Our Many Names, 1993.

Aristotle. *Rhetoric* and *Poetics*. Trans. W. Rhys Roberts. New York: Modern Library, 1954.

Atiyah, Michael. "100 Years of Mathematics." *Normat* 48 (2000): 123–26.

Baker, Russell. "Once Again." *New York Times*, April 1, 1981, national edition, 29.

Bakhtin, Mikhail (writing as V. V. Volosinov). *Marxism and the Philosophy of Language*. Trans. Ladislav Matejka and J. R. Titunik. San Diego: Academic Press, 1973.

Baldwin, Charles Sears. *Reniassance Literary Theory and Practice: Classicism in the Rhetoric and Poetic of Italy, France, and England 1400–1600*. Gloucester, Mass.: Peter Smith, 1959.

Barber, David. *The Presidential Character: Predicting Performance in the White House.* 4th ed. Englewood Cliffs, N.J.: Prentice-Hall, 1992.

Baugh, John. *Black Street Speech: Its History, Structure, and Survival.* Austin: University of Texas Press, 1983.

Beer, Colin G. "Homology, Analogy, and Ethology." *Human Development* 27 (1984): 297–308.

Big Business. Directed by J. Wesley Horne. Performed by Stan Laurel, Oliver Hardy, and James Finlayson. Metro-Goldwyn-Mayer, 1929.

Bizzell, Patricia, and Bruce Herzberg, eds. *The Rhetorical Tradition: Readings from Classical Times to the Present.* Boston: Bedford Books, 1990.

Brennan, Walter. "Homology as a Platonic Device in the Thought of Mircea Eliade." *Listening: Journal of Religion and Culture* 21 (1986): 79–93.

Broder, David S. "Direct Access: David Broder." January 19, 1999. *Washingtonpost.com Direct Access.* <http://www.washingtonpost.com/wp-srv/politics/talk/zforum/broder 011999.htm>.

———. "End of a Dream." *Washington Post,* April 1, 1981, national edition, A21.

———. "Rise in Reagan's Popularity Seen, With Little Impact on Hill Prospects." *Washington Post,* April 1, 1981, national edition, A7.

Brummett, Barry. "Burkean Comedy and Tragedy, Illustrated in Reactions to the Arrest of John DeLorean." *Central States Speech Journal* 35 (1984): 217–27.

———. "Burkean Scapegoating, Mortification, and Transcendence in Presidential Campaign Rhetoric." *Central States Speech Journal* 32 (1981): 254–64.

———. "Burke's Representative Anecdote as a Method in Media Criticism." *Critical Studies in Mass Communication* 1 (1984): 161–76.

———. "Electric Literature as Equipment for Living: Haunted House Films." *Critical Studies in Mass Communication* 2 (1985): 247–261.

———. "The Homology Hypothesis: Pornography on the VCR." *Critical Studies in Mass Communication* 5 (1988): 202–16.

———. "The Representative Anecdote as a Burkean Method, Applied to Evangelical Rhetoric." *Southern Speech Communication Journal* 50 (1984): 1–23.

———. *Rhetoric in Popular Culture.* New York: St. Martin's Press, 1994.

———. *Rhetoric of Machine Aesthetics.* Westport, Conn.: Praeger, 1999.

———. *Rhetorical Dimensions of Popular Culture.* Tuscaloosa: University of Alabama Press, 1991.

———. "Symbolic Form, Burkean Scapegoating, and Rhetorical Exigency in Alioto's Response to the Zebra Murders." *Western Journal of Speech Communication* 44 (1980): 64–73.

"Bullets Again." *Detroit Free Press,* March 31, 1981, national edition, 4B.

Burke, Kenneth. *Attitudes toward History.* (1937). 3rd ed. Berkeley: University of California Press, 1984.

———. *Counter-Statement.* Berkeley: University of California Press, 1968.

———. *A Grammar of Motives.* Berkeley: University of California Press, 1962.

———. *Language as Symbolic Action.* Berkeley: University of California Press, 1966.

——. *Permanence and Change*. Indianapolis: Bobbs-Merrill, 1965.

——. *The Philosophy of Literary Form*. (1941). 3rd ed. Berkeley: University of California Press, 1973.

——. *A Rhetoric of Motives*. Berkeley: University of California Press, 1962.

——. *The Rhetoric of Religion*. Berkeley: University of California Press, 1961.

Burns, James MacGregor. *Leadership*. New York: Harper and Row, 1978.

"Bush, Cabinet Reagan Aides Weighed, Rejected Invoking 25th Amendment." *Indianapolis Star*, April 1, 1981, national edition, 7.

"Business Halts." *San Francisco Examiner*, November 24, 1963, national edition, 1.

Campbell, George. *The Philosophy of Rhetoric*. Carbondale: Southern Illinois University Press, 1963.

Campbell, Joseph. *The Hero with a Thousand Faces*. Princeton: Princeton University Press, 1973.

Campbell, Karlyn Kohrs, and Kathleen Hall Jamieson. *Form and Genre: Shaping Rhetorical Action*. Falls Church, Va.: National Communication Association, 1978.

Cannon, Lou. "Reagan Staff Plan for Interim Rule: 'Business as Usual.'" *Washington Post*, April 1, 1981, national edition, A1.

Capon, Robert Farrar. *Party Spirit: Some Entertaining Principles*. New York: William Morrow, 1979.

——. *The Supper of the Lamb: A Culinary Reflection*. Garden City, N.Y.: Doubleday, 1969.

Carspecken, Phil Francis. "Intersubjective Structure and Systems of Practice in School-Community Relations." Technical report, ERIC ED 322245, 1990.

Castiglione, Baldassare. *The Book of the Courtier*. Trans. George Bull. New York: Penguin, 1976.

Chant, Christopher. *The New Encyclopedia of Handguns and Small Arms*. London: Multimedia Books, Ltd./Prion, 1986.

"Cool in Crisis." *Indianapolis Star*, April 2, 1981, national edition, 22.

Cooper, Jeff. *The Art of the Rifle*. Boulder, Colo.: Paladin Press, 1997.

Coutant, L. A. "Baldesar Castiglione." In *Encyclopedia of Rhetoric and Composition: Communication from Ancient Times to the Information Age*, edited by Theresa Enos, 97–98. New York: Garland, 1996.

Covino, William A., and David A. Jolliffe. *Rhetoric: Concepts, Definitions, Boundaries*. Boston: Allyn and Bacon, 1995.

Critchley, Simon. "Das Ding: Lacan and Levinas." *Research in Phenomenology* 28 (1998): 72–90.

Cronin, Thomas E. "The Presidency Public Relations Script." In *The Presidency Reappraised*, edited by Rexford G. Tugwell and Thomas E. Cronin, 160–179. New York: Praeger, 1974.

Denham, A. E. "Envisioning the Good: Iris Murdoch's Moral Psychology." *Modern Fiction Studies* 47 (2001): 602–29.

"Devil Involved, Oral Roberts Says." *Detroit Free Press*, April 1, 1981, national edition, 4B.

Dickens, Charles. (1843). *A Christmas Carol*. New York: Bantam, 1966.

"'Didn't Skip a Beat,' Officials Say of U.S." *Indianapolis Star*, April 1, 1981, national edition, 7.

"Down from the Highest Mountaintop." *Time*, August 19, 1974, 42.

Drumline. Directed by Charles Stone III. Performed by Nick Cannon, Zoe Saldana, Leonard Roberts, and Orlando Jones. Fox, 2002.

Ehninger, Douglas. "On Systems of Rhetoric." In *Contemporary Theories of Rhetoric: Selected Readings*, edited by Richard L. Johannesen, 327–39. New York: Harper and Row, 1971.

Eliade, Mircea. *The Sacred and the Profane: The Nature of Religion*. New York: Harcourt, Brace, 1959.

Evans, Nicholas. *The Horse Whisperer*. New York: Dell Books, 1996.

Evans, Robert, and Robert Novak. "Reagan: The Vital Spark." *Washington Post*, April 1, 1981, national edition, A21.

Ezell, Edward C. *Handguns of the World*. New York: Barnes and Noble, 1991.

Fenno, Richard F., Jr. "The President's Cabinet." In *Perspectives on the Presidency*, edited by Aaron Wildavsky, 312–26. Boston: Little, Brown, 1975.

Finer, Herman. *The Presidency*. Chicago: University of Chicago Press, 1960.

Fisher, M. F. K. *The Art of Eating*. New York: Collier Books, 1990.

Fisher, Walter. *Human Communication as Narration: Toward a Philosophy of Reason, Value, and Action*. Columbia: University of South Carolina Press, 1987.

———. "Reaffirmation and Subversion of the American Dream." *Quarterly Journal of Speech* 59 (1973): 160–67.

Fiske, John. "The Discourses of TV Quiz Shows or, School + Luck = Success + Sex." *Central States Speech Journal* 34 (1983): 139–50.

———. *Understanding Popular Culture*. Boston: Unwin Hyman, 1989.

Fiske, John, and John Hartley. *Reading Television*. London: Methuen, 1978.

"A Ford Foreign Policy." *National Review*, August 30, 1974, 958–59.

"Ford: 'Our Nightmare Is Over.'" *Time*, August 19, 1974, 13.

"Ford Sets His Course." *U.S. News and World Report*, August 26, 1974, 15.

Gabler, Neal. *Life, the Movie: How Entertainment Conquered Reality*. New York: Alfred A. Knopf, 1998.

Gallagher, Hugh. "Presidents, Congress, and the Legislative Functions." In *The Presidency Reappraised*, edited by Rexford G. Tugwell and Thomas E. Cronin, 215–31. New York: Praeger, 1974.

Gates, Henry Louis, Jr. *The Signifying Monkey: A Theory of Afro-American Literary Criticism*. New York: Oxford University Press, 1988.

Gauss, Christian. "Introduction." In Niccolò Machiavelli, *The Prince*, translated by E. R. P. Vincent, 7–32. New York: New American Library, 1952.

Gellatly, Angus. "Why the Young Child Has Neither a Theory of Mind Nor a Theory of Anything Else." *Human Development* 40 (1997): 32–58.

Get on the Bus. Directed by Spike Lee. Performed by Ossie Davis, Charles Dutton, et. al. Columbia Pictures, 1996.

Gibson, William. *Count Zero*. New York: Ace Books, 1987.

———. *Mona Lisa Overdrive*. New York: Bantam, 1988.

———. *Neuromancer*. New York: Ace Books, 1984.

Gilbert, Olive. *Narrative of Sojourner Truth*. Mineola, N.Y.: Dover, 1997.

Golden, James L., and Edward P. J. Corbett. *The Rhetoric of Blair, Campbell, and Whately.* New York: Holt, Rinehart and Winston, 1968.

Goldmann, Lucien. "Introduction to the Problems of a Sociology of the Novel." *Telos* 18 (1973/1974): 122–35.

"The Government Still Lives." *Time,* November 29, 1963, 21.

Gramsci, Antonio. *Selections from the Prison Notebooks.* Ed. and trans. Quintin Hoare and Geoffrey N. Smith. New York: International Publishers, 1971.

Grande, Lance, and Olivier Rieppel. *Interpreting the Hierarchy of Nature: From Systematic Patterns to Evolutionary Process Theories.* San Diego: Academic Press, 1994.

Griffiths, Paul E. "Darwinism, Process Structuralism, and Natural Kinds." *Philosophy of Science* 63 (1996): S1–S9.

"Haig Action Touches off Concern Abroad." *Indianapolis Star,* April 3, 1981, national edition, 12.

Hariman, Robert. *Political Style: The Artistry of Power.* Chicago: University of Chicago Press, 1995.

Hart, Roderick P. *The Sound of Leadership: Presidential Communication in the Modern Age.* Chicago: University of Chicago Press, 1987.

Hebdige, Dick. *Subculture: The Meaning of Style.* London: Methuen, 1979.

Hecht, Michael L., Mary Jane Collier, and Sidney A. Ribeau. *African American Communication: Ethnic Identity and Cultural Interpretation.* Newbury Park, Calif.: Sage, 1993.

Hilton, Peter John, and Shaun Wylie. *Homology Theory: An Introduction to Algebraic Topology.* London: Cambridge University Press, 1965.

hooks, bell. *Art on My Mind: Visual Politics.* New York: New Press, 1995.

———. *Black Looks: Race and Representation.* Boston: South End Press, 1992.

The Horse Whisperer. Directed by Robert Redford. Performed by Robert Redford, Kristin Scott Thomas, Scarlett Johansson, Sam Neill, and Dianne Wiest. Buena Vista, 1998.

Hutchins, F. G. "Presidential Autocracy in America." In *The Presidency Reappraised,* edited by Rexford G. Tugwell and Thomas E. Cronin, 30–59. New York: Praeger, 1974.

"'I Am in Control' Haig Told Newsmen during Early Crisis." *Indianapolis Star,* March 31, 1981, national edition, 10A.

"'I Will Do My Best'—Johnson." *San Francisco Examiner,* November 23, 1963, national edition.

"Instantly—New Finger on Nuclear Trigger." *San Francisco Examiner,* November 23, 1963, national edition, 1.

James, Henry. (1881). *Portrait of a Lady.* New York: Airmont Publishing Co., 1966.

Jameson, Fredric. *The Political Unconscious: Narrative as a Socially Symbolic Act.* Ithaca: Cornell University Press, 1981.

Jamieson, Kathleen Hall. *Packaging the Presidency: A History and Criticism of Presidential Campaign Advertising.* New York: Oxford University Press, 1996.

Jardine, N. "The Concept of Homology in Biology." *British Journal for the Philosophy of Science* 18 (1967): 125–39.

Jeanneret, Michel. *A Feast of Words: Banquets and Table Talk in the Renaissance.* Chicago: University of Chicago Press, 1991.

"John F. Kennedy." *San Francisco Examiner,* November 23, 1963, national edition, A1.

Kahn, Victoria. "Humanist Rhetoric." In *Rhetoric: Concepts, Definitions, Boundaries,* edited by William A. Covino and David A. Jolliffe, 229–42. Boston: Allyn and Bacon, 1995.

Kaiser, Robert G. "Direct Access: State of the Union." *Washingtonpost.com Direct Access.* <http://www.washingtonpost.com/wp-srv/politics/talk/zforum/kaiser012099.htm>.

Kavanagh, Thomas. "The Libertine's Bluff: Cards and Culture in Eighteenth-Century France." *Eighteenth-Century Studies* 33 (2000): 505–21.

Keep, Christopher, and Don Randall. "Action, Empire, and Narrative in Arthur Conan Doyle's *The Sign of Four.*" *Novel* 32 (1999): 207–21.

Kendall, Gavin, and Gary Wickham. *Understanding Culture: Cultural Studies, Order, Ordering.* London: Sage, 2001.

King, Margaret L. *Women of the Renaissance.* Chicago: University of Chicago Press, 1991.

Kittler, Friedrich. *Gramophone, Film, Typewriter.* Trans. Geoffrey Winthrop-Young and Michael Wutz. Stanford: Stanford University Press, 1999.

Kramer, Reinhold. "Section 8 of the Charter and English-Canadian Fiction." *Dalhousie Review* 78 (1998): 385–413.

Labov, William. *Language in the Inner City: Studies in the Black English Vernacular.* Philadelphia: University of Pennsylvania Press, 1972.

Lakoff, George, and Mark Johnson. *Metaphors We Live By.* Chicago: University of Chicago Press, 1980.

Lane, Michael, ed. *Introduction to Structuralism.* New York: Basic Books, 1970.

Langer, Susanne. *Philosophy in a New Key: A Study in the Symbolism of Reason, Rite, and Art.* 3rd ed. Cambridge: Harvard University Press, 1957.

"Lawmakers Back to Work." *Indianapolis Star,* April 1, 1981, national edition, 6.

Leach, Edmund. "Structuralism in Social Anthropology." In *Structuralism: An Introduction,* edited by David Robey, 37–56. London: Oxford University Press, 1973.

Lescaze, Lee. "Reagan, in Good Spirits, Making a Fast Recovery." *Washington Post,* April 1, 1981, national edition, A12+.

Levine, Phillippa. "Rereading the 1890s: Venereal Disease as 'Constitutional Crisis' in Britain and British India." *Journal of Asian Studies* 55 (1996): 585–612.

Lévi-Strauss, Claude. *The Raw and the Cooked.* New York: Harper and Row, 1969.

———. *Symbolic Anthropology.* New York: Basic Books, 1963.

Lewis, Anthony. "A Lonely Crowd." *New York Times,* April 1, 1981, national edition, 25.

Livers, Keith. "Scatology and Eschatology: The Recovery of the Flesh in Andrei Platonov's *Happy Moscow.*" *Slavic Review* 59 (2000): 154–82.

Lockard, Joe. "Impeachable Orgasms." *Bad Subjects: Political Education for Everyday Life.* January 17, 1999. <http://eserver.org/bs/editors/1999-01-17.html>.

Locke, John. *An Essay Concerning Human Understanding.* Amherst, N.Y.: Prometheus, 1995.

The Longest Yard. Directed by Robert Aldrich. Performed by Burt Reynolds, Eddie Albert, Harry Caesar, Michael Conrad, and John Steadman. Paramount, 1974.

Lorenz, Konrad Z. "Analogy as a Source of Knowledge." *Science* 185 (1974): 229–34.

Machiavelli, Niccolò. *The Prince.* Trans. E. R. P. Vincent. New York: New American Library, 1952.

Majors, Richard, and Janet Mancini Billson. *Cool Pose: The Dilemmas of Black Manhood in America*. New York: Simon and Schuster, 1993.

Malamud, Margaret. "Gender and Spiritual Self-Fashioning: The Master-Disciple Relationship in Classical Sufism." *Journal of the American Academy of Religion* 64 (1996): 89–117.

Maranda, Pierre. "Anthropological Analytics." In *The Logic of Culture*, edited by Ino Rossi, 23–41. New York: J. F. Bergin, 1982.

Martinez, Ronald. "Mourning Beatrice: The Rhetoric of Threnody in the *Vita Nuova*." *Modern Language Notes* 113 (1998): 1–29.

Meskell, Lynn. "Cycles of Life and Death: Narrative Homology and Archaeological Realities." *World Archaeology* 31 (2000): 405–41.

Miller, Toby, and Alec McHoul. *Popular Culture and Everyday Life*. London: Sage, 1998.

"A New President." *U.S. News and World Report*, August 19, 1974, 14.

"Newsgram." *U.S. News and World Report*, August 16, 1974, 12.

"Newsgram." *U.S. News and World Report*, August 19, 1974, 7.

Nichols, Bill. *Ideology and the Image*. Bloomington: Indiana University Press, 1981.

Noble, Kenneth B. "Market and Business Relieved." *New York Times*, April 1, 1981, national edition, 3.

Ogden, C. K., and I. A. Richards. *The Meaning of Meaning*. New York: Harcourt, Brace, 1923.

Olson, Kathryn M. "Detecting a Common Interpretive Framework for Impersonal Violence: The Homology in Participants' Rhetoric on Sport Hunting, 'Hate Crimes,' and Stranger Rape." *Southern Communication Journal* 67 (2002): 215–44.

Osborn, Michael. "The Evolution of the Archetypal Sea in Rhetoric and Poetic." *Quarterly Journal of Speech* 63 (1977): 347–63.

Painter, Nell Irvin. *Sojourner Truth: A Life, A Symbol*. New York: W. W. Norton, 1996.

Peaden, Catherine Hobbs. "John Locke." In *Encyclopedia of Rhetoric and Composition: Communication from Ancient Times to the Information Age*, edited by Theresa Enos, 396–99. New York: Garland, 1996.

Pfau, Thomas. "The Voice of Critique: Aesthetic Cognition after Kant." *Modern Language Quarterly* 60 (1999): 321–52.

Piccirillo, Mary S. "On the Authenticity of Televisual Experience: A Critical Exploration of Para-Social Closure." *Critical Studies in Mass Communication* 3 (1986): 337–55.

Pigg, Daniel F. "Figuring Subjectivity in *Piers Plowman*, the *Parson's Tale*, and *Retraction*: Authorial Insertion and Identity Poetics." *Style* 31 (1997): 428–39.

Plett, Heinrich F. "Renaissance Rhetoric." In *Encyclopedia of Rhetoric*, edited by Thomas O. Sloane, 672–83. Oxford, UK: Oxford University Press, 2001.

Porter, Dennis. "Soap Time: Thoughts on a Commodity Art Form." In *Television: The Critical View*, 3rd ed., edited by Horace Newcomb, 122–31. New York: Oxford University Press, 1982.

"The Presidency under Glass." *New York Times*, April 1, 1981, national edition, 28.

Pritchett, C. Herman. "The President's Constitutional Position." In *The Presidency Reappraised*, edited by Rexford G. Tugwell and Thomas E. Cronin, 11–23. New York: Praeger, 1974.

Quine, Willard Van Orman. "Progress on Two Fronts." *Journal of Philosophy* 93 (1996): 159–63.

Raines, Howell. "Meeting at Hospital." *New York Times,* April 1, 1981, national edition, 1.

———. "Reagan Sees Aides and Acts on Trade; Continues to Gain." *New York Times,* April 2, 1981, national edition, 1.

"Raw." *WWE Live.* World Wrestling Entertainment, Inc. The Nashville Network. March 3, 2003.

"Reagan Looks Robust after Surgery, in Good Spirits." *Indianapolis Star,* April 1, 1981, national edition, 1.

"Reagan Shows the Nation That He's Still in Charge." *Detroit Free Press,* April 1, 1981, national edition, A1.

Reedy, George. *The Presidency in Flux.* New York: Columbia University Press, 1973.

Reston, James. "The Crisis Manager Takes the Empty Chair." *New York Times,* April 1, 1981, national edition, 29.

Revel, Nicole. "'As if in a Dream . . .': Epics and Shamanism among Hunters. Palawan Island, the Philippines." Trans. Jennifer Curtiss. *Diogenes* 181 (1998): 7–30.

Richards, I. A. *The Philosophy of Rhetoric.* New York: Oxford University Press, 1936.

Roberts, Monty. *The Man Who Listens to Horses.* New York: Ballantine, 1998.

Rossiter, Clinton. *The American Presidency.* New York: Harcourt, Brace, 1956.

Rotman, Brian. "Thinking Dia-grams: Mathematics, Writing, and Virtual Reality." *South Atlantic Quarterly* 94 (Spring 1995): 389–415.

Rushdie, Salman. *Midnight's Children: A Novel.* New York: Knopf, 1981.

Rybczynski, Witold. *Home: A Short History of an Idea.* New York: Viking, 1986.

Safire, William. "One Fell Short." *New York Times,* April 1, 1981, national edition, 25.

Schaffner, Kenneth F. "Model Organisms and Behavioral Genetics: A Rejoinder." *Philosophy of Science* 65 (1998): 276–88.

Schleiner, Winfried. "Early Modern Controversies about the One-Sex Model." *Renaissance Quarterly* 53 (2000): 180–90.

Schlesinger, Arthur M., Jr. *The Imperial Presidency.* New York: Replica Books, 1998.

Schram, Martin, and Michael Gerter. "Haig's Actions Again Raise Concern over His Conduct." *Washington Post,* April 1, 1981, national edition, A1.

Sedgwick, David W. "Presidential Pornography III." *The C. G. Jung Page.* Winter 1999. <http://www.cgjungpage.org/editorial/sedg4.html>.

"Seven Days in August." *Newsweek,* August 19, 1974, 14.

Shedd, Meredith. "'Ut Sculptura Descriptio': Ekphrasis in Emeric-David's Recherses Sur L'art Statuaire." *Gazette Des Beaux Arts* 135 (2000): 315–24.

Sidey, Hugh. "Trying to Ensure an Epitaph." *Time,* August 19, 1974, 15B.

Sjöö, Monica, and Barbara Mor. *The Great Cosmic Mother: Rediscovering the Religion of the Earth,* 2nd ed. San Francisco: HarperSanFrancisco, 1991.

Sklar, Robert. "The Fonz, Laverne, Shirley, and the Great American Class Struggle." In *Television: The Critical View,* 3rd ed., edited by Horace Newcomb, 77–88. New York: Oxford University Press, 1982.

Skowronek, Stephen. *The Politics Presidents Make: Leadership from John Adams to George Bush.* Cambridge, Mass.: Belknap, 1993.

Sloane, Thomas O., ed. *Encyclopedia of Rhetoric*. New York: Oxford University Press, 2001.

Smith, Graham, ed. *Military Small Arms*. London: Salamander Books, 1994

Smitherman, Geneva. *Black Talk: Words and Phrases from the Hood to the Amen Corner*. Boston: Houghton Mifflin, 1994.

Stallybrass, Peter, and Allon White. *The Politics and Poetics of Transgression*. Ithaca: Cornell University Press, 1986.

Stanford, Miles J. *Fox's Book of Martyrs*. Ed. William Byron Forbush. Grand Rapids, Mich.: Zondervan, 1967.

"A Strong President." *Indianapolis Star*, April 1, 1981, national edition, 10.

"Stunned Eisenhower Brands Slaying as a Despicable Act." *Washington Post*, November 23, 1963, national edition, A11.

Talk, DC. *Jesus Freaks*. Tulsa, Okla.: Albury, 1999.

Thal, Donna J. "Language and Cognition in Normal and Late-Talking Toddlers." *Topics in Language Disorders* 11 (1991): 33–42.

"Time for Healing." *Time*, August 19, 1974, 10.

Truth, Sojourner, and Olive Gilbert. *Narrative of Sojourner Truth*. Mineola, N.Y.: Dover, 1997.

Tugwell, Rexford G., and Thomas E. Cronin. *The Presidency Reappraised*. New York: Praeger, 1974.

Two Tars. Directed by James Parrott. Performed by Stan Laurel, Oliver Hardy, Edgar Kennedy, Ruby Blaine, and Thelma Hill. Metro-Goldwyn-Mayer, 1929.

Wagner, Michael. "Local Leaders Are Stunned: 'It's a Sad, Sad Commentary.'" *Detroit Free Press*, March 31, 1981, national edition, 10A.

Weisman, Stevan R. "White House Aides Assert Weinberger Was Upset When Haig Took Charge." *New York Times*, April 1, 1981, national edition, 14.

"What Ford Will Do as President." *U.S. News and World Report*, August 19, 1974, 21.

"Who's in Charge?" *Atlanta Constitution*, April 1, 1981, national edition, 4A.

"Who's Minding the Store?" *New York Times*, April 1, 1981, national edition, 28.

Will, George F. "Glimpsing a Skull Beneath the Skin of Life." *Indianapolis Star*, April 3, 1981, national edition, 24.

Williams, Raymond. *Marxism and Literature*. New York: Oxford University Press, 1977.

Willis, Paul. *Profane Culture*. London: Routledge and Kegan Paul, 1978.

Wilson, Jack A. "Ontological Butcher: Organism Concepts and Biological Generalizations." *Philosophy of Science* 67 (2000): S301–S311.

World Socialist Web Site. "On the Starr Investigation." October 9, 1998. <http://www.wsws.org/correspo/1998/oct1998/cor3-019.shtml>.

———. "Week One of the Impeachment Trial." January 19, 1999. <http://www.wsws.org/correspo/1999/jan1999/cor3-j19.shtml>.

Young, Bruce A. "On the Necessity of an Archetypal Concept in Morphology: With Special Reference to the Concepts of 'Structure' and 'Homology.'" *Biology and Philosophy* 8 (1993): 225–48.

Zhuk, A. B. *The Illustrated Encyclopedia of Handguns*. Translated by. N. N. Bobrov. London: Greenhill Books, 1995.

Index